THE CONTEMPLATIVE MIND
IN THE SCHOLARSHIP OF
TEACHING AND LEARNING

SCHOLARSHIP OF TEACHING AND LEARNING

Editors
Jennifer Meta Robinson
Whitney M. Schlegel
Mary Taylor Huber

THE CONTEMPLATIVE MIND IN THE SCHOLARSHIP OF TEACHING AND LEARNING

Patricia Owen-Smith

Indiana University Press

This book is a publication of

Indiana University Press
Office of Scholarly Publishing
Herman B Wells Library 350
1320 East 10th Street
Bloomington, Indiana 47405 USA

iupress.indiana.edu

Manufactured in the United States of America

Library of Congress Cataloging-in-Publication Data

Names: Owen-Smith, Patti L., [date]
Title: The contemplative mind in the scholarship of teaching and
    learning / Patricia Owen-Smith.
Description: Bloomington, Indiana : Indiana University Press,
    2018. | Series: Scholarship of teaching and learning | Includes
    bibliographical references and index.
Identifiers: LCCN 2017015149 (print) | LCCN 2017042594 (ebook) |
    ISBN 9780253031785 (eb) | ISBN 9780253031761 (cl : alk. paper) |
    ISBN 9780253031778 (pb : alk. paper)
Subjects: LCSH: College teaching—Philosophy. | Reflective teaching. |
    Reflective learning. | Education, Higher—Aims and objectives.
Classification: LCC LB2331 (ebook) | LCC LB2331 .O94 2018 (print) |
    DDC 378.1/25—dc23
LC record available at https://lccn.loc.gov/2017015149

1 2 3 4 5   23 22 21 20 19 18

For my mother, Gilda Vilona Owen, whose contemplative spirit guided me from the first moments of my life and whose contemplative legacy remains forever in my heart

For my students, who indulged, guided, taught, and accompanied me on this contemplative journey

Contents

Acknowledgments

I THANK Dr. Pat Hutchings and Dr. Mary Huber, Carnegie Foundation senior scholars who were my omnipresent cheerleaders and wise, intelligent, and caring mentors; Mr. Eugene Rackley and his generous Oxford College Career Development Award, which not only supported my writing but affirmed my identity as a contemplative scholar; Dr. Grant Carlson, a deeply caring and tender surgeon, a contemplative in his own right, who healed me and sent me on my way to complete this book; Oxford College of Emory University, my beloved home institution, which raised me professionally and supports me in ways too numerous to count; the Carnegie Academy for the Scholarship of Teaching and Learning and the Association for Contemplative Mind in Higher Education, which so beautifully model the ways in which academic institutions can indeed be compassionate, thoughtful, and soulful; and finally my life partner, Dr. Paul Smith, who patiently and generously keeps the home fires burning, and my daughter, Dr. Ashli Owen-Smith, who will always remain the grace note in my life. I am grateful to all of them.

THE CONTEMPLATIVE MIND
IN THE SCHOLARSHIP OF
TEACHING AND LEARNING

Introduction

Envisioning the Contemplative Commons

> How young we are when we start wondering about it all, the nature of the journey and of the final destination.
> —Robert Coles, *The Spiritual Life of Children*

THIS BOOK IS about the return to and understanding of the *contemplative* in higher education. Specifically, it is about the place of contemplative knowing and contemplative practices within the scholarship of teaching and learning (SoTL) framework. The Association for Contemplative Mind in Higher Education (ACMHE) and SoTL share a commitment to improving the quality of teaching and learning, and both seek to transform higher education. The philosophical underpinnings of the two movements reveal some similar historical junctures. Both call for radical shifts in thought and practice in an effort to recover important dimensions of learning and knowing that have been lost in higher education.

Lee Shulman, president emeritus of the Carnegie Foundation for the Advancement of Teaching, from which SoTL emerged, articulates a taxonomy, or what he calls a "table of learning" (2002). Fundamental to this taxonomy are "engagement and motivation," "knowledge and understanding," "performance and action," "reflection and critique," "judgment and design," and "commitment and identity." According to Shulman, this heuristic argues for "the mutually interdependent facets of an educated person's life of mind, of emotion, and of action" (42). Shulman centers on "commitment" as a major kind of learning, one that "is both moving inward and connecting outward [and is] the highest attainment an educated person can achieve" (41).

Contemplative educators also focus on practices of mind and emotion that draw on the human capacity to know, specifically through stillness, awareness, attention, mindfulness, and reflection. A contemplative pedagogy is one that emphasizes "interior qualities of lifelong impact, such as self-knowledge and ethical cultivation" (Grace 2011, 99). Daniel Barbezat and Mirabai Bush note that all contemplative practices "place the student in the center of his or her learning so the student can connect his or her inner world to the outer world" (2014, 5–6). Therefore, both contemplative and SoTL educators prioritize the transformation of habits of the mind, deepening of attention and insight, understanding of self as influenced by both interiority and exteriority, and commitment to and reflection on the experiential. They observe these factors as cardinal processes in teaching and learning.

Although contemplative and SoTL perspectives have important differences, they also have an obvious camaraderie and dance between them. Remarkably, they seem to disengage from one another despite our entering the world as students and learners who know and understand through contemplative means. Without hesitation we begin our lives with the ability to perceive, feel, experience, and explore the world with a contemplative lens. Young children sit, stare, see, question, ponder, think, and wonder. They are knowledge builders and scientists. Sadly, the majority of us begin to lose ourselves as knowers and learners at a very specific juncture in our developmental and educational journeys. Just as our contemplative selves emerge early in life, so do they leave us early in life, and just as our excitement and joy in learning and knowing begin in our first seconds of life, so do they often decline. Both developmental and educational psychologists remind us that in most cases these losses occur when we begin school and the alienation of the contemplative from teaching and learning begins.

Modern educational systems, from kindergarten through graduate school, impose a set of restrictions and mandates that disallow the flourishing of contemplation and deep learning. We are no longer given time and space for imagination, curiosity, and creativity and for the unfolding of what we have always had. The stillness and quiet necessary for thought development and deep intellectual inquiry become nonproductive, a wasting of time, and a squandering of resources. Students learn clearly that they may not stand in the gap of their experiences, pause, and consider. In learning these rules well, we lose our ability to attend mindfully and to reflect, or in the words of Robert Coles (1990, 335), to wonder about it all. These losses result in costs that are profound for both the individual and the world we inhabit. Many of our educational reformers argue that the higher education we know today seems to reflect this legacy of loss.

Contemplative knowing as intimately linked to learning was not always absent from our educational models and cultural histories. Deeply rooted in our wisdom and spiritual traditions, contemplative practices are definitive components in Buddhist and Taoist meditation, Hindu yoga forms, Christian contemplative prayer, Sufi metaphysical reflection, and the Jewish mystical school of thought, Kabbalah. Each of these focuses on an intentional and deepened awareness (Hart 2004). Contemplative methods also find expression in the words of many educational philosophers, poets, artists, and scientists who held tightly to their contemplative lens of childhood. Some historians point out that the Greek philosophers were the first to acknowledge contemplation as a way of knowing. Plato's dialogue and koans are but two of many such examples.

Contemplative modes were also central to the monastic schools and the ways of teaching and learning born in those schools. Augustine, Seneca, and Montaigne relied on forms of contemplative reflection. Like Plato, Augustine and Seneca used the oral dialogue for self-inquiry, and Montaigne's writing practice was a type of contemplative autobiography (Stock 2012). Einstein clearly practiced a contemplative approach in his articulation of the stages of insight and imagination, pointing out that "imagination is more important than knowledge. . . . [K]nowledge is limited . . . imagination encircles the world" (Zajonc 2012). Similarly, Isaac Newton often talked of truth as first requiring a commitment to contemplation. Newton observed that if he had contributed to public service at all, it was because of his "patient thought" (Burtt 1954, 285). Psychologist, philosopher, and educator William James noted the significance of contemplative awareness and attention in observing that "genius, in truth, means little more than the faculty of perceiving in an unhabitual way" (1890, 110). Rainer Maria Rilke's poetry emerged from his distinct ability to look, attend, and see into the heart of something, perhaps best captured in what may be one of his most profound credos: "Live the questions now, perhaps then, someday, you will gradually, without noticing, live into the answer" (1903, 21).

The integration of contemplative knowing into the American school system was born in the works of such educational innovators as Horace Mann ([1840] 1989), Maria Montessori (1967), John Dewey (1984), and Rudolf Steiner (2002). In virtually all of his writing, Horace Mann emphasized inspiration as a major dimension of learning, while Maria Montessori envisioned thought as parts of the soul. John Dewey spoke of the "audacity of imagination" as the basis for every great advancement in science (1984, 247). Similarly, Steiner (2002) saw the sense of imagination and responsibility as the very "nerve" of education. One of the most influential educational theorists in the twentieth century, Paulo Freire (1970, 1990), stressed pedagogical contemplation and reflection as requisites for liberation and the transformation of the world. He also admonished teachers "to make it possible for the students to become themselves" (1990, 181). The Nobel laureate Barbara McClintock modeled the use of contemplative practices, urging her biology students at Harvard to contemplate their material, "to take the time and look . . . to hear what the material has to say to you" and to develop "a feeling for the organism" (quoted in Keller 1983, 206, 198).

These educational reformers and innovators clearly recognized the integration of our exterior and interior worlds in knowledge construction and posited models for contemplation in teaching and learning. Contemplation as a way of knowing, therefore, is deeply embedded in the work of many of the greatest thinkers, educators, and reformers who played critical roles in epistemologies of knowing. Their legacy is apparent in the current work of educators such as Parker Palmer, Alexander and Helen Astin, Art Zajonc, Mirabai Bush, Daniel Barbezat, Tobin Hart, Laura Rendon, and Mary Rose O'Reilley, each of whom has written eloquently about honoring interiority through contemplative knowing, and all are careful examiners of the processes of teaching and learning.

Educational reform movements, particularly SoTL, also reflect this legacy. SoTL has provided a guiding light for teachers who are inviting curiosity, imagination, insight, creativity, attention, collaboration, self-authored inquiry, and citizenship back into their classrooms through such pedagogies as service and experiential learning, problem- and team-based learning, reflective writing, deep reading, dialogue and inquiry, and so on. The American educator and former president of the Carnegie Foundation for the Advancement of Teaching Ernest Boyer reminds us that academic scholarship before 1906 "referred to a variety of creative work carried on in a variety of places, and its integrity was measured by the ability to think, communicate, and learn" (1990, 15). However, he also observed that 1906 marked the date when the mandate for research entered higher education and the subsequent shift away from creative thought and deep learning. Boyer emphasized a scholarship of integration, often returning to Mark Van Doren's notion that "the connectedness of things is what the educator contemplates to the limit of his capacity" (1997, 25). Connectedness leads to wisdom, according to Boyer. While Boyer might not have identified as a contemplative, the creative learning processes that he addresses and his call for a place from which thought and wisdom might emerge engage the contemplative in unambiguous ways. Lee Shulman also emphasizes requisites for higher education that include "nurturing the moral and spiritual development, the civic engagement, and the socialization of students" (quoted in Tell 2001, 6). Again, the processes that he addresses are deeply embedded in a contemplative perspective.

The conversations begun with Plato, Newton, Freire, and their legatees do, in fact, continue and are vital components in the teaching lives of many faculty members today. Just as many contemplative educators have benefited from this legacy, so has the SoTL community. The trajectories established by Boyer and Shulman, together with the work of Carnegie senior scholars Pat Hutchings and Mary Huber, contributed to the notion of Cognitive Affective Learning, which was first introduced in the Carnegie Academy for the Scholarship of Teaching and Learning. This emphasis on subjective and affective dimensions as critical and necessary aspects of the learning process affirmed the contemplative perspective that the intellect rests in the mind and the heart (Owen-Smith 2004). In reviewing the 141 projects of Carnegie scholars from 1998 through 2005, I found that a substantive number centered on components of contemplative knowing. These include projects that focused on cooperative problem solving and reflection; epiphanies in learning and affective development; the aesthetics of biology; experiences of learning based in student voice, participation, reciprocity, and trust; resiliency and the nature of human behaviors; effects of experience and values on the delivery of justice; emotional aspects of learning; and the integration of applied ethics in education. These projects included strategies, practices, or approaches that might be considered contemplative. Carnegie scholars were selected for the integrity of their project proposals. Therefore, some components of contemplative knowing were recognized and valued in SoTL by at least 1998 in spite of a vocabulary that was different from what contemplative educators might use today.

Despite this history, one that clearly suggests theoretical and pedagogical commonalities between contemplative and SoTL education, several substantive differences exist. Such differences might inform the disengagement that many SoTL and contemplative practitioners have with one another. The ancient roots of contemplative practices are central to these differences in that they profoundly shape pedagogical constructs and clearly differentiate their methods from other ways of knowing and learning. This history offers an understanding of contemplative practices and a reason that these practices are missing in many classrooms and in SoTL discourse. At the risk of reducing contemplative methods to an oversimplified summary of characteristics and perspectives, I believe it is important to observe those features that mark contemplative education as fundamentally distinct from other educational practices such as SoTL. Edward Sarath speaks to the centrality of the "inner-outer union" in contemplative education, one that acknowledges the interior and exterior facets of the individual. Like most contemplative educators, Sarath recognizes first-, second-, and third-person viewpoints within this inner-outer union, arguing that "much of contemplative education may be seen as the addition of a first-person interior realm—with meditation being a key first-person methodology—to the largely third-person confinement lamented by a long legacy of educational thinkers" (2014, 362). The first-person perspective espoused by contemplative educators stands in stark contrast to the dominance of third-person learning emblematic of traditional educational paradigms, including SoTL. Similarly, Jing Lin (2013) speaks of a contemplative education as wisdom based, drawn from the world's spiritual traditions, and centered in the cultivation of abilities emanating from the heart and the soul of every student. Therefore, emphasis is placed on working with the internal self. Barbezat and Bush (2014) hold that the defining characteristic of contemplative methods is students' introspection and cultivation of attentiveness to themselves and to those relationships of which they are a part.

A second differentiating quality and one central to contemplative education is the role of meditation. The practice of meditation, for most contemplative scholars, is the practice of mindfulness, described by Arthur Ledoux (1998) as "the cultivation of bare attention: the ability to focus on any aspect of life whatsoever with this calm concentration." For Olen Gunnlaugson and colleagues (2014) mindfulness nurtures a supple and attentive state of mind allowing us to know something more deeply. Mindfulness, therefore, cultivates an inner technology of knowing, serves as a pedagogical method par excellence, and is the aim of contemplative education.

All contemplative practices have an inward emphasis that affords both insight and connection. Barbezat and Bush (2014) see four major objectives: (1) focus and attention building, (2) contemplation and introspection that are unambiguously incorporated into course content, (3) compassion, connection to others, and an abiding sense of both the moral and the spiritual features of education, and (4) inquiry into the nature of the mind and acquisition of personal meaning, creativity, and insight. While many educators privilege focus and attention, contemplation, introspection, compassion, and connection and inquiry into the moral and spiritual features of knowing, personal meaning, and insight are not included in most current educational paradigms. As the following chapters note, many classrooms and SoTL practice and research display few such emphases.

Just as the historical roots of contemplative education are significant in explicating a major difference between contemplative and SoTL approaches, so are the historical roots of SoTL. Despite SoTL having introduced new and welcomed ways of thinking about teaching and learning, it nevertheless remained grounded in a traditional educational paradigm, resulting in a discourse emanating from this paradigm. From its formal introduction in 1990, SoTL's focus has emphasized the production and understanding of teaching and student learning as scholarly work supported by articulated classroom goals and evidence. However, for the most part, little attention has been given to the types of learning desired, specifically those focused on the interior-exterior union, and their associated venues for access. Consequently, those who welcome internal dimensions such as insight, imagination, attention, and spirituality into their classrooms and teaching lives feel a sense of impoverishment. Access to a contemplative pedagogical perspective, one that unabashedly addresses such dimensions, remains elusive or poorly defined, and educators interested in such dimensions are left to wander. In his query about SoTL as mirrored in the values we as teachers hold, the SoTL scholar Richard Gale (2009) argues that SoTL should have a place for questions about how students learn affective dimensions such as empathy, tolerance, equity, and social justice. However, he also observes that such questions are often absent from what teachers see in research and scholarly writing. This absence in SoTL maintains a literature that fails to privilege and articulate such questions, but it also precludes ways of responding to and assessing such questions. Some SoTL educators have begun to ask such questions, but many remain unfamiliar with, resistant to, or intimidated by contemplative practices. The good news for SoTL practitioners who wish to include a contemplative stance in their pedagogical approaches is that contemplative methods can be adapted to most of their current practices, many of which the following chapters describe.

Teachers have long sought an understanding of internal processes and their relationship to learning. How is it, then, that the valuing of contemplative knowledge and practices continues to be marginalized in institutions of higher learning? Why is it that contemplative and SoTL practices fail to demonstrate the ways they are intimately linked with one another in complex yet interesting ways that potentially expand their individual canons? Is this separation the result of a calculated, reductionist, or parochial decision, and if so, why? How might discourse between the two articulate important differences that exist, and what might we learn from these differences? SoTL's emphasis on integrative, holistic, experiential, and transformative learning and the associated pedagogies of engagement are grounded in a desire to deepen student learning and student understanding of self. However, are practices that undergird deep learning and self-understanding missing in SoTL conversations, or might we recognize such practices as disguised in a different vocabulary? Might the hallmarks of contemplative practices such as mindfulness, silence, compassionate listening, introspection, and self-reflection also be pedagogies engaged and supported by SoTL? How might we define contemplative knowing in the context of university goals and accountability mandates? How might we define it in the context of teaching and learning centers? If contemplative practices are to find credibility in higher education, might they do so through SoTL? What evidence do we have for contemplative practices in the classroom, and what do we need? How might SoTL provide models for investigating some of these practices, and how might contemplative methods of assessment expand SoTL's understanding and definitions of outcomes? Finally, if today's university is "without a soul," as the former Harvard dean Harry Lewis (2006) argues, is there not an urgency for an explicit contemplative stance in higher education, and how might this inform and be informed by a SoTL narrative?

The following chapters explore these questions to create a bridge between contemplative practices in higher education and SoTL. Shulman has consistently talked of the necessity for reconnection among our disciplinary narratives to end a "pedagogical solitude" (2004a, 140). If we connect SoTL and contemplative education and if they intersect, what might this look like and how might this offer the changes needed in the academy of the twenty-first century?

Chapter 1 briefly covers the histories of contemplative education and SoTL and defines and differentiates current conceptions of epistemology, theory, and pedagogy that have evolved from them. What does a contemplative education mean at this point in time, and what are the curricular components, rationale, and embedded assumptions of such an education? Is there a case to be made for such an education in the secular university? Given the trends in higher education today, such as the requirement of professional readiness and the development of marketable skills, how might the contemplative perspective find its place in students' education? The SoTL framework provides a systematic way of approaching these questions in its emphasis on a "teaching commons," or communal dialogue; evidence through assessment; and use of evidence to design and refine pedagogical approaches (Huber and Hutchings 2005). This framework as it pertains to pedagogy remains underdeveloped in today's contemplative movement. At the same time, the role of contemplative methods in deepening learning remains unacknowledged by many teaching and learning scholars despite their using pedagogies that might be considered contemplative. Chapter 1 calls for an integration of the contemplative and the SoTL perspectives as a necessary response to the profound issues that currently exist in higher education.

Chapter 2 examines contemplative systems of inquiry and classroom practices through the voices and practices of today's college and university teachers. The practices are situated in a variety of contexts. For example, many college and university teachers incorporate a single contemplative practice in their discipline-specific courses, such as meditation, concentrated reflection, contemplative reading and writing, and imagery. Others have developed semester-long courses that concentrate on contemplative ways of knowing as the central method of the course. The Contemplative Practice Fellowship Program, a collaboration between the Center for Contemplative Mind in Society and the Fetzer Institute, was an important contributor to course development and to increasing the number of teachers committed to methods of contemplative study. Still other institutions, such as the US Military Academy at West Point, the University of Michigan, and Brown University, have established contemplative programs, and the entire curriculum of Naropa University is grounded in a contemplative liberal arts education. Each of these courses, programs, and institutions provides a model for understanding how contemplative knowing informs teaching and learning.

Chapter 3 explores the hurdles and challenges often reported as impenetrable barriers to the development of contemplative practices in the classroom. Brian Stock (2012) reminds us that even the Greek philosophers were accused of subversive practices in their use of contemplation. Current criticisms, such as "unscientific," "irrational," and "a privileging of religiosity," often dominate discussions of the contemplative in higher education. Many of these criticisms are grounded in the discomfort of interrupting and interrogating deeply held beliefs about the purpose of the academy. Some criticisms emanate from a pedagogic vision that clearly excludes inner ways of knowing. Still other concerns focus on the dearth of systematic assessment and the necessary evidence. Despite these arguments, interest in contemplative dimensions is growing, as evidenced in the number of faculty members who are incorporating contemplative practices into their classrooms. The inaugural 2012 International Symposia for Contemplative Studies, sponsored by twenty-five organizations, hosted over seven hundred neuroscientists, social scientists, and contemplative scholars from around the world who shared their research. In October 2016, the Association for Contemplative Mind in Higher Education hosted its eighth yearly conference, Mindfulness, MOOCs and Money in Higher Education: Contemplative Possibilities and Promise, where Judith Simmer-Brown observed that eight thousand academics are now associated with the Center for Contemplative Mind.

Chapter 4 reviews current research on contemplative practices as it intersects with teaching and learning. SoTL and contemplative researchers share many of the same methodological approaches, such as qualitative approaches. However, the measurement of such dimensions as awareness, consciousness, and internality creates the need for additional approaches. As with all research, an array of limitations and challenges is associated with particular methods. Central to this discussion is the difficulty of assessing inner dimensions of knowing in an educational system that privileges outer knowing and research designs based on objectivism. It should not be surprising, therefore, that much current research on contemplative practices focuses on their relationship to brain activity, specifically meditation and the immediate physiological changes that it triggers. Tobin Hart (2004) extends these research findings to the classroom, arguing that these physiological changes are critical to learning in that they improve concentration, empathy, perception; lessen stress and anxiety; and increase effective performance. Although some research assesses these dimensions' relationship to contemplative practices in the classroom, it is at best limited. The Britton Lab of Brown University is an example of a research laboratory that focuses on the effects of contemplative practices on cognitive, emotional, and physiological well-being. Hal Roth (2012) refers to this approach as one grounded in third-person methods (traditional scientific inquiry) with first-person approaches (contemplative inquiry). Still, others are creating a bridge between the traditional methods of research and transpersonal and heuristic approaches in the assessment of contemplative modes. Laura Rendon describes this method as working "at the center and at the edge . . . blending methods, perspectives, and discourses to push the envelope of what constitutes academic research and what is involved in uncovering the truth" (2009, 155).

Chapter 5 envisages an academy for the twenty-first century and the associated issues that permeate a reimagined higher education. A modern skill set is now required, one that transcends the procurement-of-information-only emphasis in the service of an ethical and compassionate position grounded in wisdom. Contemplative methods are requisites for the creation and transformation of an academy that best meets the needs of today's students, staff, faculty, and administrators and communities beyond the campus gates. Central to this discussion is consideration of how the contemplative vision might be better articulated, interrogated, and strengthened. Specific attention is given in the discussion to a revisioning of contemplative definitions as they relate to teaching and learning communities, reimagining of the traditional research paradigm, reconsidering of curricula for a global and transcultural world, reconciling with the conundrum of technology, and programmatic integrating of contemplative courses as an essential to widening the contemplative perspective in higher education.

These chapters consider how the integration of contemplative and SoTL practices provides critical opportunities for one another, opportunities yet to be tapped in a cohesive, systematic, and comprehensive manner. It is not my intent to reduce and oversimplify the critical differentiating elements of these important perspectives. Unquestionably, there are substantive differences. Rather, the aim is to demonstrate their complementarity and potential for deepening students' development and understanding of the self as learner, knower, and citizen of the world. Certainly, the bequeathing of these ways of knowing to the next generation of students is not only our responsibility as teachers entrusted with their intellectual and affective development but a necessity and moral mandate for a new world order.

Finally, in keeping with my identity as a contemplative educator, I wrote this book from a first-, second-, and third-person position. I teach in a similar manner. My classrooms are filled with personal stories and experiences, collaborative dialogue, and the material of my own discipline. Students' first-hand experiences and perspectives are valued in these classes just as are their collaborative dialogues. Regrettably, the first-person perspective has been written out of academic discourse, and although discussion is emphasized in many classes, the second-person "we" perspective—the one that includes others—is fragile and often missing. The absence of first- and second-person perspectives contributes to a disengagement from others and the sense of isolation experienced by many students in today's classrooms. It also contributes to a fallacious understanding of knowledge as that imposed and received rather than constructed and shared. My conventional training as a developmental psychologist compels me to use the third-person perspective when appropriate, and I have used it often throughout the book. However, my identification as a contemplative encourages a personal narrative, just as my commitment to SoTL and its emphasis on a community of scholars requires the second-person perspective of "we."

1 A Historical Review

There's always been a conflict between the exterior, social self and the interior, private one. The struggle to reconcile them is central to the human experience, one of the great themes of philosophy, literature, and art.

—William Powers, *Hamlet's Blackberry*

DEFINITIONS OF EDUCATIONAL practices, pedagogy, and epistemology, as well as accompanying criticisms, derive from their respective historical and cultural contexts. Contemplative and SoTL perspectives are no exception. These perspectives' histories yield critical information and understanding about their place in higher education and their relationship with one another. Contemplative education and SoTL both have ancient roots despite being often considered innovative and new. For example, many of today's questions, debates, and perspectives about the role of higher education, specifically in current analyses and evaluations of contemplative modes and SoTL, are the same as those that began in ancient Rome. Training for an occupation or profession versus training for personal and intellectual fulfillment; the role, responsibility, and relationship of the university to the broader society; and the place of interior and spiritual dimensions of learning are just a few of the discussions that began many centuries ago. These same debates and questions also frame the *integration* of contemplative and SoTL modes explored in this chapter.

As noted in the introduction, SoTL began in 1990 with the Carnegie Foundation's publication of Ernest Boyer's (1990) *Scholarship Reconsidered: Priorities of the Professoriate*. Lee Shulman, who followed Boyer as president of the Carnegie Foundation, expanded Boyer's notion from the scholarship of teaching to the scholarship of teaching and learning. Boyer's and Shulman's conceptions of teaching and learning, and later senior scholar Pat Hutchings's, were the basis for the launch of the Carnegie Academy for the Scholarship of Teaching and Learning (CASTL) in 1998, whose major mission was to support teaching and learning initiatives. While these developments are relatively new, the narrative inherent in Boyer's and Shulman's work is one that began over three hundred years ago when attention to and questions about teaching and learning began in the United States (Fuhrmann and Grasha 1983). SoTL is often defined as centered on "problem posing" about an issue of teaching or learning (Cambridge 2000) and constructed around an "ethic of inquiry" and a "taxonomy of questions"

(Hutchings 2000, 2, 4). Central to such definitions is the role and significance of "reflective critique" and a "critical self-reflection" that lead to transformative learning (Musolino and Mostrom 2005, 52).

The Center for Contemplative Mind in Society began its development in 1991, giving birth to its academic program in 2008, the Association for Contemplative Mind in Higher Education (ACMHE). However, contemplative education began as early as the fifth century BCE with the Sophists, or teachers of wisdom (Lucas 1994), and flourished in the monastic and cathedral schools of the twelfth century CE. Like SoTL practitioners, contemplative educators describe intellectual examination as "inquiry into the nature of things" (Barbezat and Bush 2014, xiii). Tobin Hart (2004) expands this definition to include *how* we know as opposed to what we know, and Arthur Zajonc describes contemplative education as a venue for a deeper understanding of subjects and ways of living (Kaleem 2014).

Questions about teaching and learning in the construction of knowledge, therefore, are an integral part of the evolution of higher education and clearly echoed in SoTL and ACMHE. While the elements of and context for questions raised by SoTL and contemplative educators are dissimilar in some important ways, they are nevertheless derived from many shared conceptions of learning as a process of inquiry that is holistic and integrative, and each is circumscribed by criticisms that are, more often than not, similar in tone. Zajonc, former director of the Center for Contemplative Mind in Society, of which the ACMHE is part, and Lee Shulman, former president of the Carnegie Foundation for the Advancement of Teaching, from which SoTL emerged, are remarkably alike in terms of their understanding of the integration of exteriority and interiority in the learning process. Zajonc emphasizes the need for an education that understands the learner holistically:

> By seeing the cultivation of human experience as the basis of education, we multiply our ways of knowing ("epistemology") and enrich our understanding of the world ("ontology"). . . . If we could expand the worldview that supports education, we can find no better place to begin than by opening ourselves to the full scope of human experience. . . . Parallel to the universe of our experience is a comparably rich world of inner experience. Taken together they constitute of world of human experience. (2010, 60–61)

In a somewhat different manner, Shulman also speaks of the significance of the learner's both internal and external experience in his notion of "serious learning," or one that is based on the relationship between students' meaning construction and prior or native understanding:

> Any new learning must, in some fashion, connect with what learners already know. . . . [I]t is what I mean by "getting the inside out." As teachers, unless we can discover ways of getting the inside out and looking jointly at their prior knowledge

with our students, taking seriously what they already know and believe, instruction becomes very difficult. (1999, 12)

These understandings play a critical role in contemplative and SoTL perspectives of teaching and learning. While there is little doubt that SoTL and contemplative education have followed parallel, disconnected trajectories and that their emphases are dissimilar, they have a striking relationship. Both the disconnections between contemplative and SoTL perspectives and their relationship have the potential to deepen what each sees as its central mission and goals. The following exploration of these histories reveals how they have been disengaged from one another and at the same time embedded within one another.

While contemplative practices such as prayer, meditation, and silence are universal and rooted in virtually all spiritual and religious traditions, many of those that endured through time emerged from Asian philosophy and centered on meditative practices. Buddhism and Taoism were developed by intellectuals who were also yogis and contemplatives trained to value knowledge achieved through practices such as ethical discipline, sustaining attention, emotional alteration, and cultivation of wisdom (Walsh 1989). Because Buddhist institutions of higher learning were the most numerous and their educational practices most fully developed, the Buddhist influence on contemplative education was the most profound. The Buddhist study of the mind through the examination of thought, emotion, and consciousness contributed significantly to the methodology and content of the Buddhist "inner sciences" curriculum (Zajonc 2010). Robert Thurman notes that the Buddhist goals of empowerment and liberating transformation in an educational context have remained constant and carefully preserved through the years in the mountains of Tibet (cited in Buell 1999), and they endure in the villages of Southeast Asia. Therefore, a split between monasticism and education did not occur in Buddhist civilizations as it did in the West, and this history becomes important in understanding the circuitous trajectory of the contemplative in Western intellectual inquiry.

In the West, contemplative activity as critical to learning also began in monastic schools and in the Greek philosophers' notion of insight as the heart of knowledge. However, when European universities established themselves as alternatives to the monasteries and the cathedral schools of the twelfth and thirteenth centuries, a critical shift took place in the curriculum. This shift was intensified with the text-centered emphasis of Renaissance humanism and the evolution of the disciplines associated with the Enlightenment and scientific revolution (Buell 1999). The contemplative curriculum of the monasteries was replaced by one that emphasized logic and science. Contemplative activity at that point became the domain of monastic and religious life and, therefore, separated from the university. Contemplation as an important dimension of inquiry and knowing was considered to be a threat to the integrity of the modern university. Committed students of the contemplative life left the universities of Oxford and Cambridge in search of institutions that provided a contemplative hospitality that for the most part was religious (Stock 2012). Contemplative knowing that centered on interiority, spirituality, empathy, and wisdom was lost in favor of Aristotelian logic, contributing to the split between contemplative practices and academic study that we still see today. Zajonc observes that by the sixteenth century the forces of science and the Industrial Revolution began to shape education in significant ways and led to a "myopic vision of science and industry" (2010, 59).

Shulman (2004b) extends Zajonc's observation by pointing out that the psychologists and educational theorists William James, G. Stanley Hall, E. L. Thorndike, and John Dewey were the first American scientists to acknowledge internal processes in learning. However, by the turn of the nineteenth century they had succumbed to the influence of C. Lloyd Morgan's canon of 1894, which moved away from the psychological study of mental processes in learning. This shift transformed the discipline of scientific psychology in America, resulting in James's definition of psychology as the "science of mental life" (1890, 1) and John B. Watson's and later B. F. Skinner's emphasis on the science of behavior. This dismissal of interiority and internality as foundational for learning dominated learning theories during the first half of the 1900s. The consequences of this myopic vision have been profound for academic institutions, resulting in a nineteenth-century perspective of knowledge as objective and education as reducible to teaching students how to manipulate that knowledge. Mirabai Bush refers to this split as producing "a compartmentalized, fragmented way of learning and teaching, a dualistic alienation of body from mind, emotion from intellect, humans from nature, and art from science" (2011a, 223–224). Like Bush, Shulman (2004b) refers to this as an abandonment of introspection in the study of learning.

A few contemplative practices, or a secular spirituality, did exist in early Western intellectual history. Montaigne, Seneca, and Augustine were among the earliest contemplatives in their practice of reflection and self-inquiry. In her review of American contemplative education, Bush notes that William James might well have been the first American contemplative with the publication of his *Principles of Psychology* (1890) and his position that "the faculty of voluntarily bringing back a wandering attention, over and over again, is the very root of judgment, character, and will. . . . An education which should improve this faculty would be the education par excellence. But it is easier to define this ideal than to give practical directions for bringing it about" (Bush 2011b, 185).

Two significant occurrences provided fertile ground for more recent developments in contemplative education and SoTL. First, the gradual opening of Tibet that began in the 1970s allowed Western access to the Buddhist inner sciences curriculum in ways that were impossible in previous years. This accessibility offered a methodology for articulation of the contemplative and its integration into classroom practices and resulted in a heightened consciousness regarding social responsibility and citizenship. Interest in the expanded consciousness movement at Harvard in the 1970s (inspired by William James's writings), a vital element in the development of contemplative education, emerged from this political change. This movement later influenced the work of Daniel Goleman, whose book *Emotional Intelligence* (1995) became seminal in the academic community, and Richard Davidson, who established the laboratory for functional brain imaging and behavior and the laboratory for affective neuroscience at the University of Wisconsin. In fact, Goleman's concept of emotional intelligence was central to twenty-seven articles appearing in the *Journal for the Scholarship of Teaching and Learning* between 2012 and 2015.

While universities such as John F. Kennedy University (founded in 1964), the California Institute of Integral Studies (1968), and Maharishi University of Management (1971) focused on contemplative perspectives, Naropa University, founded in 1974, represents the first academic institution based on a Buddhist vision of contemplative education. Naropa emphasizes three modes of inquiry that make up a contemplative education: traditional academics, or third-person inquiry; experiential learning, or second-person inquiry; and contemplative, or first-person inquiry. In recent years a contemplative curriculum has been integrated into other universities, such as the University of Michigan, Brown University, and Lesley University. They model the integration of Eastern teaching philosophies seen in contemplative education and the Western educational traditions and practices that became the focus of SoTL. The University of Michigan's Center for Research on Learning and Teaching, the oldest teaching center in the United States, is firmly grounded in SoTL practices. Its program in creativity and consciousness studies, which examines and envisions the relationship between creativity and the growth of consciousness, exemplifies integration of exterior and interior ways of knowing and investigation. The Contemplative Studies Initiative at Brown University is committed to contemplative scientific research through its Clinical and Affective Neuroscience Laboratory, Translational Neuroscience Laboratory, and the Laboratory for Cognitive and Perceptual Learning. Brown has distinguished itself in effectively integrating third-person study with critical first-person study in its teaching methods and in its research labs. Lesley University's Center for Teaching, Learning, and Scholarship, also informed by SoTL, includes SoTL practices in investigating contemplative dimensions. This center's *Journal of Pedagogy, Pluralism and Practice* promotes "interdisciplinary thinking and [encourages] a more diverse dialogue across multiple fields of study." Many of the articles published by this journal highlight contemplative dimensions of body, mind, spirituality, identity, reflexivity, pedagogical imagination, and moral awareness. Lesley also offers a master's degree and a graduate certificate in mindfulness studies.

Several of today's signature pedagogical practices in higher education also integrate contemplative practices, and virtually all emerged during this same critical time period. The service learning model, dedicated exclusively to campus-based civic engagement and reflection, was formalized in 1969 and remains an important venue for the development of social justice. Cara Meixner observes that the contemplative practices of reflection, mindfulness, and social action encourage learners to "locate self by serving others" (2013, 317).

Like the service learning pedagogy, inquiry-based learning was also recognized in the 1960s, as new curricular design was proliferating. Embedded in an inquiry model is the notion of "deep structure learning" through experiential reflection and self-directed analysis (Roberts 2002). Similarly, the servant leadership movement in higher education that began in the 1970s resulted in the burgeoning of leadership programs and courses on most campuses today. Servant leadership programs and their accompanying practices are dedicated to developing learner characteristics that are consistently investigated in both SoTL and contemplative education: listening, empathy, awareness, stewardship, civic reflection, critical analyses, and compassionate and ethical understanding with action.

Respective programs that incentivized these particular practices also emerged. The Contemplative Practice Fellowship Program, established by the Center for Contemplative Mind in Society in 1997, was the earliest effort to reinforce the contemplative dimension of teaching and learning in higher education and craft a multidisciplinary curriculum that would include and encourage contemplative study. Central to the program was the creation of "new forms of inquiry and imaginative thinking to complement critical thinking" that will support "a more just and compassionate direction for society" (Bush 2010). The Carnegie Academy for the Scholarship of Teaching and Learning (CASTL) began in 1998, one year after the Contemplative Practice Fellowship Program. CASTL gave birth to the Carnegie Scholars Program, whose mission was to advance a scholarship of teaching and learning through individual faculty projects that would "investigate not only teacher practice but the character and depth of student learning that results (or does not) from that practice" (Hutchings and Shulman 1999, 13). Both the Contemplative Practice Fellowship and the Carnegie Scholars Programs from their inception were dedicated to the public dissemination and critical evaluation of the scholarship produced.

The second event critical to the growth of contemplative education and SoTL was the call for educational reform that began in the 1960s. This development was in part a response to Skinner's radical behaviorism and its emphasis on antimentalism and refusal to rely on nonobservable events as explanations for behavior (Richelle 1993). As the recognition grew that both internal and external events contributed to learning, revised educational theories proliferated. Central to these revisions was an expansion of ways of understanding that would include not only the cognitive but also the affective, moral, and spiritual development of students. The constructivist theory of Jean Piaget (1977) and Lev Vygotsky (1978); critical pedagogy of Paulo Freire (1970); transformative learning theory of Jack Mezirow (1981); feminist theories advanced by Carol Gilligan (1982), Mary Field Belenky and colleagues (1986), and bell hooks (1994); experiential or holistic learning theory of David Kolb (1984); and developmental theories of Robert Kegan (1982) and William Perry (1970) led to a burgeoning of questions about who students are and how they learn. These questions also led to a narrative that emphasized the growth of the whole person. Terms such as *connected knowing, interiority,* and *engagement with the self and others* introduced a new vocabulary in higher education. Pedagogies derived from these theoretical constructs began to appear in classrooms across the country.

The constructivist theorists and developmental scientists Piaget (1977) and Vygotsky (1978) posit that knowledge is constructed rather than transmitted and that it is derived from one's personal meaning-making and interpretations of subjective experiences. While Piaget is often associated with cognitive stages of development, he also discussed the "affective unconscious," arguing that while a person might be conscious of her or his thought content, there is often an ignorance of the functional and structural explanations that restrict and restrain that content. Piaget observed that with such an occurrence "there is no access to the internal mechanisms that direct [an individual's] thinking" (1977, 64). Vygotsky identified dialogue within a social context as of particular importance in the construction of learning and saw the development of "tools of the mind" as a necessary antidote to knowledge controlled and constructed by the environment. Vygotsky observed,

> Every function in the child's cultural development appears twice: first, on the social level, and later, on the individual level; first, between people (interpsychological) and then inside the child (intrapsychological). This applies equally to voluntary attention, to logical memory, and to the formation of concepts. All the higher functions originate as actual relationships between individuals. (1978, 57)

Current understanding of integrative and holistic learning is fixed not only in the philosophy of Plato and the theory of Dewey but also in the constructivist and cognitive theories of Piaget and Vygotsky.

The themes of cognitive development articulated by Piaget and Vygotsky are also reflected in Freire's critical pedagogy, whereby "knowledge emerges only through invention and re-invention, through the restless, impatient, continuing, hopeful inquiry human beings pursue in the world, with the world, and with each other" (1970, 72). Freire emphasizes pedagogical practices that lead to curiosity, self-empowerment, and transformation of the individual. For Freire, one cannot become human when inquiry, dialogue, and praxis are absent.

Influenced by Freire's (1973) concept of "conscientization" and critical consciousness, Mezirow's (1981) transformative theory centers on meaning-making and a "meaning perspective" as essential to transformative learning. In the past two decades, Mezirow has refined and revised his original theory of 1981. These revisions and further refinements mirror some of the changes in other theoretical conceptions of teaching and learning, specifically the holistic view of the learner. For example, in 1985 Mezirow expanded his emphasis on the three domains of learning (technical, practical, and emancipatory) seen in his original theory to include dialogical and self-reflective learning as critical in perspective transformation. Mezirow further refined his notion of "habits of mind" to not only embrace the cognitive dimensions but also offer an "alternate language" of imagination, intuition, dreams, inspiration, awareness, empathy, and transcendence (2000, 229). While transformative theory is often attributed to Freire (1970) and Mezirow (1981), John Dirkx (1998), Mary Rose O'Reilley (1998), Tobin Hart (2004), Laura Rendon (2009), Parker Palmer and Arthur Zajonc (2010), Alexander Astin, Helen Astin, and Jennifer Lindholm (2011), and Lisa Baumgartner (2012) have also revised Mezirow's understanding of "transformation" in substantive ways and in a manner that reflects a contemplative perspective at its core.

In contrast to Mezirow's theory, which focused on individual transformation, feminist theory is grounded in social transformation. Many feminist scholars situate their work in one of two bodies of literature: (1) women's connectedness to others as critical in knowledge building (Gilligan 1982; Belenky et al. 1986) and (2) a critical pedagogy that challenges patriarchy and power relations (hooks 1989). Like Freire's critical pedagogy, feminist theories emphasize a participatory epistemology in which the student's positionality, identity, and voice, undergirded by self-reflexivity and self-reflection, are salient in the construction of knowledge. Elizabeth Tisdell observes that positionality and identity as constantly evolving are directly connected to the affective and spiritual domain in that this domain "emphasizes the movement toward greater authenticity and the ongoing development of authentic identity" (2003, 207). Service and experiential learning practices emerged from feminist epistemologies, as do activist contemplative practices, which facilitate the development of intellectual capacities and the knowledge of the self as a human being (Rendon 2009).

Kolb's (1984) experiential theory focuses on four environments conducive to learning: the affective, symbolic, perceptual, and behavioral. Similar to Freire's and Piaget's theories, experiential learning theory holds that "learning is a holistic process involving the integrated functioning of the total person—thinking, feeling, perceiving, and behaving" (Kolb and Kolb 2005, 194). According to Alice Kolb and David Kolb (2005), the learner moves through the cyclical process of reflection and action, feeling and thinking.

Like Kolb and Kolb and Mezirow, the developmental theorists Kegan (1982) and Perry (1970) emphasize meaning-making as occurring in stages of development. Kegan notes that through "orders of consciousness" there is a "personal unfolding" of the learner in the shaping of experiences that mature into more complex mental systems (1994, 7, 9). Therefore, for Kegan this results in epistemological changes that have implications for the context in which these changes occur. Kegan calls for "holding environments," or a supportive space, a supportive classroom, where students are nurtured, or "held," as they move through these developmental changes (43). Akin to Kegan and influenced by Piaget, Perry also emphasizes "an intellectual Pilgrim's Progress" (1970, 3), or a developmental journey marked by epistemological shifts. Integrated within Perry's model is the focus on empathy in teaching and learning. According to

Perry, "Providing students with opportunities to discover and refine their own powers [is] the first prerequisite [for] the student's experience of being *met*" (1985, 5; emphasis in original).

This review of contemporary educational theories is by no means exhaustive. But the work of these particular theorists is a historical representation of modern educational reform and a conceptualization of the learner as an experiencing, thinking, and feeling human being, an idea central to contemplative perspectives and to many SoTL practitioners. The recognition of the learner as having an exterior *and* interior self is imagined in virtually all the major theories of learning produced in the last four decades as are many of the pedagogies derived from this vision. The origins of inquiry-based learning, experiential and service learning, dialogical communication, integrative and holistic learning, interdisciplinary learning, and collaborative learning, as well as introspection and attention processes, are firmly grounded in Freire's notion of a critical pedagogy, Piaget's affective development model, Vygotsky's "tools of the mind," Mezirow's "alternate language," and the participatory epistemology of Belenky and colleagues and Gilligan. Simulations and field experiences; textual readings; visualization; and problem solving through listening, reflection, writing, journaling, and collaborative group work, now common approaches in many college and university classrooms, are situated in the theories of Kolb, Kegan, and Perry. Each has conceptualized education as focused on the mind, body, *and* spirit of the student.

While theoretical attention to the whole student as a learner and knower is well substantiated in higher education, many of the actual classroom practices associated with these theories continue to be partially understood, underdeveloped, and inadequately engaged. For example, service learning courses should offer one of the clearest means for deepening learning, exploring self and personal beliefs, and broadening an awareness of social injustices. In many ways a well-executed service learning pedagogy *is* a contemplative practice. However, that the requisites of time, reflection, and mindfulness are often missing or partially constructed in the service learning classroom continues to be a central criticism of the service learning pedagogy. Service learning students, therefore, can have a well-crafted course but miss the meaning of this experience, an experience that leads to the understanding of self and others. Thus, a reification of stereotypes, a poorly articulated understanding of social issues, and an exacerbation of power differentials among groups can result (Furco 2011).

An inquiry-based learning pedagogy is plagued by some of the same issues observed in service learning. Virginia Lee (2004) defines the inquiry pedagogy as encompassing strategies that promote independent investigation as well as curiosity, initiative, critical thinking, imagination, and maturity. However, these dimensions are too often weakened by the rapidity of attention given to the method of inquiry. Akin to service learning, inquiry-based learning is a process, not a product-oriented approach, and yet many teachers still view themselves as what Trae Stewart calls "intelligence expert(s)" who interpret and enforce correctness of a product (2011, 38). Ellen Langer refers to this as a "mindlessness" in which we fail to attend to process but concentrate instead on ends (1997, xxiii). Therefore, more times than not, students see knowledge as restricted to one meaning and one that is self-irrelevant.

Process-oriented practices, including the most recent pedagogies of engagement, require a mindfulness that makes deep learning possible. Daniel Barbezat and Mirabai Bush define such mindful processes as those that "support mental stability" and by necessity allow focus and attention development, inquiry into one's own interiority, exploration of personal meaning, and the deepening of compassion and connection to others (2014, 11). Yet description and discussion of these introspective practices as integral to and undergirding pedagogies of engagement are often absent in college and university classes. My review of disciplinary journals, teaching and learning conferences, and professional conferences in the past decade clearly shows a dearth of use and assessment of introspective processes in the classroom. While SoTL scholars and researchers are committed theoretically to holistic learning, many of the actual practices studied and assessed by these same scholars are those that lack the introspection necessary for these practices to flourish.

Contemplative educators have embraced practices that center on interiority as the critical source for personal and intellectual growth and the strengthening of exterior ways of understanding. The teacher, poet, and writer Mary Rose O'Reilley notes that some classroom practices "crush the soul" and consistently asks, "What spaces [might we] create in the classroom that will allow students freedom to nourish an inner life?" (1998, 3). The professor and psychiatrist Robert Coles observes that the fundamental moral and spiritual questions asked by both children and adults are those that reside within our interiority. He sees "overwrought language and overwrought theory" as the place where we lose our humanity and where our sensibilities die (quoted in Swick 2010). The economics professor Daniel Barbezat (2015), emphasizes awareness, attention, and introspection as critical to the student's comprehension of course material and development of self-awareness. Arthur Zajonc, a professor of physics and the former director of the Center for Contemplative Mind in Society, asks if an education of critical reasoning, writing, speaking, and scientific and quantitative analysis is sufficient. He suggests that "the sharpening of our intellects with the systematic cultivation of our hearts [might be] of equal if not greater importance" (2006, 2). Tobin Hart (2010), a professor of psychology, advocates "a new kind of liberal arts . . . that brings us to the center of our *humanitas* . . . [and unlocks] virtue, genius, and delight." Olen Gunnlaugson and colleagues consider the contemplative dimensions of "presence, discernment, and equanimity" as those that might transform "disengaged forms of academic analysis and disenchanted and instrumental habits of mind and life" (2014, 5).

While contemplative educators have articulated specific practices for accessing the interior and the spiritual, they often fail to expand their conversations beyond the parochial contemplative gates. Although impressive assessment is occurring in the laboratory on the physiological outcomes of meditation, evaluations of specific classroom pedagogies are lacking. As with SoTL's reluctance to engage the contemplative in its public and scholarly conversations and practices, ACMHE has neglected SoTL methods, research, and signature pedagogies. The ACMHE's past six conferences reflect little incorporation of SoTL approaches in spite of ACMHE's commitment to teaching and learning in higher education. SoTL's expertise in these areas could potentially yield an expanded consciousness about the significance of introspective methods to deep learning, particularly to those outside the contemplative walls. Similarly, SoTL's well-developed assessment approaches could offer another tool for evaluating the integration of exterior and interior methods. Neither the SoTL nor contemplative education movements appear to draw on the other for support, elaboration, and expansion of each's programs. Each seems to exist in a well-insulated silo in which exterior and interior ways of knowing are often estranged rather than complementary. Susan Burggraf and Peter Grossenbacher summarize the potential of this complementarity:

> Traditional modes of inquiry in the liberal arts, such as analytical and critical thinking, require intellectual engagement with text, laboratory experimentation, and so on. Due to their inward focus, contemplative pedagogical methods can enrich and complement the disciplinary modes of inquiry already used in the liberal arts by enhancing the learner's personal connection with the subject matter. (2007, 1)

Zajonc (2008) also acknowledges the significance of analysis and critical thinking in education but points to the importance of contemplative and reflective practices in helping students locate and cultivate all the capacities they might have. The failure to uncover these capacities results in a partial knowing, one that lacks the depth afforded by access to the interior self.

The integration of the contemplative into teaching and learning is an urgent and particularly profound need in today's colleges and universities. Three major factors might explicate this need. The first factor relates to the current climate of higher education. The corporatization of colleges and universities and the resulting emphasis on professional rather than liberal studies contributes to creating students and teachers who are frantic, frightened, and often blinded by a societal value system that is at odds with their intuitive knowing. Students are pressured into choices and goals at a time when many are developmentally ill prepared; many have no sense of self or confidence in their agency and authenticity. Both teachers and students are hyperventilating through course materials. A national study of spirituality in higher education by researchers at the Higher Education Research Institute, a research and policy organization on postsecondary education at UCLA, offers evidence for what students need and teachers and schools fail to provide (Astin, Astin, and Lindholm 2011). Three-fourths of the 112,232 first-year students surveyed in institutions across the United States reported that they are "searching for meaning/purpose in life," a search not addressed in today's curriculum. The researchers expand on this finding by pointing out that today's students are preoccupied with the "big questions" of life such as "Who am I?"

"What are my most deeply felt values?" "Do I have a mission or purpose in my life?" "Why am I in college?" "What kind of person do I want to become?" "What sort of world do I want to create?" (1). In other words, they are asking permission to contemplate and make meaning out of their classroom experiences.

William Powers observes that while the human struggle to reconcile our exterior and interior selves has existed through the ages, "the balance has tilted decisively in one direction. We hear the voices of others, and are directed by those voices, rather than by our own. We don't turn inward as often or as easily as we used to" (2010, 3). According to Daniel Holland, the adoption of corporate values represents a "careerist" rather than "visionary" perspective at the very time an alternative to the corporate culture is required (2006, 1843). Hart modulates Holland's perspective on corporatization in noting that "the goal of training people for the marketplace is honorable and reasonable, but it is incomplete" (2012, 28).

The second factor, related to the first, is an epistemological, pedagogical, and ethical one. The academy's commitment to educating the *whole* student and to *social responsibility* is highlighted by the majority of today's institutions. An examination of college and university mission statements clearly reveals these commitments. They include phrases such as "formation of a complete individual for a world in flux" (Bowdoin College), "leading change to improve society and to help solve the world's greatest problems" (University of North Carolina), "confronting the human condition and human experience" (Emory University), "social transformation and service to the world" (Harvard University), developing "compassionate graduates and the discovery of solutions to human problems" (Howard University), "instillation of a sense of responsibility for each other and for the broader world" (Dartmouth College), and "promoting the public welfare by exercising an influence in behalf of humanity and civilization" (Stanford University). These statements derive from the history of higher education discussed above, one that conceptualizes education as attending to the cognitive and affective dimensions of the student and that unambiguously asserts responsibility for a just and more humane world. Yet Ira Harkavy observes that "disciplinary ethnocentrism, tribalism, [and] guildism strongly dominate American universities today and strongly work against their actually doing what they rhetorically promise to do" (2006, 14). The implementation of the mission is fraught with multiple difficulties, chief among them an inadequate understanding of practices for this implementation.

The third factor is what Daniel Pink observes as a seismic shift occurring in the advanced world. He notes that we are quickly moving away from an economy and social structure grounded in "logical, linear, computer-like capabilities of the Information Age to an economy and a society built on the inventive, empathic, big-picture capabilities of what's rising in its place, the Conceptual Age" (2005, 1). He further explains,

> The future belongs to a very different kind of person with a very different kind of mind—creators and empathizers, pattern recognizers, and meaning makers. These

people—artists, inventors, designers, storytellers, caregivers, consolers, big picture thinkers—will now reap society's richest rewards and share its greatest joys. (1–2)

Academic institutions are tasked with preparing students for this complexity and new way of thinking. The skill sets required will be markedly different from what we now know. Lisa Napora suggests that the skill set for the twenty-first century must include an education whereby students

> become empowered, informed, and responsible citizens as well as cultivat[e] complex cognitive skills (e.g., the ability to evaluate, analyze, interpret, reflect, and think critically and creatively). This contemporary skill set reflects an expansion of the goals of education beyond the acquisition of information. Many of these skills require awareness of one's own cognitive processes and the ability to regulate them (i.e., metacognition). (2011, 64)

Like Pink and Napora, Barbezat (2015) observes that the requisites for the twenty-first century will most likely include a particular skill set of accomplished listening, speaking, and connecting to the other, "a type of intra- and interpersonal awareness, compassion, focus and discernment."

As early as 2007, the formative document *College Learning for the New Global Century*, from the Association of American Colleges and Universities, reported a silence about what college graduates should know and be able to do, "yet off the public radar screen, evidence is mounting that Americans can no longer afford to ignore these questions" (8). Little seems to have changed. We are on new terrain navigating unfamiliar territory. The skills and accompanying pedagogies that we as teachers saw as important a decade ago may not be the ones necessary for students today. In fact, all the evidence unequivocally suggests they are not. The very good news is that this seismic shift affords new and unparalleled opportunities for students and teachers. It allows us to create different types of classroom spaces that access and nurture interior ways of knowing that in turn deepen exterior ways of knowing. It enables us to expand, reimagine, and reenvision our ways of being in the classroom. It also allows us to "reframe" our conceptual systems, thus changing what we see and attend to (Hobson and Morrison-Saunders 2013). As Brendan Ozawa–de Silva (2014) suggests, we might be best served by taking an expansive perspective and attending to a multiplicity of practices and methods, some of which have been marginalized and forgotten. The integration of the contemplative into SoTL is an opportunity to travel this new terrain with greater certainty.

2 Contemplative Practices in Higher Education

> Contemplative pedagogy need not involve esoteric practices. Almost any classroom exercise may be transformed into a contemplative one . . . by slowing down the activity long enough to behold—to facilitate deep attention to and intimate familiarity with—the object of study.
>
> —Rick Repetti, "The Case for a Contemplative Philosophy of Education"

A MULTIPLICITY OF definitions exist regarding contemplative education. Terms such as *contemplative pedagogy, contemplative practices, contemplative studies,* and *contemplative epistemology,* as well as *mindfulness* and *meditation practices,* are often used interchangeably. Such proliferation in terms often obfuscates rather than clarifies, makes assessment of these practices difficult, and leads to reticence embracing the practices by many outside the contemplative community. Even those within this community continually discuss the need for a careful differentiation of terms. In fact, as I write this chapter, the online discussion of the Association for Contemplative Mind in Higher Education has to do with what some contemplative scholars describe as a looseness in terminology within the field, an issue further explored in the coda. Contemplative methods can be conceptualized in a variety of ways. Victoria Smith (n.d.), for example, speaks of contemplative practices as "hygienic" and as "modes of inquiry." Hygienic practices are those that calm the mind and facilitate focusing by quieting the sympathetic and parasympathetic nervous system. As modes of inquiry or complementary ways of knowing, contemplative practices develop the life of the mind beyond intellectual dimensions and inclusive of emotions, the senses, and the self. For Harold Roth, contemplative practices use both third- and critical first-person approaches and are introduced to students in "a spirit of open inquiry," with no mandated beliefs, dogmas, or assumptions about the usefulness of these methods (2014, 100).

For the purpose of this chapter, contemplative practices are discussed as specific pedagogical exercises that may be integrated in traditional liberal arts courses. They are defined as metacognitive modes and first-person investigations that nurture inner awareness, concentration, insight, and compassion. Exercises such as silence, reflection, witnessing or beholding, listening, dialogue, journaling, and self-inquiry are prototypical. Each of these is solidly anchored in mindful attention, the sine qua non of all contemplative practices. The Center for Contemplative Mind in Society expands this definition with its tree of contemplative practices, depicted in figure 2.1. The center places practices in six clusters, while being clear that these practices are not exhaustive or definitive, with exemplars in each of the clusters: activist (volunteering, bearing witness), creative (journaling, contemplative arts), generative (meditation, visualization), movement (dance, qigong, yoga), relational (dialogue, deep listening, storytelling), ritual or cyclical (retreats, ceremonies), and stillness (quieting the mind, silence).

Many of these practices are clearly located in today's classrooms under the rubrics of transformative, critical, experiential, and engaged learning. The expanded development and assessment of specific practices associated with these rubrics have been advanced in SoTL investigations. My review of the Carnegie scholar projects, mentioned

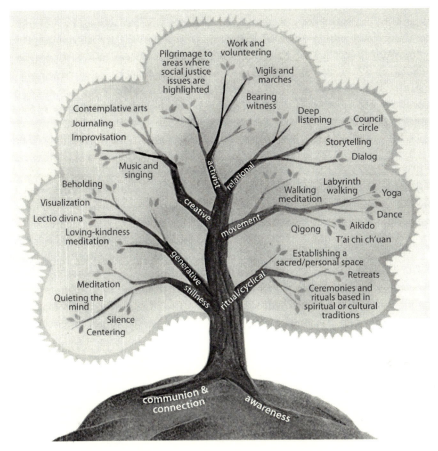

FIGURE 2.1. Tree of contemplative practices (© The Center for Contemplative Mind in Society; concept and design by Maia Duerr; illustration by Carrie Bergman)

in the introduction, illustrates some of these practices. What, then, marks such practices as introspective or contemplative? Several critical dimensions are central to this question. Tobin Hart notes that contemplative practices are located in an epistemology of inquiry that "includes the natural human capacity for knowing through silence, looking inward, pondering deeply, beholding, [and] witnessing the contents of our consciousness" (2004, 29). The epistemic question for Hart is not *what we know* but rather *how we know*. This quality of resonant knowing is located in interiority, and for Hart it is a missing link in today's curriculum and methods of teaching, "affect[ing] student performance, character, and depth of understanding" (128). Similarly, Fran Grace asks, "Without first knowing how the mind operates, how can we know anything outside of it?" (2011, 116).

Attentiveness to what one is trying to understand is the root of all contemplative practices. It stabilizes and informs the wandering mind. Juan Mah y Busch differentiates certain transformative practices from contemplative pedagogies by arguing that critical pedagogies specifically, as well as many other of the transformative modes, employ word-based, linear dialectics, whereas contemplative modes appreciate the dialogical, or a "wordless dimension of experience," one that is "inherently more relational and multidimensional than a dialectic" (2014, 126–128). Drawing from the work of the literary theorist M. M. Bakhtin, Mah y Busch discusses dialogism as consisting of numerous subjectivities that coexist; it is not about speech (though conversation can be dialogical). He suggests that while the dialectic is critical to analytic thought and discursive practices in the classroom, its limitation rests in its consistent privileging of words over wordlessness. Julia Hobson and Angus Morrison-Saunders continue the discussion by attending to the ways we consider our teaching practices. They hold that "the conceptions and system of conceptions that we use in teaching and learning change what we observe and notice" (2013, 774). They urge us to consider what is left in and what is left out of higher education's conversations about teaching and learning.

Arthur Zajonc holds that the "cultivation of attention" is central to all learning paradigms and yet, ironically, excluded by conventional pedagogy (2008, 9). This void leaves students without that which leads to creativity, insight, balance, and imagination; therefore, it leaves them without access to their interiority. Like Zajonc, Peter Grossenbacher and Alexander Rossi (2014) emphasize the importance of present-moment awareness, urging educators to understand the relevance of this information for teaching and learning. Daniel Barbezat and Mirabai Bush (2014) speak of contemplative exercises as a return to the understanding of the student as a whole person. As previously noted, they articulate four distinct objectives of contemplative practices: (1) focus and attention building that sustain mental stability, (2) location of self in the content of the course that deepens understanding of the material, (3) compassion and connection to others that lead to the moral and spiritual characteristic of education, and (4) inquiry into the nature of the self and the mind. Therefore, Barbezat and Bush see the contemplative dimension as grounded in a critical first-person inquiry, one that accesses and engages interiority, attends to the production of knowledge in a particular manner, and offers a much-needed portal for the birth of insight, creativity, and personal resonance in the classroom.

Contemplative educators call for an integral model of knowing that canvasses both interior and exterior epistemologies. For them the contemplative, first-person modes are not in conflict with the more traditional, third-person classroom approaches in many classrooms but rather complement, enrich, and expand these approaches. For example, Olen Gunnlaugson and colleagues observe that contemplative practices are transdisciplinary, and therefore, "to the extent that most higher educational settings have at least an implicit or tacit contemplative dimension . . . the foundational assumption [is] that any course can be taught with a contemplative orientation" (2014, 4). Barbezat and Bush expand on this:

> Contemplative and introspective methods are complements to traditional teaching methods . . . [offering] a range of extensions and even transformations for traditional lecture and discussion formats. Rather than abandoning or rejecting abstract, analytical thought, contemplative modes can help students more deeply understand material and can integrate third-person views better into their own lives through the examination of their own experience of the material. (2014, 83)

As discussed in the introduction, I do not intend to conflate contemplative and SoTL approaches to classroom practices or to marginalize the ways they are substantively different in some of their goals and methods. To do so would disempower a conversation that is necessary for the growth of both movements. However, many of the practices that follow are located in SoTL and in contemplative education, albeit sometimes the practices are decidedly dissimilar in how they are accessed and approached in the classroom. Remarkably, the integration of contemplative and SoTL perspectives in the classroom addresses much of what higher education espouses and yet has failed to accomplish. For example, the Association of American Colleges and Universities asks,

> How . . . do we prepare students to cultivate their own inner resources of spirit and moral courage? How do we enable them to engage moral and social dilemmas with clarity about their own values as well as the capacity to hear and respond to others' deeply held commitments? How do we prepare graduates to make difficult ethical choices in the face of competing pressures? And how, without proselytizing, do we foster students' own development of character, conscience, and examined values? (2007, 23)

Similar questions are raised by Pat Hutchings and Lee Shulman and the Carnegie Academy for the Scholarship of Teaching and Learning (CASTL):

> What are our students really learning? What do they understand deeply? What kinds of human beings are they becoming—intellectually, morally, in terms of civic

responsibility? How does our teaching affect that learning, and how might it do so more effectively? (1999, 15)

Germane to both the Association of American Colleges and Universities and CASTL questions is the centrality of interior dimensions as critical learning outcomes of a liberal education. At the heart of all of these questions are (1) the recognition that new ways of knowing and learning, those that respond to the entirety of students' lives and to the issues they now (and will) navigate, are requisites for an education in the twenty-first century and a life of meaning and depth; (2) civic, moral, and spiritual development is, in fact, a domain of higher education practices; and (3) teacher recognition that pedagogical practices that address students' both interior and exterior lives can no longer be relegated solely to spaces and individuals outside the classroom.

The following practices are those that contemplative educators see as critical in the classroom. All these are grounded in introspection and self-reflection and are important means for accessing interiority. The central core of these practices is the disruption of unproductive habits, allowing the development and maturation of awareness and the cultivation of compassion. Contemplative educators recognize that no one contemplative method fits all students, all teachers, all classes, all disciplines, and all pedagogical goals. Contemplative scholars also remind us that contemplative practices are not intended to take the place of additional types of productive pedagogical methods. However, they do maintain that a content-driven contemplative dimension can be engendered across disciplines, including science, technology, engineering, mathematics, accounting and finance, and business (Repetti 2010). SoTL practitioners will easily recognize many of the contemplative practices discussed below. In fact, much of SoTL research has been aimed toward understanding these practices more fully. Some of these practices may be less familiar or intentionally avoided or dismissed for many of the reasons discussed in Chapter 3. The intent here is to explore how contemplative practices are deeply embedded in good teaching and learning. Thus, they will resonate for SoTL practitioners in compelling and practical ways, potentially strengthening and expanding classroom practices.

Stillness and Silence

The speed, chatter, busyness, and anonymity of many of today's classrooms might contribute to a breadth of knowledge but do so at the expense of depth and meaning-making. This classroom ethos and the losses that result from it are significant barriers to interior development, self-understanding, understanding of others, and deep learning. William Powers refers to this as a "traffic jam" at the center of our lives (2010, 13). This traffic jam has enormous implications for learning. In silence, insights and analyses initially emerge, and in silence we locate our interiority and self-knowledge. As Mara Adelman says, "Without it [silence], we never feel quiet within ourselves" (2014, 59).

We are a culture that fears silence and one that is far more comfortable with noise. As Grace (2011) observes, noise is addictive in that distractions are a welcome respite from our real lives. The world of higher education embodies this comfort. To teachers professionally socialized to both privilege words and bestow them, silence can be an intimidating or uncomfortable process. Many of us see silence in the classroom as a failure to do our job, to disseminate a certain type of knowledge or generate dialogue and activity in our classroom. We may feel a responsibility for the student anxiety that often results when there are no accustomed words on which to land. Still others of us might resist silence if we interpret it as a waste of classroom time or a luxury not to be indulged in the classroom hour. Some of us feel a dis-ease in navigating silence. As Katherine Schultz (2009) notes, many teachers lack the ability to interpret and listen to student silence and, therefore, fail to see it as a method of participation and a construct for knowledge.

A substantive body of literature in higher education supports these interpretations, as reflected in the consistent problematizing of silence in the classroom. Silence is often treated as a form of student resistance, oral incompetency, or boredom and, therefore, a response to be remedied. These interpretations of silence in the context of learning, however, are not universal. Patrocinio Schweickart, for example, observes that for Filipinos silence is emblematic of cognitive activity and agency; silence "attends wisdom" (1996, 306). Many First Nations peoples speak of silence as superior to words, the single most important venue for learning, and "the sign of perfect equilibrium . . . the absolute balance of body, mind, and spirit" (Ohiyesa 2001, 7). In his study of silence in Japanese classrooms, Dat Bao found that both talk and silence are valued collectively in the Japanese academic system. He calls for "a move beyond the colonialization perspective . . . [and the] Western-dominant angle" (2015, 51). Bao found that silence in Japanese students is a powerful communication tool and one that, along with talk, offers a balance in every learning scenario. Sandra Braman (2007) discusses the historical conceptualizations of silence, pointing out that while silence is commonly thought of as an absence, there is a well-developed understanding of silence as presence resulting from a clear purpose and agency.

The call for silence in the classroom is a powerful pedagogical tool used by contemplative educators. It is the wellspring for all other contemplative practices. Although higher education is reluctant to embrace silence as an important method in teaching and learning, some have espoused it outside contemplative pedagogies. The constructivist theorist Lev Vygotsky might be one of the first to speak of silence in learning, suggesting that cognitive maturation moves from external vocalization to internal, or "silent," private speech. According to Vygotsky, "Inner speech is for oneself; external speech is for others" (1986, 225). In this conceptualization, opportunities for silence in the class are an imperative for self-awareness and learning. Likewise, Thomas Bruneau put forward the notion of "slow time," or a reflective, inner time, to think in the classroom (1973, 21). More recently, scholars such as Guy Claxton have expanded Vygotsky's and Bruneau's notions of silence by emphasizing the "knack of delicate inward attention," or focusing, a "thinking at the edge" that leads to "the development of a broad epistemic culture" in classrooms (2006, 351, 360). Gesa Kirsch speaks of the use of silence as "in line with what a number of composition scholars suggest about the power of silence as a rhetorical tool" (2009, 8). This rhetoric of silence has been popularized by many teachers, including Cheryl Glenn, professor of English at Penn State, who talks of silence as a "rhetorical art . . . a creative or ethical resource within the college classroom and for college writers" (2004, xiii). Similarly, the Bryn Mawr College lecturer in English Ann French Dalke defines silence as an alternative way of knowing that is the center of the learning process. She states, "When we do not speak, we may listen, hear, understand, even communicate in other ways. If language distorts, silence may open us to revelation" (2002, 53). George Kalamaras advances an epistemological model evolving from silence. Silence, for Kalamaras, is "a generative condition for discourse theory . . . [and] for writing theory and practice" (1994, 160). Like Kalamaras, Angelo Caranfa (2004) also posits a model of education based on silence. He urges instructors to find ways to use silence as a major pedagogical mode.

The theoretical approaches discussed above offer an important understanding of silence, but the question remains: How do these epistemologies translate into practical approaches in the classroom? In his theory of education grounded in silence, Caranfa points out that reading and writing are two practices that support his model in that they are ways to know the self. According to Caranfa, "It is the silence of reading and writing that engages the students in the process of self-understanding. . . . During these solitary reflections, we bring together reflective and imaginative thinking" (2004, 229). The history professor Robert Zaretsky (2013) describes the use of silence in the context of sustained "pauses," imagining that such pauses might "bump [his students] into new thoughts not just about history but also their own selves [and] better prepare them to bump into other selves: be they historical actors, fictional characters or our fellow men and women." In her ecology class the professor of pedagogy Barbara Patterson uses a pause as the initial step in contemplative practices, a close observation of what is arising in the self. "By stretching open the spaces that might prematurely fill with conclusions, contemplative pedagogies [that begin with a pause] make room for discipline based content" (2011, 158). Silent pauses, therefore, are used by many teachers for a variety of reasons. They afford a respite, a slowing down for noticings, or a focus on what has just been said, read, or heard. The pause of silence provides an unmonitored space for reflection, creativity, and imagination with no interruption or imposition.

Ros Ollin's (2008) research on "silent pedagogy" centers on the instructor's silence in the classroom. Some teachers reported their own silence during software slideshow presentations in which they showed images without words. One teacher reported that if she had communicated effectively on the slide, "vocalisation was extraneous." Other teachers reported that this approach "made students think for themselves, rather than being told or guided by words" (2008, 273). Ollin also speaks of movement and activity in the classroom as potentially a silent pedagogy:

> Kinaesthetic activities, such as sculpting in clay or the use of drawing, rather than talking, were described by a number of participants as a means of developing a fresh perspective: "Drawing your problems, drawing your ideas rather than talking about it." Here it was suggested that silent visual representation enabled students to engage in creative activity without the need for a vocalised performance, which might tend to steer them towards producing what was conventionally expected. This "creative silent space" provided an opportunity to take a fresh look at an idea or an issue. (273)

Communal silence is another mode of classroom stillness. The West Point professor of poetry Marilyn Nelson begins all her classes with a five-minute period of silence, what she sees as relevant to teaching poetry as a "slow art." She describes this process and its relationship to the course: "They turn off the lights, loosen their ties; some of them take off their shoes and sit cross-legged on the floor. I set the timer. We close our eyes; we enter silence" (2001, 548). From this place of silence her military cadets begin to write their poetry. Nelson reflects on her contemplative stance and this experience of silence in teaching poetry in a military institution: "I hope that by teaching these twenty-eight cadets how to find and hold interior quiet, I am giving them the where-withal of wise conflict resolution. Perhaps poetry will help them to lead others toward peace" (552). Edward Sarath, a professor of music and the chair of the Department of Jazz and Contemporary Improvisation at the University of Michigan, has designed a transpersonal approach to improvisation in which students silently contemplate before a performance that is part of the course. He constructed what he refers to as "Silence Studies" in his classes and uses silence as an aspect of the music itself (2003a, 205).

Some instructors incorporate silence as an important epilogue to the viewing of a film. Following a film that typically exposes the "-isms we carry around with us," the University of Toronto professor Edmund O'Sullivan, uses a "spot check," or a four- to five-minute silent period, with the caution that students practice composure and a centeredness. O'Sullivan describes the after experience of sitting in silence:

> Without cross-talk we invited people to go around and speak. People felt like they could be authentic and speak from where they were. . . . These things have to be dis-cussed and worked through. We don't have to push away controversy to have peace. An energy developed out of this that allowed people to see what others actually think, rather than what they think they think. (2003, 189)

For O'Sullivan silence was a necessary prior process to interrogation of the film's meaning.

Like Nelson, Sarath, and O'Sullivan, I, too, use a communal silence in virtually all my psychology and women's studies classes and introduce this notion of silence initially through music. I explain to my students that the manner of entering the activity of learning is important. For me music and silence are critical doors to what will follow in the classroom. Music provides both a context for silence and a hospitable way to introduce it. Initially, students are more likely and prepared to sit in silence when contemplative music is playing. While I refrain from the use of many words, I do remind students before the music begins to breathe deeply and concentrate on the in and out movement of the breath, processes that are more likely to facilitate attention and awareness. From that groundwork I gradually move toward minutes of silence, without music and without my guidance, in the sixty- to seventy-five-minute class. The request for a moment of silence at any point during the hour is any class member's call. Often, I will ask for a minute of silence if circumstances warrant, but as the class progresses through the semester, students find their own comfort in calling for silence when they feel the need. If I use presentation software on a given day, I insert a slide labeled "Sevasana in Our Classroom," which students learn to recognize as a silent moment to reflect on and consider what we have been discussing thus far in class. *Sevasana* is the final pose in the yogic tradition, whereby one relaxes, allowing the body to process the postures completed. Similarly, I will ask students to sit in silence and consider what they are hearing. Following the silences in the classroom, we might talk about why silence was needed, what we found from it, and what we might do because of it. Sometimes we will write about it. However, more times than not, we will merely let the experience be and move on. Just as the moment and spirit of the class determine our call for and welcoming of silence, so do they govern the nature of its ending. The practice of silence helps us both engage and disengage according to what the moment requires.

Many punctuate the start of silence or a pause with a meditation bell. David Borker, professor of accounting and management at Manhattanville College, uses a bell to introduce silence in his classes. On the first day, he offers this simple directive:

> I would like you to consider a short practice we could do at the beginning and end of class that involves ringing a bell like this one three times. [*ring bell once*] Some students have found that it helps them to reduce stress and focus better during the class. Would you be interested in trying it out for a while? (2013b, 52)

If there is interest, Borker explains how the process will work in the classroom and why it is being offered. In his classes at Naropa University, Richard Brown also uses the mindfulness bell at intervals during the classroom hour. He urges his students to simply "listen to the sound of the bell [and] when thoughts or emotions arise while listening return to the sound itself" (2011, 82). Brown's students adjust easily to the rhythm when used regularly, and the class settles in to appreciate the "gaps."

Research on silence and learning is still in its infancy. Hart (2009) categorizes neuroscience research on the basis of breakthrough or clarity, experiences that he sees as corresponding to silence. Increased alpha wave activity is correlated with silence and stillness and appears to be related to the experience of insight and epiphanies, whereas clarity corresponds to neural synchrony and an increase in large-scale brain coordination that occurs during silence. Likewise, George Prochnik (2011) notes that fMRI studies of individuals in silent states demonstrate an enhanced ability to discriminate between important and unimportant stimuli. Ollin's 2008 qualitative research study with teachers indicated that the use of silence in teaching and learning can be multimodal and, therefore, not limited to the absence of talk. These included (1) writing in silence for "the opportunity for more measured thought and a more permanent record of that thinking," (2) visual silence, or "visual images used without vocalization and visual images used without verbalization," and (3) spatial silence, or "a giving space for students to think or feel, by removing the immediacy of the teacher's presence," and a space to silently "settle in, for example, to a new situation, a new experience or task" (272–274).

Part of the difficulty in measuring the effects and process of silence and, therefore, one of the reasons for the dearth in research might be unclear definitions of what silence means in the classroom. Many of the robust approaches to the measurement of silence are those that are confounded with meditation (Lutz et al. 2004). Therefore, the question that arises has to do with the relationship between silence and meditation. Are they identical, similar, derivative, or separate processes, and what defines each? Most contemplative scholars would suggest that meditation has as its primary goal the training of attention and consciousness of present experiences. Silence in the classroom can afford this type of awareness. Jack Miller (1994) argues that silence and meditation are integrally linked, particularly in creativity and insight. Silence as a pedagogical method in the classroom may be, in fact, a secular form of meditation, an opening into reflection, imagination, creativity, and self-awareness, all of which are in the service of learning. Sandra Braman (2007) posits a series of research questions, many germane to higher education: How does the contemplative practice of silence affect knowledge identification, memory, and amalgamation? What might be the circumstances in which silence in interpersonal settings such as the classroom is most productive? What conditions might prevent the productivity of silence? Exploration of such questions is necessary to support and protect silence as an integral practice in the classroom.

Mindfulness and Attention

Mindfulness is born and matures in silence. It is an attention to and beholding of our interior selves, a noticing of what is present in that self and in the moment. As such, it is a witnessing of our subjectivity that leads to an interruption and transcendence of our habitual perspectives and a freedom from our inflexible thought patterns. Contemplative scholars are quick to differentiate mindfulness from concentration. One of the enduring definitions of secular mindfulness is from Jon Kabat-Zinn, who speaks of it as "paying attention in a particular way: on purpose, in the present moment, and non-judgmentally" (1994, 4). Robert Roeser and Stephen Peck's review of research into mindfulness practices suggests that most human beings do not automatically develop this type of concentration and awareness unless they participate in some specific mental practice, which they call "contemplative" (2009, 128).

Ironically, many educational researchers point out that mindfulness is a type of cognitive training, and yet there has been little substantive discussion or practice of this element aside from within contemplative education. Mindfulness is both a venue for as well as a result of learning. In some important ways the study of mindfulness as it intersects with learning began with the work of the educational psychologist Ellen Langer, who articulated the ramifications of mindfulness for learning:

> When we are mindful, we implicitly or explicitly view a situation from several perspectives, see information presented in the situation as novel, attend to the context in which we are perceiving the information, and eventually create new categories through which this information may be understood. (1997, 111)

Although Grant Wiggins and Jay McTighe (2005) do not address mindfulness in learning, they are key scholars in curricular design. According to them, teachers must structure their classroom around the single question What are the desired results? Through their notions of "backward design" (8) and sequencing, Wiggins and McTighe argue that three stages are central to the design of courses: identify desired results, decide what will be appropriate evidence, and determine relevant learning experiences. Therefore, if deep understanding and learning of course material are the goals and if students are to see course material as relevant to the self and self-development, we must construct activities, approaches, and so on, that enable reaching these goals. In this type of paradigm, mindfulness and attention are the initial imperatives for meeting the goals of deep learning and understanding. Patterson (2011) underscores this observation when noting that contemplative pedagogies are most effective when they are sequenced starting with focused attention.

Kevanne Sanger and Dusana Dorjee expand the importance of mindful attention in the classroom by pointing to attention as a "key modulator of cognitive processing," allowing a differentiation between task-relevant and task-irrelevant stimuli (2015, 700). Similarly, Daniel Siegel speaks of cognitive mindfulness as the ability "to be open to contexts, embrace novel ways of perceiving, distinguish subtle differences in ideas, and create new categories of thinking" (2011, 48). Siegel argues that this type of mindfulness results in an improvement in how we think and how we approach the learning process. According to David Sable, mindful attention in the framework of higher education is "a complement to discursive analysis, an unbiased investigation of experience" (2014, 2). Therefore, mindfulness trains the mind to notice. Rick Repetti, assistant professor of philosophy at Kingsborough Community College in Brooklyn, points out that the many philosophical arguments presented in his classes lend themselves to the contemplative method of mindfulness, such as "imagining being a prisoner in Plato's cave, living in a Matrix-like illusion, or engaging in some philosophical role reversal" (2010, 9). He suggests that envisioning these roles through mindfulness is a more enriching and personally relevant experience for his students and one that develops their understanding of philosophical tenets more fully.

Barbezat and Bush refer to mindfulness as "the essential contemplative practice for the academy" (2014, 98). However, when one considers its cognitive correlates (well-developed discriminative abilities, deep understanding, awareness of the moment, increased concentration, and consciousness of other perspectives), mindfulness is the par excellence practice of *all* classroom practices. In a discussion of mindfulness Deborah Schoeberlein and Suki Sheth include its effects on teachers and point to the benefit of greater enhancement of their responsiveness to students as well as improved focus and awareness in the classroom: "When teachers are fully present, they teach better. When students are fully present, the quality of their learning is better" (2009, xi). The development of mindful attention can be cultivated in classrooms. As noted above, sitting in silence, if only for a few minutes at a time throughout the class hour, provides the first site through which access to the moment and to the self is possible.

Many mindfulness practices in the classroom have been shown to increase such capacities as perspective taking, empathy, and compassion. While these capacities are critical to developing citizenship in students, they are particularly germane to service learning and social justice pedagogies. Current research emanating from Stanford, Emory, and the University of Wisconsin has identified specific brain circuitry that controls compassion and finds that mindfulness practices strengthen this circuitry, leading to greater altruism and care for others (Suttie 2015). Most of institutional mission statements affirm the importance of these capacities and their development through curricula.

While mindfulness practices might seem more easily situated in humanities and social science classrooms, they are being increasingly integrated into science and mathematics courses. The Bryn Mawr chemistry professor Michelle Francl acknowledges that *contemplative scientist* might, in fact, sound like an oxymoron in a society that equates scientific methods with objectivity and denial of the personal. However, as Francl (n.d.) observes,

> a curriculum that includes contemplative practices has the potential not to merely produce scientists, but to allow scientists to engage in forming themselves. . . . The world cries out for reflective scientists, who can intentionally create a space in which to see their work in its full context—scientific, cultural, political and personal. Embedding contemplative practices, then, not just in any course, but in a course that is seen as rigorous and fundamental to the discipline, lets students grow as scientists

in a culture that acknowledges that such ways of seeing and relating to the world are useful for their work and not incongruent with what a scientist should be.

Francl uses a stillness exercise to quiet the mind and prepare for the classroom work that follows, what she calls "stilling to start: listening out." She observes that this exercise fosters patience with and attentiveness to the tasks at hand. The Harvard professor of physics and the history of science Gerald Holton (1998, xviii) refers to such a process as an "unforced pace" and a measure of "self-direction of the scientific imagination" that permits researchers to derive personal sources of inspiration that have been silenced by the scientific community.

As Barbezat and Bush point out, science courses demonstrate the exploratory and research nature of mindfulness practices. Mindful practices are imperatives for "the education of reflective scientists" (2014, 103). They highlight the work of the Amherst professor of physics Arthur Zajonc, who urges his students to generate a mindful attention to both natural and human-made objects, asking them to focus on some object in great detail, close their eyes, and imagine it with the same attention to detail. He then has students repeat this cycle until they have a vibrant image of the object in their mind. For Zajonc, such an exercise shifts students' awareness and approach to their work in transformative ways. Zajonc maintains that "the same values of clarity, integrity, and collegiality can infuse contemplative education as have supported natural scientific exploration" (2009, 16).

Susan Burggraf and Peter Grossenbacher (2007), professors of psychology at Naropa University, discuss their use of mindful attention as a laboratory approach in a psychology of perception course and a social psychology course. They point out that a mindful, reflective methodology enhances the learning laboratory by blending customary scientific inquiry (third-person methods) with contemplative inquiry (first-person methods). Like Zajonc, they urge their students to attend mindfully to their experiences in the same way that a biologist might use a microscope. According to Burggraf and Grossenbacher,

> Students come to appreciate the extent to which their usual conscious awareness of sensations [as in the case of the psychology of perception course] is drastically restricted. Such observations and inferences provide experiential insight into the research and theory standard in this field. (2007, 5)

Justin Brody (2016), mathematics and computer science professor at Goucher College and director of the college's Laboratory for Computational Cognition, incorporates contemplative methods to explore the mathematical infinite. In his course Contemplating Infinity, Brody teaches analytic meditation to his students as a method for deliberating Cantor's theorem, Godel's theorem, and Zeno's paradoxes. In his course syllabus, he describes analytic meditation as a form of mindfulness in which "an idea is processed using a[n] interplay of analytic and intuitive approaches. [Thus], it has the potential to provide both technical and intuitive insights into a question." Frank Wolcott, visiting professor of mathematics at Lawrence University, also approaches the teaching of mathematics with an emphasis on contemplative dimensions. He sees mindfulness in the classroom as a critical experiential context both in the teaching of mathematics and in mathematical research. In his introductory differential equations class, Wolcott integrates mindful reflection. He urges teachers of mathematics to consider how the doing of mathematics might include the experiential, and "reflecting on process was part of your process" (2013, 92). As he points out, mathematics can be a struggle for many students because it is often stripped of its humanity. Honoring student experience through contemplative reflection returns such humanity to the mathematics classroom, making it accessible and rich.

In an experiment on mindfulness and multitasking supported by the National Science Foundation, David Levy and his colleagues (2012) found an increased time on task and a decreased number of task switches following mindfulness training compared with no training. They also cite improved task memory. Levy describes mindfulness as a way to increase student awareness when texting, e-mailing, using Facebook, and using other digital practices. He asks students to observe the amount of time spent on such activities, how it affects their emotional states, and how it affects their attention. Levy argues that mindfulness training can educate students on the effects of multitasking and disproportionate reliance on technology, thus increasing awareness of experiences to cultivate and those to minimize (e.g., weariness, anxiety, lucidity, or calmness). "Once we observe and reflect, we can begin to see the kinds of choices we habitually make and why we make them. We are then in a position to evaluate these patterns . . . [and] to imagine alternative ways of behaving" (Levy 2016, 23).

I began incorporating mindfulness into my classroom as a SoTL practitioner. As a result of my Carnegie scholar project that investigated epiphanies in learning, I became increasingly aware of the importance that attention had for sudden moments of understanding in the learning process. This was long before my identification as a contemplative educator. Initially through silence and music at the beginning of class, I introduced my students to the notion that momentarily *just sitting* in purposive quiet is crucial to deep learning and critical analyses and to the cultivation of what Hart refers to as "an inner technology of knowing" (2004, 3). I have continued this process for more than two decades, and as I become more mindful, so does the classroom practice. I now invite my students to check in with their interior selves and be present to what they find there. I prompt them to notice what they are experiencing in their heads and their hearts and urge them to listen carefully and compassionately. The majority of my classes incorporate a service learning component. Therefore, I also remind students that we cannot consider, interrupt, and challenge oppressive systems until we are fully aware of them, pay attention to them, and reflect on them with a clarity of consciousness. Similarly, other contemplative scholars see such attention and mindfulness as not only critical components in learning but vehicles for ameliorating the ills of the world.

In his discussion of contemplative ecology, the Loyola Marymount professor Douglas Christie emphasizes the centrality of attention as a contemplative process "for deepening awareness and growing ethical maturity . . . oriented toward helping us see and inhabit and tend to the world fully and deeply" (2013, xi).

While focused and mindful attention is considered to be of critical importance in learning, it is seldom methodically nurtured in traditional classrooms. Consequently, it is little studied. However, a body of research is accumulating. As early as 1997 Michael Murphy, Steven Donovan, and Eugene Taylor demonstrated that mindful attention is related to perceptual and cognitive competencies. Shauna Shapiro, Kirk Brown, and Alexander Astin reviewed evidence relevant to meditation and its relationship to traditional classroom goals. *Meditation* in their report is an umbrella term that encompasses all mindfulness training exercises that have "the common goal of training an individual's attention and awareness so that consciousness becomes more finely attuned to events and experiences in the present" (2008, 6–7). It seems apparent that these features are paramount in learning and knowing. Shapiro, Brown, and Astin discuss three key research findings on mindfulness as relevant to cognitive and academic performance: (1) mindfulness encourages the ability for preparedness and attention orientation, (2) mindfulness suggests an increase in the ability to accurately and quickly process information, and (3) concentrative-based meditation ("disciplined, single-pointed focus attention") may have a positive impact on academic achievement (7). More recently, a number of the Contemplative Practice fellows, instructors who have incorporated mindfulness practices into their courses, have reported cognitive transformations in their students. Mirabai Bush summarizes these cognitive processes as "increased concentration, greater capacity for synthetic thinking, conceptual flexibility, and an appreciation for a different type of intellectual process" (2011a, 188).

Because of the momentum in developmental neuroscience a substantive number of studies are focusing on essential neurocognitive mechanisms. For example, Sanger and Dorjee (2015) note that studies concentrating on the relationship between attention performance and mindfulness training demonstrate improvements in disengaging and reengaging attention, retaining sensitivity to external stimuli, and monitoring conflict between thought, action, and emotion. Some of this research has focused particularly on adolescents and young adults of college age. Catherine Bradshaw and colleagues (2012) point to high levels of brain neuroplasticity and changes in the structure of the brain during this developmental period that make intervention strategies particularly effective. For example, Stefan Friedel and colleagues (2015) found that adolescents and young adults with higher levels of mindfulness demonstrated less thinning of the insula, a region of the cortex critical to self-regulation (i.e., maintaining self-control, managing negative emotions, and sustaining goal-directed behavior).

Students increasingly report stress, test-taking anxiety, depression, attention deficit hyperactivity disorder, and other mental disorders, and academic institutions are confronted with tasks unlike those in the past. A 2014 survey by the Association for

University and College Counseling Center Directors found that more than half the students seeking help from counseling centers have severe psychological problems, an increase of 13 percent in just two years (Reetz, Krylowicz, and Mistler 2014). As I write this chapter, four campus shootings perpetrated by students have just occurred. Teachers are also faced with challenges in the classroom. Mindfulness practices such as sitting in silence, stillness, and breath concentration may no longer be framed as extraneous to course goals, simply interesting, or just a popular innovation known as "Mc-Mindfulness" (Hyland 2016, 97) but rather as a requisite for the psychological, physical, emotional, and intellectual health of this generation of students. Current research supports this imperative. Aslak Hjeltnes and colleagues' (2015) qualitative study of mindfulness training for university students summarized five relevant themes reported by the student participants following eight weeks of mindfulness training: (1) locating an inner calm, (2) understanding that anxiety is experienced by many students and that it is not a solitary experience, (3) understanding how to focus in learning situations, (4) reframing fear and anxiety as curiosity in academic learning, and (5) experiencing greater self-acceptance when facing problematic situations. Likewise, Viviane Bueno and colleagues (2015) found that mindfulness practices improved sustained attention and executive control in young adults with attention deficit hyperactivity disorder.

The training of mindfulness in the college classroom, particularly if that classroom is filled with students in late adolescence and early adulthood, may be not only developmentally advantageous but also vital for efficient learning and the maturation of habits of the mind. It also offers opportunity for the growth of compassion for self and others, a quality promised in almost all academic mission statements. Silence and mindful attention are the critical components and common denominators in each of the practices that follow. The faculty members associated with many of these practices represent both large universities and small colleges and effectively demonstrate how these practices offer a balance to the rational and analytic aspects of disciplines and courses. They also implement contemplative practices in a variety of ways in the classroom.

Reflection

Reflection is perhaps one of the most used (and overused) terms and practices in teaching and learning discourse. Most teachers have an intuitive understanding that allowing students to pause for careful thought is a requisite for deep learning and meaning-making. It is embedded in all critical analyses and thinking. Grossenbacher and Rossi (2014) speak of reflection as metacognitive in that it incorporates an awareness of one's own mental processes. Terry Hyland (2016) states that self-awareness and knowing as well as compassion and empathy become rooted in academic courses through reflection. In *The Mindful Brain* Siegel calls reflection the "fourth R of education" and discusses how it "embeds self-knowing and empathy in the curriculum." He observes that "in neural terms . . . reflection would essentially be an education that develops the prefrontal cortex . . . our 'cortex humanitas,' the neural hub of our humanity" (2011, 261–262). Similarly, Feng Deng and colleagues hold that reflection is a crucial aspect to changing students' views of the nature of science, enabling them "to gain ample metacognitive experiences that may facilitate the process of conceptual change" (2011, 984). Sable further defines reflection by differentiating *reflection on action* and *reflection in action*, with the latter being "a particular kind of affective dimension, a reflexive disposition," that requires a mindfulness and an awareness of both interiority and exteriority (2014, 3). Reflection is an essential for all pedagogies, particularly team- and problem-based learning, inquiry-based learning, critical textual discourse, dialogue, and experiential activities. According to Donald Schön (1987), reflection is the significant dimension for all critical thinking.

Perhaps no pedagogy privileges the central role of reflection more than service learning. Paradoxically, it is the quality of reflection that remains at the center of controversy about the service learning pedagogy. The service learning researchers Robert Bringle and Julie Hatcher, define service learning as the "intentional consideration of an experience . . . [with the] presumption [that] community service does not in and of itself produce learning" (1999, 180). Their point is an important one. The provision of an experience in the classroom without consideration of its meaning is simply an experience that may or may not yield significance and worth.

While the discourse around reflection in teaching and learning is profuse, a fully developed understanding of what reflection is and how to introduce and structure associated processes into the classroom is often missing. Certainly, reflection and reflective critique are critical to the definition of SoTL as well as assessment of practices. SoTL scholars such as Carolin Kreber (2006) identify reflection as a crucial practice in SoTL. However, many of these same scholars admittedly state that the method itself remains poorly defined, comprehended, and conceptualized. Too, much of the focus in the SoTL literature is on teacher reflection. Surprisingly few studies are on student reflection and ways to implement it in the classroom. Some teachers report that they feel unprepared to facilitate students' deep analyses of material. Still others are uncomfortable with both the silence and the pauses that careful reflection necessitates. While many teachers are diligent in constructing reflective opportunities for the student, they fail to ensure that students make meaning and that they derive understanding of self and others. Teachers often assume that students make the connections they as teachers make. Most teachers have not been professionally socialized for these skills. Ellen Rose casts a different analysis. In her essay on the nature of thought in the twenty-first century, she suggests that much of the difficulty with the implementation of reflection in today's classroom is due to it being a "form of deep sustained thought for which the necessary conditions are solitude and slowness . . . [and] in our digital-cellular-online-robotic-information-saturated-hyper society, solitude and slowness are increasingly difficult to come by" (2013, 3–4).

Teachers ask students to reflect on the profound ideas of the disciplines they teach and the connections students see to their lives and the lives of others without proper preparation and time for this reflection. In this respect, teachers profoundly disserve students. Many of my own advisees point out that while they are consistently expected to reflect in their classes, they do not know how to reflect or are unclear as to what the term actually means. One result of this fragmented use of reflection is an increase in student anxiety, sense of failure, and confusion around meaning-making and analyses.

Numerous difficulties with reflective processes are located in failure to attend to dimensions of thinking and learning that are the initial requisites for and components of reflection, dimensions located in contemplative practices. Deborah Middleton, for example, differentiates contemplative reflection from the more traditional practice of reflection as being "a slower, deeper and more embodied process . . . [that brings] the student into a much more detailed relationship with their experience; reflecting at length on individual moments rather than generalizing" (2014). John Baugher expands this differentiation by suggesting that contemplative reflection centers on "the *how* and the *what* of the reflecting," urging teachers to consider how they might guide their students (2014b). Rose offers ways to nurture reflection in the classroom through the provision of the following:

1. Attention to the language used in the classroom: "Language . . . is the basic material with which the reflective mind works."
2. "Appreciation for the indeterminate products of the reflective intellect."
3. "Moments of silent withdrawal" and occasions for writing and reading that are not evaluated.
4. "Reflection-then-action" that inspires students to engage "in activities and experiences that are informed by their reflection." (2013, 103)

Although Rose is a professor of education who does not identify as a contemplative scholar, her guidelines for reflection are deeply embedded in the contemplative practice of reflection emphasized by Middleton, Baugher, and other contemplative educators. In an effort to accentuate the commonality among reflection practices Iddo Oberski (2014) suggests that other student-centered approaches might be excellent portals into contemplative pedagogy, such as allowing students to periodically sit quietly during the course of a lecture for the purpose of writing, listening with intention, reading, summarizing, or doing a short meditation.

While reflection is a complex, incomplete, and often flawed classroom process, emerging research and scholarship offer important perspectives and subsequent guidelines. Gina Musolino and Elizabeth Mostrom's (2005) overview of reflective strategies in SoTL and the assessment of these strategies is a reminder of the importance of reflection in SoTL and in virtually all contemplative approaches. The following reflective practices, grounded in both the contemplative and the SoTL perspectives, address the fragmented and problematic aspects of reflection, thereby deepening it in concrete ways.

Listening

The University of Maryland professor of communication and law Andrew Wolvin, observes the difficulty in teaching people to listen:

> Unfortunately, listening has come to be viewed, at least in American society, as a passive, simple act that we just do. The word "just" is all too frequently used to describe listening in the admonition "Just listen." This reduces listening, then, to the non-active, receptor, part of human communication. (2010, 1)

This passive approach to listening confounds our understanding of its significance in the learning process and lends itself to the multiplicity of definitions that we find in the pedagogical literature. Researchers and scholars often focus on listening as discriminative, critical, evaluative, empathic, or therapeutic, framing one or more of these under the umbrella of passive or active listening. As a classroom practice, deep listening facilitates a witnessing of both cognitive and affective dimensions with focus on what is heard. The Center for Contemplative Mind in Society articulates deep listening as a process that

> trains [students] to pay full attention to the sound of the words, while abandoning such habits as planning their next statement or interrupting the speaker. It is attentive rather than reactive listening. Such listening not only increases retention of material but encourages insight and the making of meaning. (n.d., "Deep Listening")

Concentrative listening to the self and to others brings a conscious lucidity. In listening we honor and care for ourselves and one another. However, it is a difficult process to acquire, and thus few of us take the time or know how to hear ourselves and others. We are socialized away from deep listening just as we are socialized away from silence. There is another reason also. As Norman Fischer says, listening can be dangerous and risky: "It might cause you to hear something that you don't like, to consider its validity, and therefore to think something you never thought before" (2003, 44). To choose not to listen and, therefore, not to see absolves us of our responsibility to act.

Mary Rose O'Reilley discusses listening by suggesting the possibility of "*listen[ing] someone into existence.* . . . Good teachers listen this way, as do terrific grandfathers and similar heroes of the spirit. The critical hearer, by contrast, crushes our spirits, leaves us with that sense of inner defeat" (1998, 21; emphasis in original). The voice of classrooms is often one of critique and criticism. Many of our students have grown accustomed to listening only to teacher censorship. Some also perceive judgment on the part of their peers. They are distrustful of and, at times, devastated by honest communication; they are fearful of both hearing the other and being heard by the other. They are well conditioned to this paradigm.

Contemplative listening empowers students to know and understand, to see their own agency in the construction of knowledge. It is a return to the first-person investigation that has been marginalized in teaching and learning arenas—often to students' peril. According to Hart, teachers can guide students in deep listening through various exercises that promote a careful reading or consideration of a passage or a viewing of a piece of art. For example, he suggests the following prompts to students in response to a textual reading:

> Observe the images that arise in your mind, the feelings in your body, thoughts, emotions, meanings, sounds, tastes, movement, symbols, shapes, or anything else that arises. How does your body want to move? How does this resonate within you? What do you want to do as you listen deeply? What story can you tell about this? Sit silently for several moments and just notice without judgment. (2004, 36)

David Borker (2013a), argues that deep listening practices in his classes afford a consciousness about the value-laden ethical frameworks that are used to explain economic outcomes. For Borker, the integration of deep and mindful listening allows an openness of the mind that in turn facilitates students' ability to find their own ethical framework.

Deep listening can also occur with others. Attention to and a mindfulness of experiences in each moment are central to communication and community with others. Charles Scott refers to these as "dialogical virtues," suggesting that the dialogical encounter, or turning to the other, is grounded in mindful listening (2014, 327). John Stewart and Milt Thomas (1995) describe dialogical listening as having four characteristics: (1) shared conversation that is open ended and unrestrained, (2) humility, trust, and recognition of the other as one who makes choices, (3) a focus on what is occurring between partners in a cocreation process, and (4) a presence to the process and to the partner. Carolyn Klein and Ann Gleig at Rice University see listening as a major venue for deepening relationality. Through their use of A. H. Almaas's Diamond Approach, a method of teaching in which students reflect aloud in the classroom about their own inquiry into a personal experience, Klein and Gleig describe this experience as "an opportunity to learn about the impact of another's presence on" students (2011, 191). In examining this approach to relationality, they state,

> we had three interrelated aspects in mind: relationship to self, to other, and to knowledge. In this context, many students reported a new recognition of how habitually self-critical they were and how restrictive this was, inside and outside the classroom. (191)

Shu-chin Wu, an Agnes Scott College history professor, describes a deep listening exercise used in one of her courses on the Vietnam War. In the format of a classroom debate she drew from the principles of Buddhist and Vietnamese scholar Thich Nhat Han to encourage students "to be open, non-judgmental, and unassuming, and to have the intent to understand rather than to criticize . . . to reiterate their opponents' arguments to demonstrate that they truly understand the entirety of the other side's perspective before they articulate their disagreements" (2011, 214). She reports that as the debate proceeded, classroom dynamics shifted. Students began to speak and listen with compassion and clearness that resulted in an intimate encounter with their own views and those of others with differing views. For Wu, the debate experience offered her students a contemplative space that made possible a greater understanding of history.

George Catalano (2012) emphasizes the importance of listening in his bioengineering course at Binghamton University, arguing that listening generates insight. In his initial class meeting with students Catalano explains that his fluid mechanics course will be taught from a different perspective from what they are familiar with in engineering and describes the development of "imaginative insight" (155) as the ultimate goal of the course and the critical element for bioengineers and all scientists. He proposes a research question that centers on contemplative listening as fostering a deeper understanding of course material as well as a mixed-methods approach to an analysis of both quantitative and qualitative data.

In an effort to partner with my students in more effective listening, I have constructed an exercise that I call mindful dyadic dialogue. I use this regularly in virtually all my courses but find it particularly helpful in my service learning courses as an intimate and safe way to discuss community experiences. There are many frameworks such as this one, and the one I offer is an amalgam of these. Central to the exercise is a full presence to the partner in a silent, nonjudgmental mode of listening carefully and intentionally for three minutes. Roles are then exchanged, so that the listener becomes the speaker for the next three minutes. I remind my students that in dialogue we are called on to be vulnerable with, humble to, and trusting of the person who is listening. As the listener, we are required to practice acceptance, compassion, and care. This is not an easy method for students—although as I sit in faculty meetings, I am reminded that this is very difficult for faculty members also! Mindful dialogical listening is particularly effective for classrooms in which difficult dialogues occur and are necessary. Deep listening is also helpful for the group work that so many SoTL practitioners construct in classes. Problem- and team-based groups, debates, fishbowl activities, and discussion groups as well as other cooperative learning group practices are significantly deepened when there is a careful integration of mindful listening.

Teachers can also benefit from contemplative listening practices. Louis Komjathy (2011) points out that many of us are listening to institutional restrictions, student apathy or anger, and our own uncertainties and reactions, all of which can be overcome through a contemplative perspective. He urges instructors to listen to something else and attend to what they are actually hearing and to what lies beneath appearances. This type of deep listening on the part of the teacher can only benefit the student's personal and academic development.

The method of wait time in the classroom has been an effective means for intentional listening, particularly for me as an instructor. I wait at least five seconds after asking a question or receiving a comment before responding to it. This method is not new. Richard Brown (2014) summarizes studies on wait time that have been done since the 1970s and points out that this method demonstrates an increase in student response, deeper understanding of content, more flexible and sophisticated student-teacher interactions, more complex information processing, and improvement in academic achievement scores. Wait time becomes a contemplative practice when it affords a mindfulness about speech and a respect for the listener that can change the class atmosphere. For Brown, wait time allows "teaching from the spaces between." He draws from the words of a professor who describes the experience of wait time:

> I chose to back off, just quit talking so much about what I think I know on the topic and to invite "intelligent space" to participate. Students' voices were timid as they entered the space. Then I noticed more voices appearing around the topic. There was more space in the discussion, more room for the other people in the class. I felt a little lighter, a little freer and immense gratitude for my willingness to just relax a little. (2014, 277)

The significance of deep listening in teaching and learning appears in the work of many scholars, from psychology and philosophy to the performance arts. However, as early as 1952 in his article published by the National Council of Teachers of English, Harold Anderson observed that there was a paucity of research on listening and its role in the classroom. The same remains true today with a few exceptions that focus on the role of listening in ESL and foreign language classes and those that are centered on active listening and the goal of understanding and interpreting another's meaning. Graham Bodie and Margaret Fitch-Hauser (2010) note that the current instruments and scales to assess listening still remain flawed. Andrew Wolvin calls for a quantitative and qualitative, mixed-methods approach, necessary to an understanding of "one of the most, if not the most, complex of all human behaviors" (2010, 2).

Like all other contemplative pedagogies, deep listening is a practice and is cultivated slowly, particularly in today's busyness. However, I am struck by the grace and willingness of students to engage in deep listening exercises and then practice them with commitment. I am a more careful and intentional listener with the use of wait time and in practicing my own listening skills along with my students. We become a more thoughtful and respectful class and more engaged community practitioners because of it.

Contemplative Reading

Ironically, while reading is central to the education of college students, it is also a pedagogy fraught with problems and challenges. The 2014 National Survey of Student

Engagement reported that the development of literacy skills in the majority of colleges and universities is restricted to issues of plagiarism, citations, and improvement of information sources. Over 60 percent of students appear to read information uncritically. A contributing factor to this type of indiscriminant reading may be how teachers position reading in our classrooms. Mark Sample (2011) suggests that one of the most significant errors made by college instructors is the privileging of only one type of literacy, silent reading, over all others. Societal valuing of constant activity, emphasis on breadth at the expense of depth, and the transition to a digital culture in which speed is favored over careful pondering shape our conceptualization of reading in the classroom. These characteristics are also antithetical to the critical literacy skills necessary for success in the twenty-first century (i.e., problem solving, critical thinking, effective communication, on-task attention, and compassion and care for others). Maryanne Wolf and Mirit Barzillai observe that reflective reading shapes the brain and thought, contributing to advanced metacognitive skills. They suggest that

> by the time the expert reader has comprehended a text at a deep level, all four lobes and both hemispheres of the brain have contributed significantly to this extraordinary act—a neural reflection of the many processes involved. . . . [H]ow deeply we read shape[s] both the brain and the thinker. (2009, 34)

Some teachers are now recognizing that reflective reading enhances sophisticated cognitive development and complex reasoning. This approach is often referred to in the teaching and learning literature as deep reading, slow reading, or text rendering. In the contemplative tradition this type of reading is referred to as the *lectio divina*, or what Repetti (2010) refers to as a text-based mindfulness. The tradition of *lectio divina* is an adaptation from early Judaism's way to read and interpret the Hebrew Bible. In the Christian tradition it became known as contemplative reading and had its origins in monasticism. The *lectio divina* requires a concentrative focus on a sentence or paragraph, a type of dwelling on the words. Typically, students are asked to read and reread passages, noticing what resonates for them. Many of today's contemplative scholars, in both secular and faith-based institutions, point to the use of the *lectio divina* as not only a way to challenge and halt the chaotic speed reading of today's college student but also a method for deep personal reflection and connection.

Susan Wegner, professor of art history at Bowdoin College, describes the use of the *lectio divina* in her classes. Her students reflect on medieval manuscripts and then respond through journal writing, thinking, or drawing, followed by "finding something from the text that connects to oneself, a word or an image, and then making some sort of reply, be it a vocal or silent" (2003, 199). David Kahane, professor of political science at the University of Alberta, incorporates the *lectio divina* in his classes, using it not only for textual readings but also as a venue for viewing photographs:

Following this contemplative reading or seeing, students might be asked to free-write to capture what had come to them, or simply to talk in groups about the experience. Students frequently expressed surprise at the meaning that they stumbled across in this way, and the connections they were able to make. . . . [The] *lectio divina* suspended some of the students' intimidation and self-monitoring, and allowed them to tap into new levels of meaning, experience and insight. (2014, 127)

Rhonda Magee, professor of law at the University of San Francisco, centers much of her work on the incorporation of the pedagogy of race into the legal education literature. She emphasizes the preparation of students for a diverse world, arguing that certain contemplative practices encourage "a slowing down and single tasking" that lead to deepened critical analyses and inquiry. One such practice Magee refers to as "contemplative group reading," or the *lectio divina*. She points out that this type of reading "assists us in seeing one another more effectively, and sets the stage for more effective working together" (2016, 46).

The *lectio divina* has been a significant pedagogy in my own courses, all of which incorporate the service learning pedagogy. Before students begin their community work and in the first few weeks of the semester, I introduce the concept of a social justice–based, service learning course through selected readings about justice, care, activism, and service. Using specific sections from Paul Loeb's *The Impossible Will Take a Little While* (2004) and *Soul of a Citizen* (1999), we recite a selection together, with each person reading a few lines or a paragraph. We then read it again silently to ourselves, each choosing a specific paragraph that is important or resonates on a personal level. We then read our own selection again. I am careful to choose those sections that are directly related to their community placements and justice issues. I continue with this method throughout the semester as a prologue to our monthly community service discussions and as a context for meaningful discourse. At times we talk about these noticings from the selections, sometimes we write about them, and sometimes we merely sit with them. Like Kahane (2014) I have also used photographs in the same manner. I find that the *lectio divina* method both allows a deeper understanding of course material and its connection to the community experience and contextualizes a thoughtful, contemplative discourse about social justice. Like many contemplative teachers who use the method of *lectio divina* as a secular practice, I have adapted the traditional scriptural approach to one that is centered on social justice readings.

Dorothe Bach and John Alexander, humanities instructors at the University of Virginia, assessed their use of reflective reading from data collected through anonymous end-of-semester course evaluations. They write that "for the overwhelming majority of the class the process of deep reflection was both empowering and affirming" and that anonymous comments from students indicated that deep reading was seen as a way to depict what contemplative scholars call the "self-authoring mind" (2015, 30). Similarly, my students report both a joy from reading to understand and an affirmation of a competency they seem to believe they did not have. Like many other contemplative practices, the *lectio divina* arouses personal agency and perspective, curiosity, and inquiry in an unhurried space. The secular integration of the *lectio divina* as reflective reading in classrooms is a penetrant and inspiring method. In a workshop at the 2015 annual Association for Contemplative Mind in Higher Education conference, I and other faculty members from around the country read "Letter from Birmingham Jail." Through the *lectio divina* method, virtually all of us reported experiences of hearing and feeling Dr. Martin Luther King's famous words in new and profound ways (even though most of us had read and even taught these words many times before). We were paying attention in a specific manner and, according to Bach and Alexander, "intentionally shifting [our] focus to a particular type of engagement with the written word . . . [resulting in] an invitation to notice habits of mind and to exercise conscious choice" (2015, 20). Certainly, this is a process many of us wish for our students.

Contemplative Writing

All classroom writing is potentially a contemplative practice. Pat Schneider describes writing as "an intentional, particular inner act . . . an inward looking, listening" (2013, 12). Like many contemplative pedagogies, thoughtful writing involves the process of inquiry that reflects the content and nature of the mind, a communication with the other, and the expression of self. The Stony Brook University professor of English Pat Belanoff refers to reflective writing as producing important metacognitive activity in that there is "a close examination of or reconstruction of one's thinking during the whole process of writing a paper or putting together a portfolio" (2001, 411). This type of writing can occur in a variety of venues, such as portfolios, journals, one-minute papers, and so on. Therefore, writing can both advance contemplative practices in classrooms and benefit from these practices.

Freewriting adds an unparalleled dimension to those courses punctuated by difficult dialogues. Popularized by Peter Elbow (1998), freewriting is a method of writing that is nonstop for a period of time. As Elbow points out, freewriting provides no feedback or editing; it is a "writing without teachers." Similarly, Kahane observes that freewriting as contemplative inquiry "allows writing without so much scripting and conscious control; you get into the flow of an idea or impulse and write things that you didn't know you had to say" (2014, 126). This approach to writing affords students the opportunity to observe their emotions and reactions and then reflect on the rawness of these experiences in an unmonitored writing space. In spite of efforts to make the classroom a place of safety for all students, it is not always experienced as such, particularly when controversial issues are discussed, often the case in some classes. Freewriting provides an avenue for the expression of confusion, sadness, disagreement, shame, frustration, and compassion. Rick Repetti notes that freewriting is a gateway "to let loose the floodgates of creative thought" and a way to "go 'meta,'" in that there is reflection on process and engagement in the activity (2010, 5).

In assigning freewriting assignments I typically collect them but will not grade them or respond to them other than with a comment of appreciation when I return them. At times this has been difficult for me, particularly if a student has expressed a misunderstanding, a blatant prejudice, or a reliance on a stereotype. I am learning to develop patience with this process and allow students to acquire critical consciousness in their own time. I ask students to choose several of their freewritings for inclusion in their final portfolios, which are graded. I remind them that they do not need to submit one if for some reason they are uncomfortable with its contents and that they may remove a part of a freewriting before submission should they so choose.

Like freewriting, journal writing offers the potential for the exploration of interiority and the development of confidence in writing. It is also a response to what Gayl Walker observes is "the innate need to express ourselves, to discover who we are, to bring meaning to the situations in our lives, and tell our stories" (2001, 108). Many instructors in a variety of disciplines incorporate the journal as a method that uses first-person narratives about one's experience; it is storytelling in the most poignant form. Journaling can offer another way to reflect on a problem discussed in class or respond to difficult or controversial texts read in class. It is also of great value in an inquiry-based learning pedagogy that centers on students' exploration of questions, problems, and concerns for which there is often no single answer. The difficulties associated with inquiry-based courses often relate to insufficient scaffolding and attention to a product rather than a process-oriented approach. Most educational research demonstrates that effective scaffolding reduces cognitive load and allows students to learn complex material. For those of us who have introduced inquiry-based learning into our classrooms, the lesson learned (often painfully) is that we cannot simply ask students, particularly undergraduates, to be inquirers without giving them both the structure and a process to become inquirers. Contemplative, exploratory journaling can be the first step toward an examination and inquiry into a subject.

Christy I. Wenger (2015), professor of English, rhetoric, and composition at Shepherd University, uses contemplative approaches in her first-year composition classes as a way of encouraging her students to become attentive to their writing in a manner that deepens their rhetorical work. She is careful to point out that some teachers make the assumption that their students know how to attend mindfully and that they deliberately choose not to engage such processes. However, evidence suggests that the contemplative dimension to learning is a skill that must be developed and practiced. Rehearsed attention, according to Wenger, promotes a "flexible mind," one of the required "habits of the mind" reported to be necessary for success in college writing by the Framework for Success in Postsecondary Writing (109). This habit is necessary not only for writing but for all learning regardless of the discipline.

For the Bentley University professor of English Gesa Kirsch, writing invites what is "at the edge of their [students'] consciousness" (2009, 3). It serves as a venue for the deep human need to derive some sense out of a disordered world. She posits that deep thinking and engagement as well as sound research emerge when students write about what is personally significant to them. Jacqueline Royster and Gesa Kirsch describe a major goal for their undergraduate writing students as creation of a space in which contemplation and reflection are a serious endeavor and one that can enable formable writing. They invite their students to go on "archival adventures" in order to, they say,

> encourage exploration, visits to new places, attention to historical and cultural artifacts, and reflections on the research process; that is, I try to invite students to come to a place where reflection, contemplation, and observation meet. . . . The invitation to attend to inward and outward journeys as well as lived experiences often leads students to passionate, thoughtful, and powerful research and writing. (2012, 96)

Michael Heller, professor of English at Roanoke College, emphasizes the significance of personal inquiry in his classes. Journaling, for him, is an example of a classroom that honors the inward life. Heller (2009) constructs three questions for journal writing: "What matters here?" "Where are you now?" and "What do you know now?" He reminds us that such questions are behind all traditional research. Heller expands this thinking to the teaching of the contemplative or lyric essay. This type of essay inspires ownership and appreciation of the inner life as an imaginative source. As Heller (2009) states,

> So it's not that we want to deny this outward life or textual knowledge. But we want students to combine the outward life and textual knowledge with seeing their own experience inwardly as a resource. Our text is the self, the community, and the world.

Writing, specifically journals and portfolios, provides an important source of assessment. In their survey of transformative and spiritual dimensions of higher education, Maia Duerr, Arthur Zajonc, and Diane Dana (2003) report that journals and portfolios are among the most popular methods for assessing student learning using contemplative methods. For example, SoTL practitioners Maureen Hall and Olivia Archibald investigated writing as a contemplative practice in their undergraduate and graduate courses, asking "How does a practice of reflective writing in the classroom inform students' value of the need for reflection and reflective writing within the classroom and within their lives?" (2008, 7). Their data sources included student journals, e-mails sent to each other and to the professors, end-of-course evaluations, and other course-linked materials. Using Krathwohl's taxonomy of the affective domain, an assessment for describing the development of values about objects and concepts, they found that over 90 percent of their students moved to at least a level-three stage by the end of the semester, indicating they can compare and contrast new information with their current ideas and thoughts and engage in critical thinking. Hall and Archibald also articulate three themes that emerged from the data. Contemplative writing afforded the development of greater focus in the classroom, reduction of stress in the classroom and in students' personal lives, and enhancement of students' identities as writers.

The linguist Robin Lakoff (1973) refers to college writing as the currency of the university. Yet teachers of writing continue to bemoan that many methods for teaching college writing are often unfruitful and writing assignments ineffective. Paradoxically, a review of descriptive statements posited by college and university writing centers indicates an understanding of writing as being grounded in contemplative dimensions. For example, numerous writing centers acknowledge that effective writing is the product of locating personal agency in the writing process (Vassar College, n.d.), illuminating process and empowering the writer's voice and self-awareness (Evergreen State College, n.d.), expanding ideas of literacy and composition beyond traditional models and geographic boundaries (Michigan State University, n.d.), and understanding the student's relationship with writing (i.e., "What's working for you, and what's holding you back?" and "What restrains or inspires you as a writer[?]") (Indiana University–Purdue University Indianapolis, n.d.). However, the championing of these contemplative dimensions as necessary for writing does not always translate into actual contemplative writing practices. Contemplation and reflection guide us toward deepening our writing pedagogies. They remind us of the significance of pondering, noticing, and stillness for effective writing. They urge us to remember that writing comes from the silent speech within and is accessed only in slow time. Ralph Waldo Emerson observed that the writer is an explorer. To write well, students need the time to explore both their internal and their external worlds. Contemplation makes this journey of exploration possible and, thus, responds effectually to many of the issues raised by teachers of writing.

Contemplative Arts

The Center for Contemplative Mind in Society sees contemplative arts as divided into two categories: one that emphasizes process and one that emphasizes product. In both cases, the practitioner's commitment is the same: to engage in the creative process with contemplative mindfulness and attention. Piper Murray (2006) suggests that all the arts are essentially contemplative, a way for human beings to encounter their wholeness and their longing to relate to something greater than the self. Contemplative arts are woven into secular disciplines, the classroom, and the curriculum as a whole in a variety of ways.

The performer, choreographer, professor, and past president of Naropa University Barbara Dilley observes that "the great struggle in the contemplative arts classroom has been doing less" (quoted in Murray 2006, 15). More specifically, she refers to her contemplative perspective in dance as the discovery of "movement in the moment" and "spontaneous composition," places where imagination shows up. In her memoir Dilley (2014) argues that training in dance is multilevel and composed of both outer disciplines and inner experiences. She urged her students to engage in movement research by considering how the mind, body, and spirit interlace. Like Dilley, Stephanie Briggs (2015), assistant professor of English at the Community College of Baltimore County, integrates and investigates the use of movement and multidisciplinary mindfulness practices in the college classroom. Briggs draws on the research-to-performance methodology to assess this intersection of contemplative perspectives with improvisation and performance.

Peter Schneider, a professor of architecture at the University of Colorado in Denver, teaches architecture as both a body of knowledge and a contemplative art. He urges his students to engage in "design imagination" that begins with sensory awareness of their interior and outer worlds and is followed by creatively and then contemplatively reimagining it. Schneider's goal is to design with mindfulness (Murray 2006, 3).

Joel Upton, professor of fine arts and art history at Amherst College, frames all his courses around the same question. In a world where art is accessed within seconds through a walk by in a museum or from the internet, how might his students contemplate a work of art, set aside their characteristic ways of perceiving art, and consider the dilemma of being human that determines artistic composition. Upton structures his courses around three contemplative processes: (1) writing assignments that promote deep engagement with the particular work of art, (2) a "beholding," or attention to a work of art, for a substantive length of time, and (3) a final essay assignment in which students write about a piece of art to which they have attended for the entire semester through research and analyses of the art. For Upton, the use of "contemplative practice amounts to a radical reclaiming of art at its human core" (quoted in Murray 2006, 9).

Vijay Kanagala and Laura Rendon speak of "birthing internal images" through what they call the *"cajita* project" (2013). Designed by Alberto Pulido at the University of San Diego, a *cajita* is a personal reflective box that students create out of artifacts that might symbolize identity journeys, life stories, political and philosophical commentaries, and so on. Rendon describes the cajita as a "creative knowledge canvas" and "a cultural autobiographical story" and argues that if students are to participate in the world in a socially conscious and intelligent manner, they need to appreciate who they are and, therefore, become "reflective scholar-practitioners" (2009, 43). The cajita becomes a means for self-reflection and for moving more deeply into internal and external learning. For Rendon, this type of examined experience creates a place that values "inner knowing (deep wisdom, wonder, sense of the sacred, intuition, and emotions) as well as outer knowing (intellectual reasoning, rationality, and objectivity)" (27). The cajita offers possibilities for personal and social justice reflection. Systemic injustices as depicted in artifacts chosen by students allow a deeper consciousness about these systems. I use the cajita in my service learning classes. Students often bring to class artifacts from their community placements (e.g., drawings from elementary school children, autobiographies written by residents in a local prison, letters to students from occupants in halfway houses and group homes). Each of these could be used in a cajita with an accompanying reflective narrative and presentation to class members.

Similar to Rendon's and Pulido's work with the cajita is the talisman exercise. I have also applied this exercise to my own classes. Students bring an object that is meaningful to them and share its story with class members. Each student tells a story and leaves the object on the "table of inspiration" (Center for Contemplative Mind in Society 2012). Many students in my service learning classes, when permitted by the school or agency, will bring photos of children whom they are tutoring or residents in an assisted-living facility with whom they have developed a relationship. Some bring brochures about a nonprofit agency or small pebbles presented to them by preschool children. One student who was engaged to be married brought a wedding quilt made by women in a senior citizen retirement center who wanted her to have it as a memory of them. The student talked at length about this great act of generosity on the part of women who had very little power by societal standards but had great power in terms of their wisdom. We covered our table of inspiration with this quilt. The list of examples is exhaustive, but each is centered on how the object is related to personal experience in the context of the course. The construction of these objects, whether in a cajita or on the table of inspiration, provides an important method for substantive, contemplative thinking about each person's experience and how this experience informs deep learning of course material.

Service Learning

Just as contemplative arts can be conceptualized as a practice, so might a well-crafted service learning course. Service learning courses are grounded in a theory and practice of engaged, meaningful learning and should develop social justice and responsibility. Both service learning and contemplative practices call us to be mindful of the world in a certain manner. Therefore, it would seem axiomatic that they should complement, inform, and deepen one another. Marshall Welch and Kent Koth use the breath as a descriptive metaphor for this relationship:

> As we inhale we find inspiration, we nurture our spirit, and we search for meaning; yet none of us can survive by merely inhaling. Likewise, we cannot survive by focusing solely on our own spiritual [contemplative] journey as we risk moving into a pattern of self-absorption and narcissism. In short, we cannot be just *in*spired. To survive, we must also exhale, we must engage the world. In exhaling we connect with others. At our best, in exhaling we find ways to serve and learn from others. (2009, 3)

Ai Zhang argues that contemplative service learning can shape a curriculum so as to provide students with "a foundation for internal cultivation and self-development and external experiences to make students capable and socially oriented working professionals who can make a positive impact on society" (2013, 185). Naropa University describes its contemplative service learning program as one that intentionally "joins wisdom and insight with skillful action by engaging and empowering students, faculty, and community members in compassionate selfless service" (n.d., "Transpersonal").

Deep, intentional, and authentic reflection is the sine qua non component of a well-constructed service learning course, one that honors and integrates social justice and compassion for self and others. Scholars of the service learning pedagogy argue that this approach to student reflection must be at the core of and consistently integrated into all service learning courses. Yet in his review of approaches to service learning in the classroom Trae Stewart (2011) observes that very few of these methods emphasize contemplative and interior dimensions as significant to meaning-making. When they are considered, they remain secondary to the traditional approaches of reflection. The marginalization of these dimensions may, in fact, contribute to the many criticisms and hurdles that have plagued the service learning pedagogy. Chief among these hurdles are (1) the challenge inherent in the intensity of service learning experiences for students and instructors, (2) an academic culture that is based on a traditional pedagogy, one that fails to speak to the wholeness of human beings and one that privileges the rational and intellectual at the expense of self-examination and the development of an ethic of care, and (3) a superficial approach to meaning-making and social justice. Service learning as a contemplative practice offers a corrective and ameliorative response to these hurdles and criticisms by reframing and deepening reflective approaches. Contemplative reflection is a countermeasure to the "extrospective reflection . . . [born out of a] historicist reductionism that assumes that these experiences are epistemologically invalid" (Stewart 2011, 59).

As noted above, I use many of these practices for the reflective process. However, I think of my service learning classes as synonymous with the contemplative practice of *beholding* and *bearing witness*, a critical dimension in the contemplative perspective. I remind my service learning students that their role is to *behold* and *bear witness* to their experiences in their respective community placements. In beholding an experience, I continuously emphasize the question What do you see? The Center for Contemplative Mind in Society points out that "seeing" and attentiveness are the first steps toward the development of care and the "the foundation of an ethical awareness, the beginning of an ethical stance" (n.d., "Contemplative"). However, I remind my students that beholding is not an end in itself in service learning experience. We must be present to and responsible for that experience, to bear witness. Deborah Dunn, professor of communication studies at Westmont College, suggests that to bear witness is to assume some responsibility for what is seen:

> Perhaps this responsibility will lead to an account that can be shared with others, a joining in the enactment of future actions and accounts, or a way of speaking to the

cultural and social significance. In any event, bearing witness requires the witness to own a stance in relation to what one has seen. (2014, 41)

Like Dunn, I want my students to understand that beholding and bearing witness is an abiding service to others. To see and honor the stories and conditions of other human beings is moral and ethical action, the central goal of a service learning pedagogy. Assessments of the service learning component focus on each student's beholding and bearing witness in their discourse and writing.

The literature and research on service learning as a contemplative practice in higher education remains slim. However, as Steven Emmanuel suggests, service learning may be the one pedagogical approach that bridges the gap between contemplation and social justice activism in spite of the notion that contemplation and action have often been understood as opposites. By mindfully contemplating such questions as "How do we identify communities in need of service? What is our place in these communities? [and] What is the relationship between server and served?" students have a deeper and more transformative experience (Murray 2008, 4). Recent studies have focused on the place of multiculturalism and contemplative practice in facilitating students' identities as social change agents (Rendon 2009), mindfulness as a method to access and understand community engagement experiences (Stewart 2011), how contemplative practices address problems embedded in the service learning and social justice relationship (Owen-Smith 2016), and deep reflection and exploration of identity as venues for understanding positionality and privilege (Mitchell et al. 2015). As more contemplative scholars engage in service learning research and social justice mindfulness, we can anticipate an increasing body of research and a heightened consciousness supportive of the integration of a contemplative pedagogy within a service learning, social justice education.

Space

Mary Rose O'Reilley (1998), retired teacher of English at St. Thomas University, asks how we might make spaces in classrooms that will allow students the freedom to nurture an inner life. We have many examples for filling spaces and gaps in classrooms but almost none for their creation. William Powers uses e-mail as analogy for the lack of space in our lives. In both the composing and the reading of e-mails, the central point is "almost *not* to be thoughtful, not to pause and reflect. To eliminate the gaps" (2010, 53; emphasis added). O'Reilley draws from developmental theorists, such as Robert Coles, who insist that the inner lives of students are central to cognitive development. How do we access these inner lives when classrooms are filled, overflowing, and often deafening with verbosity? Mindfulness practices such as the ones discussed above are important means for creating spaces; they afford an atmosphere of respect in the classroom. However, the creation of a contemplative space from which other practices might unfold is also a practice in and of itself. When we as a community of learners (both instructors and students) construct space in our classroom hour through moments of silence, mindful attention, reflection, listening, writing, and reading, we also build an openness that facilitates the prologue for a deep learning process. Mah y Busch, professor of English at Loyola Marymount University, describes classroom space:

> Spaciousness is not a place at all. It is a quality. A living quality of experience. Whether we describe political liberation or the moment a student, in sudden realization, gasps "a-ha," what we actually appreciate in each example is the quality of spaciousness that has occurred. It is not the degree of depth or distance. Spaciousness is the quality of having enough room. (2014, 129)

Renee Hill, philosophy professor at Virginia State University, casts an additional understanding of space. Hill turns to the work of Bradford Grant, Howard University professor of architecture, who emphasizes that "negative space" is "the space above, under, between, and around objects, like the three dimensional dough left behind once the gingerbread cookies have been removed. The 'not object' space" (quoted in Hill 2014, 135). Hill expands Grant's conceptualization by suggesting that we squander our negative spaces by filling them with our busyness and harried lives and fail to notice the space that is present. The classroom structure is no exception. Teachers have been acculturated to fill up the room with activity and their words. We might ponder the questions How much space may we allow in our classrooms? and Where do we hold contemplative practices if there is no such space? How do we engage in O'Reilley's notion of "the practice of [classroom] hospitality" if we are not fully present to the spaciousness of the moment, one another, the self (1998, 8)? To construct space in classrooms is not to abandon irresponsibly the work of the classroom or to marginalize the lecture, discussion groups, learning teams, and all other pedagogical methods held dear by teachers. Rather, it is a pause (perhaps just a moment), a breath, and a deepening of presence that allows contemplative practices, as well as all classroom methods, to flourish.

This chapter examines contemplative methods through the voices and practices of college and university teachers. Some of these instructors are contemplative educators with a long history of experience with the contemplative perspective. Other instructors have very little experience with contemplative education, and yet their approach to teaching offers contemplative potential. All are committed to what Zajonc calls a "re-imagination of knowing" (2006, 1744). As Daniel Barbezat and Allison Pingree (2012) observe, a rich tradition of experiential education in the academy focuses on the student's personal connection to learning; therefore, introspective practices are not unfamiliar in higher education. In fact, SoTL practitioners have highlighted some of these practices in both their teaching and their assessment. However, the distinguishing feature of contemplative practices is the emphasis on the student's self-examination and the cultivation of this awareness of self and others. It is a way of knowing that attends to personal resonance and meaning-making. In his acclaimed book *What the Best College Students Do*, educational researcher Ken Bain describes creative, imaginative, compassionate, and aware college students as "examining their lives and coming to appreciate the qualities and perspectives that only they could muster. Self-examination [leads] students to understand those passions that would excite their soul" (2004, 46). Contemplative methods are powerful facilitators of these attributes born in self-examination and awareness. They expand and deepen what most excellent teachers continue to do well.

3 Challenges and Replies to Contemplative Methods

> There's no place for this in the academy. This is spirituality in the classroom. This is Buddhism Lite. Meditative silence is a home for the demonic. How can you grade inner experience? This is pseudoscience. You can do the same thing with Prozac. How do you justify having students pay all those tuition dollars to do . . . nothing?
>
> —John Gravois, "Meditate on It"

IN THE EPIGRAPH that begins this chapter, John Gravois summarizes some of the more extreme responses to contemplative practices. Some of these criticisms are punctuated by cynicism, annoyance, and misunderstanding. Many are situated in a general angst around transformative education and in the specific place of introspection and interiority in the classroom. However, some criticisms also raise legitimate and thought-provoking questions, many of which have endured throughout time. The conflict between the exterior and interior selves is an ancient one. The articulation of this struggle throughout history has centered primarily on the intrapsychic, idiosyncratic, and profoundly personal processes of individual development. As William Powers (2010) reminds us, such struggles are clearly reflected in literature, art, psychology, and philosophy. Responses to the integration of the contemplative into higher education replicate this struggle on a systemic and institutional level. The privileging of exteriority and the marginalization of interiority in the academy in general and in classroom structure more specifically contribute significantly to a substantive number of challenges for the contemplative movement.

Some of these same critiques and questions are recognizable to SoTL practitioners, who share a transformational agenda with contemplative educators. In this respect contemplative education and SoTL are situated in a polemic about definitions of academic integrity and rigor, assessment, classroom efficiency, student agency, and the appropriateness of affective and introspective dimensions in teaching and learning. The struggle for academic legitimacy by both contemplative and SoTL movements is primarily due to this polemic. At times the two movements have disengaged from one another, either consciously or unconsciously, lest each abdicate its fundamental pedagogical principles in the service of the other. However, both can inform and challenge one another in interesting and complex ways so as to illuminate, expand, and strengthen understanding of transformative education and inquiry. By joining forces, contemplative and SoTL movements can respond more effectively to the following challenges.

Challenges to the integration of contemplative practices in higher education lie in (1) institutional structures that are inhospitable to the inclusion of introspective and contemplative dimensions in teaching and learning, (2) ambiguous language, and (3) the ethics of, for example, emotionality and religiosity in the classroom, fidelity to the contemplative tradition, teacher preparation, pedagogical intention, and assessment of interior dimensions. This chapter articulates the important questions raised about the place of contemplative practices in higher education and responds to them to further conversations by transformative and contemplative educators.

Institutional Structures

The majority of educators committed to transformative pedagogies in the United States agree that preparing students for judicious participation in a democracy is central to their mission. Phyllis Robinson (2004) furthers this perspective by suggesting that contemplative practices are central to transformative and integrative learning. There is both an urgent need for and resistance to transformative education. In spite of the need for practices that will ground and deepen learning, there is a reluctance to implement them and a struggle to assess them. The confusion and trepidation around the actual notion of the "contemplative" in higher education is merely an extension of this opposition. The palpable discomfort is maintained by the very structure of an academy that is struggling with its identity, confronting external demands from its stakeholders, and holding tightly to a model of education that seems at odds with learning in the twenty-first century.

Some critics suggest that the dominance of today's economic imperialism (Gilead 2012) and resulting pressure for "measurable economically-rendered aims" (Ergas 2015a, 205) lead to an infertile ground for all pedagogies that challenge tradition but particularly for those grounded in contemplative and introspective approaches. Similarly, Maia Duerr speaks to the difficulty of integrating contemplative practices at a time when there is "an American propensity toward consumerism, the tendency to turn everything into a commodity and to look for an 'easy fix'" (2011, 28). In Duerr, Arthur Zajonc, and Dianne Dana's (2003) survey of transformative and spiritual dimensions of higher education, some of the interviewees observed a historically embedded productivity issue in American education. Students were prepared for the marketplace, and this preparatory mission endures today at the expense of valuing transformative classroom methods. As Lourdes Arguelles observes, secular institutions approach learning in a manner that "is designed to do away with any kind of transpersonal imminent dimension of knowing. Positivism reigns in the academy" (quoted in Duerr, Zajonc, and Dana 2003, 203). A bifurcation has resulted from such conversations so that market preparation and introspective knowing become antithetically positioned. There appears to be an unwillingness to consider that both can and should exist in higher education as students prepare for the twenty-first century.

Transformative methods ask us to suspend our typical approaches to understanding in the service of a different approach to learning, knowing, and assessment. Emphases on affective, introspective, and spiritual development through mindfulness, silent reflections, listening, and first-person perspectives are particularly alien to today's academic culture and thereby pose a challenge. Mark Wallace at Swarthmore College observes that a learning that fails to support the canon of an objective, value-free education engenders fear, which is the most significant barrier to transformative, contemplative, and introspective practices (cited in Duerr, Zajonc, and Dana 2003). Whether the anxiety around these practices emanates from fear, as Wallace suggests, or simply a misunderstanding or fundamental pedagogical disagreement, transformative methods nevertheless enter the classroom as a "dangerous pedagogy" (Gardner, Calderwood, and Torosyan 2007, 13). Elizabeth Gardner, Patricia Calderwood, and Roben Torosyan (2007) explain the "danger" as due specifically to the unravelling of the student-teacher power relationships. Student agency and leadership in the classroom disrupts the status quo, the privileging of the teacher's authority over all others. Authentic partnerships between students and teachers introduce a new climate to the classroom and one that can be uncomfortable and unfamiliar for the most well-seasoned teacher.

Others see risks with contemplative pedagogies for a different set of reasons. For many administrators and teachers the introduction of the contemplative in the public university legitimizes religious practices and, therefore, essentially fails to separate church from state. Daniel Barbezat and Mirabai Bush contend that one of the most vocal criticisms of classroom contemplative practices is that "religious views are being rolled in within the Trojan horse of secular ideas of 'attention' and 'mindfulness'" (2014, 78). However, they remind us that contemplative practices require no particular belief but, rather, allow students to explore their own interiority and accompanying processes. Contemplative methods complement and extend the analytic and abstract. Kirsten Song and Glenn Muschert (2014), argue that mindfulness practices must be separated from their religious associations in the secular university and that this separation can facilitate Western education's development of a more unbiased perspective and epistemology toward mindfulness practices and their applications. Charles Burack cautions that care should be taken in maintaining a "pluralistic classroom," one that is free from any indoctrination of students to a particular worldview (2014, 47). However, Oren Ergas, in an online discussion forum, put forth a different perspective:

> The "accusation" of "mindfulness" or contemplation as advocacy within an educational context in that sense must always be located within the claim that the

teaching of math or history, Law, or Economics are other forms of advocacy. They are choices made, and as such—they could have been otherwise. . . . This of course hearkens back to notorious dualisms of cognition/affect, body/mind, ethics/science etc. because there is a very strong and misguided belief held by many that if we stick with math, science, history, etc. either in school or in university lecture halls then we are somehow avoiding ethics or avoiding the proselyting of certain beliefs. . . . That is utter falsehood. (2015b)

For Ergas, advocacy in classrooms cannot be circumvented regardless of what is being taught. Feminist scholars have long held to this notion. Therefore, it is not contemplative methods that are being advocated so much as it is the understanding of self, compassion for others, and the locating of meaning in our lives, all of which are critical dimensions for character development and are seen by most colleges and universities as embedded in their mission statements. Harold Roth (2015) differentiates advocacy from inquiry, pointing out that we must engage knowledge-based inquiry through contemplative methods that follow rigorous cognitive constructions and that will stand the tests for legitimacy in the disciplines we teach and learn.

Many critics point to the abdication of depth for breadth, process for product and the resulting abandonment of the informational model of teaching as being the major danger of new pedagogies. Administrators and teachers who have been professionally acculturated in a very different type of paradigm find discomfort in the expenditure of time required by such methods. Unlearning what is known and well practiced is a difficult, time-consuming process on many levels. Teachers often report that the investment of time in the restructuring of their classrooms contributes to a drain on their teaching lives. The law professor Rhonda Magee (2016), observes that the legitimacy of taking time away from classroom approaches that are culturally and institutionally approved is a major challenge even for the most tenacious and fearless of teachers. Susan Wegner, associate professor of art history at Bowdoin College, puts it this way:

There is not really any room built into the curriculum for such lavish use of time— periods of silence—spending time on something not graded. There is so much pressure on the faculty to cover material. . . . [I]t makes for a hurried, frenzied, busied rush to just acquire stuff and catch up. (Quoted in Duerr, Zajonc, and Dana 2003, 202)

Without institutional, administrative, and financial support and with little attention to radical curriculum reform and development, teachers seeking to explore and implement transformative pedagogies are left to struggle in isolation.

Some see these deficits and challenges as opportunities for the introduction of transformative and contemplative pedagogies into the curriculum. For example, Tobin Hart (2004) calls on contemplative educators to participate actively in the conversation of higher education. He advises contemplative scholars to formulate a rationale and gather supportive evidence for methods that address the actual concerns hovering over higher education today. Susan Burggraf sees the secularization of contemplative practices as producing a "new hybrid," a junction between the academic disciplines and introspective methods that, in turn, offers ways of living in a complex and pluralistic world (2011, 245). Concomitantly, Jeffrey Bernstein suggests that "satisfying our external stakeholders in an academy under siege requires to a large extent that we demonstrate that we are paying greater attention to teaching and to how our students learn" (2012, 3). In discussing the principles of good practice in teaching, Peter Felten (2013) calls for a demystification and clarification of SoTL to help us do the work of educating students. Certainly, the parochialism and insularity that often exist in marginalized groups of scholars such as SoTL and contemplative practitioners contribute to this mystery and lack of clarity. An unproductive cyclical relationship can exist between these educators and the institution at large. Often there is an assumption that the institution is inevitably unwelcoming to such pedagogies. Therefore, the tendency on the part of some transformative and contemplative educators is to remain in circles in which the language and philosophy are understood and accepted. This in itself can create an inhospitable tenor toward the institution that furthers suspicion from institutional administrators toward creative and innovative educators. The cycle repeats, and opportunities for connections are lost. In an effort to address this immobility and communicative gap Connie Schroeder, an instructional development scholar at the University of Wisconsin in Milwaukee, calls for a process that identifies intersections, "connective tissue," between movements such as SoTL and other institutional initiatives:

> SoTL involvement with institutional reform requires leaping from a classroom context level to some type of meaningful alignment between SoTL work and institutional level initiatives. . . . [I]t is a time of bringing SoTL work to bear upon the problem of improving the institution in terms of the initiative at hand. (2007, 3)

Teaching and learning centers have made a significant response to Schroeder's admonition to provide this "connective tissue." Contemplative scholars Daniel Barbezat and Allison Pingree (2012) also see teaching and learning centers as a major support for contemplative education in that they afford an infrastructure and legitimize approaches to learning that might be seen as suspect. Naropa University's program and several other contemplative programs, such as the one at Brown University, are prototypes for linking contemplative approaches of the classroom with institutional initiatives. Yet for the most part contemplative pedagogy in the classroom remains sidelined from institutional initiatives and rarely supported by teaching and learning centers. In important ways, SoTL's experience and deftness in developing teaching and learning centers as a way to confront institutional marginalization can offer a hand to contemplative educators struggling with this marginal position.

Language Ambiguity

Like most nascent fields of study, contemplative education has struggled with an ambiguous language. Many definitions of *mindfulness* currently exist, producing a lack of consensus among contemplative scholars as to what the word means. While definitions of *mindful learning and teaching, contemplative epistemology,* and *mindfulness theory* continue to evolve and develop, they still lack refinement. This multiplicity of definitions adds confusion about contemplative methods. Antoine Lutz and colleagues (2015) observe that the confusion is also the product of the breadth of settings in which the definitions are used. Psychology, cognitive neuroscience, psychiatry, preventive medicine, and education all use contemplative approaches. According to Lutz and colleagues this diverse landscape leads to a tension in framing a single and universally accepted definition. Juan Mah y Busch points to a paradox in discussing contemplative language. He observes that while contemplative practices refer to pedagogy and pedagogy is typically associated with words, the contemplative practitioner "relishes in the wordless, though tangible, dimensions of experience. This is why it defies definition" (2014, 127).

A substantive difficulty for contemplative educators is the translation of terms rooted in the wisdom traditions to a secular language. However, Burggraf (2011) sees the secularization of language as offering a host of opportunities. Secularization provides a portal for learning from many traditions, developing a common language, averting the marginalization of contemplative studies, and allowing accessibility to all individuals. In the seminal report on the Contemplative Net Project, a qualitative study sponsored by the Center for Contemplative Mind in Society, research participants underscored the importance of "meeting people where they're at," or trying to "gear their teaching methodology and content to the particular group of people they were working with" (Duerr 2004, 118). According to Duerr (2011), the task for contemplative educators is to locate an appropriate language for presenting and formatting contemplative methods and develop a willingness to adapt classroom goals and approaches that will support the context for contemplative practices. According to this report, one of the most remarkable findings as related to language was a reluctance to embrace the word *spiritual* because of its limiting connotation. Robert Gass, one of the research participants, described the language he used in his seminars:

> I make a great effort to use very everyday commonsense language, which is why I continually have people at the end of these say, "You know for ten years or twenty years, I've been totally turned off to do anything spiritual." And all of a sudden I get "This helps our life so much." I'm deeply committed to a spiritual path, but I'm not wedded to the words of spirituality. It's the thing itself. . . . [I]t's not the words. (Quoted in Duerr 2011, 116)

Other participants reported being strategic in their choice of words around mindfulness exercises introduced in class, using such phrases as "strategies for learning readiness" as opposed to contemplative practices and "writing exercises" in the place of journaling. However, some participants expressed a clear comfort with a language grounded in spirituality. As Meg Wheatley said,

> As the world has grown more accepting of even speaking the words of spirit, soul, love, wholeness, that's created more room for us. And then also I have to say that as I get older, I'm just clearer about what's important and so I can become the voice for it rather than having to wait for someone's approval of it. (Quoted in Duerr 2002, 66)

Burack uses a range of terminologies for introducing contemplative practices into his undergraduate psychology courses:

> I encourage students to use whatever words and images they feel comfortable with. We discuss the fact that different cultures and individuals use different words and symbols for talking about their nonordinary experiences. One person might call the experiences *religious* or *godly*, while another calls them *spiritual*, while others call them *epiphanies*, or *moments of deep connection*, or *experiences of heightened vitality*. We also discuss the unfortunate fact that wars are waged over what to call these experiences and how to understand and value them. (2014, 47)

Mirabai Bush (2011b) also offers examples of terms used for contemplative methods in secular classrooms. She suggests that some instructors of art history refer to contemplative seeing as "beholding" (196), a familiar English word that denotes appreciation and a way of engaging the senses. One philosophical anthropologist, Josef Pieper, presents contemplation as "visual perception" (quoted in Bush 2011b, 196). A professor of chemistry at Bryn Mawr College, Michelle Francl teaches the mindfulness of sound and refers to this practice as "listening out" in the service of detecting "the acoustic ecology" (quoted in Bush 2011b, 196). My own Theories of Personality course, an upper-level psychology class in which psychological theories are not only read but also practiced in an experiential context, is steeped in the contemplative. Sigmund Freud's (1955) emphasis on insights emerging from unconscious conflicts, Carl Rogers's "unconditional positive regard" in relationships ([1961] 1995, ix), Abraham Maslow's ([1962] 2014, 29) and Karen Horney's (1950, 64) human drive for "self-actualization," and Erik Erikson's (1950) existential questions and crises all employ therapeutic methods that are contemplative. Each of these examples demonstrates the use of accessible phrases from the respective instructor discipline.

Barbezat and Bush (2014) cast a different consideration of language. They emphasize the impact of contemplative language on students and argue for an awareness of how teachers use language in framing contemplative exercises. Barbezat and Bush draw on relational frame theory for understanding the intersection of language and cognition and that words can be triggers for different groups. They stress the criticality of teachers' understanding of how students have learned to associate words with particular beliefs and views. Their admonition is relevant for many pedagogical methods and disciplines. Women's and gender studies faculty have long been acutely aware of this. Nevertheless, bell hooks reminds us that how words are used in the context of dialogue is one of the easiest methods for teachers to "cross boundaries" (1994, 130). Henry Giroux delineates hooks's position:

> You can't deny that students have experiences and you can't deny that these experiences are relevant to the learning process even though you might say these experiences are limited, raw, unfruitful, or whatever. Students have memories, families, religions, languages, and cultures that give them a distinctive voice. We can critically engage that experience and we can move beyond it. But we can't deny it. (1992, 17)

As is the case with many teaching and learning approaches in higher education, the lack of a common, interdisciplinary language presents challenges. Mary Huber describes these challenges as due to "field specific engagements," or a language understood only by those in a particular field (2013, x). Contemplative pedagogy is no exception. As several of the individuals above indicated, no one contemplative language or understanding of the language fits all instructors, all students, and all disciplines. To some extent the ambiguity of contemplative language can be traced to this position. Yet it is important to recognize that engagement with the larger teaching community is productive and can potentially lead to a shared, more nuanced, and clearer language. Huber points out that the expansion of knowledge originates at "the borders of disciplinary imagination" and in "trading zones where scholars from different fields [are] exchanging insights, ideas, and findings even though the meanings and methods behind them may vary considerably" (2013, ix). Many contemplative educators remain isolated in their disciplinary contemplative work and reluctant to engage others in their vision and practice. As a participant in numerous SoTL and service learning national and international conferences every year, I typically see very few presentations of any type on contemplative practices. Contemplative scholars appear slow in furthering their work in the "trading zones" of disciplinary exchange, particularly those zones located beyond the contemplative walls. This sequestration, either chosen or imposed, will continue to contribute to a contemplative language poorly articulated and misunderstood.

Ethical Debates

Chief among ethical questions embedded in the above discussions and others is the place of emotionality in the classroom, fidelity to the contemplative tradition, teacher preparation and qualifications for the implementation of contemplative practices, the instructor's pedagogical intentions, and the grading of interior dimensions.

Emotionality in the Classroom

One of the concerns about transformative practices most often raised by teachers focuses on the emotional dimension of introspection. Classroom spaces constructed for the purpose of deep and authentic reflection can indeed cause trepidation. Teachers want to allow genuine emotion in the classroom but point out that they are unprepared to do therapy. Although a rare occurrence, introspective and contemplative processes might reveal a student who needs professional help. Some students might find personal reflection difficult if not impossible because of their history, culture, family dynamics, and so on. However, transformative teaching and learning by their nature involve substantive change. Dorothe Bach and John Alexander refer to this change as "a dissolution from established beliefs and a shift towards new meaning frameworks . . . [and, therefore,] is emotionally demanding for the person undergoing it" (2015, 32). This emotional demand applies to *both* teachers and students. For many students, the contemplative and introspective classroom can mean risks, particularly for those students acculturated to and comfortable with the traditional classroom of analyses grounded in abstraction. An invitation for first-person, experiential ways of knowing can result in student apprehension and resistance. Contemplative and introspective processes are powerful in that they can create transformations for good or for harm. Burack (2014) notes that for some students with weak psychological boundaries, such processes can profoundly disturb the ego. He therefore recommends three safety measures when implementing contemplative processes. Contemplative processes should be voluntary; students should be told they can terminate the practice if an experience becomes aversive; and the frequency, kind, and length of the practice should be limited. Many contemplative educators stress the importance of framing practices in a context of inquiry. This framework usually prevents inappropriate classroom disclosures that would best be handled in a counseling center or student affairs office. Most teachers, whether contemplative educators or not, have experienced moments in the classroom in which a student needs greater emotional support than what can be provided in the classroom hour. Incumbent on all teachers is preparation for such moments with referral resources.

John Baugher notes that the most daunting obstacle is not student emotionality but rather the teacher's trepidation about dealing with her or his own emotions. Baugher calls for a "pedagogy of witness," a term coined by the English professor Elizabeth Duntro, that is grounded in "a recognition that to create spaces for transformative learning teachers must themselves learn to be comfortable with 'holding' uncomfortable emotions—our own and those of our students—in an atmosphere of inquiry and loving kindness" (2014a, 236). Similarly, Gesa Kirsch (2009), in her exploration of classroom approaches that might allow students the freedom to develop an inner life, argues that teachers will need courage for not knowing what they might face. The reality of virtually all classroom experience is that teachers seldom know what they will encounter in the classroom. Emotions are pervasive in all classrooms whether we acknowledge this or not, have courage or not. They appear in various ways whether invited, as in the case of the contemplative classroom, or not. Students bring a multiplicity of layered experiences with accompanying emotions to the classroom.

Virtually all teachers can attest to the experience of walking into their classroom and sensing an angst, sorrow, joy, or other emotion, either from an individual student or the classroom at large. Bravery is needed to name, legitimize, and witness such responses. Beth Berila (2014, 65–67) offers support for teachers who wish to integrate contemplative practices but are fearful of the emotional consequence. She advocates practicing a mindfulness and following five principles:

1. Assume that someone in the room has suffered trauma, and behave with the requisite compassion and calm.
2. Prepare the students for possible reactions beforehand.
3. Offer the option of opting out.
4. Provide support resources.
5. Hold the space nonjudgmentally and with compassion and kindness to remain grounded and to meet students' reactions—whatever they may be.

Fidelity to the Contemplative Tradition

Contemplative methods have their roots in Buddhist, Muslim, Jewish, and Christian traditions. Some contemplative educators raise concerns that these practices might become so disconnected from their original traditions that they are reduced to simple methodologies at the expense of authentic spiritual development. Their fundamental question is how to remain faithful to the tradition of contemplative methods while introducing them in the secular academy. For example, Judith Simmer-Brown questions the ethics of using religious practices that are "divorced from their roots and contexts—such that 'mindfulness' becomes popularized as mere relaxation (like yoga has become in the United States)" (2011, 108). Similarly, Jon Kabat-Zinn specifically asks whether contemplative pedagogies might be seen as "the next promising cognitive behavioral technique, decontextualized and 'plugged' into a behaviorist paradigm, with the aim of driving behavioral change, or fixing whatever is broken" (2003, 145). Anne Harrington and John Dunne summarize concerns such as these in their substantive review of the "ethical qualms" of mindfulness practices (2015, 621). They do not question whether these practices work; rather their question is whether there is risk in divorcing them from their original ethical frameworks.

Brendan Ozawa–de Silva addresses this question in his emphasis on a "secular ethics," an approach offered by His Holiness the Dalai Lama. A secular ethics affords an expansion of contemplative practices by positioning them in a wider ethical and social paradigm, one that acknowledges the value of religious tradition yet appeals to "scientific and common sense reasons" (2014, 92). Edward Sarath responds to these criticisms by also arguing that even if the practices are removed from their spiritual roots but provide mental clarity and attention, they still reflect substantive benefits to the educational process. According to Sarath, this type of extrication can allow for the development of a spiritual self that is grounded in "an interior experience, rather than shaped by exterior, institutional, or denominational influences . . . a trans-traditional identity [that is] spiritually ecumenical [and] receptive to linkages among intellectual, creative, and other areas of life" (2003b, 229). This "trans-traditional" model has been well articulated by SoTL scholars in their development of teaching circles, teaching and learning centers, national and international conferences, and scholarly journals. Each of these venues has brought together academicians from seemingly dissimilar fields and theoretical traditions. In so doing, SoTL has located a common ground where these disciplines intersect and where authentic conversations about teaching and learning begin. As Sarath suggests, contemplative studies can also be a conduit for such intersections. If one considers the contemplative practices most often used in the classroom, many of which are discussed in the above sections, it is difficult to see compelling risks.

There is little evidence that detaching contemplative methods from their spiritual roots is a risk in the secular classroom, and there is some ambiguity around what the specific risks might be. Certainly, most contemplative educators agree that the practices introduced into the classroom must be clearly secular, developmentally suitable, culturally sensitive, supported by a mindful teacher, and grounded in evidence and pedagogical integrity. Introducing contemplative practices into a secular academy may require extricating these practices from their traditions. Hart (2004) suggests that two basic elements are essential for integrating contemplative practices into mainstream education: (1) a rationale and evidence that these methods respond to the concerns of present-day education and (2) secular methods that can be adapted to the classroom context. Such is true for all pedagogical methods introduced into the classroom. It is always incumbent on the teacher to choose methods carefully and implement them skillfully. Therefore, the critical challenge for the classroom teacher is how to introduce and integrate the practices with competency and mindfulness. Succeeding in this alone offers fidelity to the contemplative tradition even if the practices are detached from their origins.

Teacher Preparation and Qualifications

A major ethical challenge in implementing contemplative methods, and one that evolves from faithfulness to the contemplative tradition, is the growing debate around teacher preparation and qualifications for contemplative work. Simmer-Brown (2011) argues that it is necessary for instructors who implement self-reflective pedagogies to have a personal contemplative practice that in turn provides the context for the methods introduced into the classroom. Therefore, she advocates for "training standards" and an assessment of teacher preparation. She states, "Long before we bring pedagogies into our classrooms, we bring our contemplative minds to ourselves, our students, and the subject area that we teach" (111). Likewise, Barbezat and Bush (2014) argue that although many contemplative practices are simple, they necessitate an ongoing practice of one's own and familiarity with the consequences of these practices. (This agrees with those who hold that all instructors need training and experience in the respective methods they use in their classrooms whether those methods be problem-based learning, service learning, inquiry-based learning, etc.). Some contemplative scholars, however, see this position as leading to a type of "branding," "standardization," or "commercialization" and argue that these "trademarked practices . . . hold the potential for growing into hierarchical systems that limit inquiry rather than encourage it" (E. Davis 2015). Patricia Morgan (2015b) responds,

> I don't think that standardising things will necessarily produce better contemplative pedagogues or researchers, or stop the potential for harm. I think if not sensitively handled it could mean that a lot of fine contemplatives will not be able to teach, they may for example not have the funds if a situation arises where particular courses are recommended that people have to do to become accredited. As we know with many professions that have to go through strict accreditation this doesn't mean that it stops them acting unethically. It always comes back to the individuals and the context.

Embedded in this discussion is a more general concern about the consequences that might emerge from introspective methods in the classroom and teacher preparation for these consequences. Fran Grace notes that contemplative methods are not for all students for a variety of reasons. As one of her students in an honors seminar said, "Who wants to actually *look* at their life? This is a scary prospect. I'd rather *not* know what I am doing" (2011, 105). As one of my own students recently said in a contemplative seminar, "I do not want to talk about pain." This statement referred to a reading and discussion of "Letter from Birmingham Jail." Burack (2014) reminds us that introspective methods are powerful and can promote disturbances. Some students report an agitation and anxiety in confronting difficult emotions and the sound of their inner voice. However, it is often in these moments that a portal opens and that the most profound personal and academic transformations take place. Regardless, the instructor must be respectful of the student's position and the student's agency and freedom to engage the practice or not. The instructor must also be willing and prepared to travel this transformative journey should the student ask for a companion.

Pedagogical Intention

Contemplative educators argue that introspective methods enhance the educational experience of students by improving awareness, refining perceptual and observational skills, promoting risk-taking, and nurturing attitudes of curiosity and wonder (Kahane 2014). Students also express a thirst for such practices as a means for spiritual development. The UCLA Higher Education Research Institute's survey (2005) of 112,000 first-year students indicated that these students have high expectations that their institution will enhance their emotional and spiritual development. Therefore, an effective rationale for the use of contemplative practices in higher education is well established. However, it is critical that contemplative educators think carefully about and clearly articulate an intention for the use of specific methods in their respective classrooms. This is certainly true for all the choices made regarding pedagogical methods in classrooms. However, there may be a particular ethical consideration when interiority and the inner life are central to the pedagogical method chosen. Contemplative practices are nonnormative and unfamiliar for many students in the secular institution and can, in turn, produce an uncertainty and even anxiety not typically experienced with other classroom practices. Some students might respond to such approaches with a reluctance or even refusal to engage in the practice. Therefore, a greater and more deliberate explanation and delineation of contemplative practices by the teacher is needed. If the instructor is unclear about the goal of the practice and the guidelines given to students are inexplicit, more ill than good can result. Burggraf discusses the potential superficial or vague connections between practice and the classroom context:

> A class that begins with a few minutes of silent sitting and then does not connect this experience to the subsequent lecture and discussion is not, in our view, contemplative pedagogy. To the extent that contemplative practice contributes to, and is integrated with academic content or disciplinary methods and bodies of knowledge, the University's mission is served. (2011, 241)

If teachers are to confront the challenges of contemplative practices, we will need to understand the purpose of the practices that we introduce. Burack (2014) expands this point further by suggesting three student-centered goals for including contemplative practices in the classroom: focusing on precise learning outcomes; cultivating cognitive, affective, and spiritual qualities; and improving growth, development, and overall welfare. However, as he suggests, teacher-centered goals must also be grounded in an unambiguous commitment to contemplative practices as "a necessary and powerful means of expressing our holistic or integrative orientation" (2014, 38). Contemplative teachers first and foremost must be faithful to the mission of engaging the whole student and constructing practices that allow this. Grace Bullock (2015) stresses the importance of understanding why contemplative practices are taught and why the specific methods chosen make a difference. She observes that substantive evaluation of the contemplative process is impossible until a clear pedagogical intention is articulated by the teacher.

Grading Interior Dimensions

In a recent workshop presented to my own faculty (and the first one on contemplative practices), the most immediate and expected question was: How on earth do you grade this? For example, how are silence, reflection, personal meaning, and first-person investigations evaluated? These questions are particularly important ones given that today's academy is pressured with rigid standardization and assessment guidelines. Instructors are compelled to produce grades and respond to student queries about these grades. Simmer-Brown states that these dilemmas can be framed as a simple question: "How can we create an environment that supports student self-discovery if we evaluate that discovery?" (2011, 115). Gina Musolino and Elizabeth Mostrom (2005) see the evaluation of contemplative practices as potentially discouraging students' honest responses. Janet Hargreaves (2004) exemplifies these quandaries by pointing to experiences with student writing, arguing that when students are compelled to produce contemplative prose for a grade they are more likely to construct a narrative that is acceptable than honest. Essentially, how can risk-taking be encouraged in students if it has a substantive price? Therefore, the assessment of contemplative practices in the classroom poses a minefield of ethical difficulties for both the student and the instructor.

The ambiguity in contemplative language influences the evaluative language of contemplative practices. Dave Trotman (2006) argues that before a shared evaluative language can be considered, the requisite conditions for educational assessment must occur. While he admits that the assessment of imaginative practice has many challenges, he articulates specific conditions, methods, and processes for assessment:

- observed pupil responses—behaviours, reactions, expressions of mood, emotions and feelings and ideas
- recorded conversations
- pupil interactions
- forms of pupil writing—prose poetry, diaries
- pictures and images
- photography
- animations, storyboards and videos
- choreography
- composition
- improvisations and presentations (2006, 12)

Others also offer ways for assessing interior methods. In her discussion of a *sentipensante* (sensing-thinking) pedagogy, one that assesses both the cognitive and interior, affective aspects of learning, Laura Rendon's (2009) philosophy of assessment is that (1) faculty can establish academic rigor *and also* address individual growth, (2) traditional evaluative methods such as tests and papers can be accompanied by the reflective assessments of journals, contemplative writing assignments, and so on, (3) grades derived from tests should not be used punitively but rather as feedback to evaluate where a student is at particular point, and (4) faculty need to recognize that knowledge and wisdom development take time, often beyond the constraints of a semester. Rendon interviewed faculty members who were assessing interior dimensions, and education professor Sam Crowell said,

> I usually make a distinction at the beginning of every course between the essential question of evaluation and the essential question of assessment. In . . . evaluation you ask a question: Did you learn X, Y, or Z? . . . And there are means of finding out whether or not they learned X, Y, or Z. But I think a more important question for me is the assessment question, which is: What did you learn? And I build that question in several reflective assignments. What did you learn that was significant for you? Can you explain its significance? Can you explore any revelations or insights that our activities in the course—the readings, the processes, the lectures, your work with others? . . . What happened as a result of this course to your thinking and learning? (Rendon 2009, 122)

In my service learning courses, which incorporate contemplative dimensions, I evaluate students on the basis of their weekly journals, which consist of reflections about their experiences with their community placements. Using both traditional and contemplative questions derived from first-person and third-person perspectives, I prompt them to consider the following: What specific concepts from this course are applicable to my service learning experience? How has this experience supported the concept or theory we have studied? How has it raised questions about it? How might I rethink a concept or theory based on this experience? Why should I rethink this? What did I learn about others and myself? Why is it important? What will I do because of it? What impact did this experience have on me? What did I do that was effective and how was it effective? What did I do that seemed to be ineffective, and how could I have done it differently? What values or opinions that I held or decisions I made have changed through this experience? What has surprised me about the agency with which I have worked, the people I work with, and myself?

My students tend to write eloquently and with great insight. I attribute this to two factors. First, the majority of these questions center on personal, first-person experiences, which almost always produce narrative richness. I have learned to trust the extraordinary power of student voice. Second, journal entries are evaluated only in terms of whether the student responded to the prompts. I choose not to assess the quality of their responses, which would be disrespectful of their individual journeys. After many years of making this assignment, I have yet to have a student who failed to respond with integrity and generosity.

Simmer-Brown has articulated a paper-grading rubric for contemplative writing composed of three evaluations. One-third of the emphasis is on comprehension of the readings, which includes confirmation that students "have read the assignment, followed the argument, identified the evidence, and 'done their homework'" (2011, 116). Another third of the paper is grounded in "integration," which she operationalizes as the ability to reflect on what was studied via experience. The final third is constructed on the mechanics of writing, such as structure, fluency, and grammar. For Simmer-Brown, an outstanding paper is one that has successfully assimilated each of these three components. The crucial point is "to show respect for both the first- and third-person aspects of our courses, ensuring rigor that is both academic and contemplative" (116). Barbezat and Bush (2014) also point to the effectiveness of assigned papers, specifically those at the end of the course, that are evaluated on the basis of student integration of contemplative experience with course material. For example, Barbezat describes the evaluative method he uses in one of his economics courses:

> In the syllabus and early in the course, I make it clear to students that the final paper of the course will be an opportunity for them to integrate their [contemplative] experiences with the required readings. After each exercise, I give them time to write down brief notes about their experiences and insights during the exercises and create an online discussion forum for them to share their reactions, insights, and observations. . . . The assessment is based not only on their participation in the exercises but also on their ability to examine and reflect on their experience, deepening their understanding of the course material. (Barbezat and Bush 2014, 77–78)

Sharon Solloway (2014) uses two assessments that she sees as a learning method for both student and instructor. The Solloway Mindfulness Journal evaluates journal subject matter as it relates to the examination of self-awareness, and the Lectical Solloway Mindfulness Assessment focuses on how students comprehend ideas vital to mindfulness practices and measures the complexity of students' thinking about specific mindfulness themes. Each assessment yields a continuing feedback loop for instructor and student. Peter Grossenbacher and Steven Parkin view assessment of learning outcomes as an opportunity for the teacher to give encouraging feedback to the student. For example, cognitive inclusivity can be measured by the student's "variety of content," "breadth of perspectives," and "readiness to engage with additional alternative perspectives" (2006, 6). Via returned papers, instructors can ask questions about the student's individual experience and address content and language use.

Even though these approaches offer important possibilities for grading the contemplative aspects of courses, some believe that outcome-focused assessment methods may not adequately address the contemplative process. Kirsten Song and Glenn Muschert remind us that contemplative practices in the classroom present "a different *quality* of learning experience" and, therefore, may need a different quality of evaluation, one that better captures the usefulness of such practices (2014, 334; emphasis in original). Likewise, some aspects of learning can never be adequately assessed in the context of a single semester or a single year. In his presentation to the 2014 Association for Contemplative Mind in Higher Education conference, Michael Franklin discussed the "downright paralysis" that many instructors encounter as they attempt to grade subjective work. However, he sees this struggle as an opportunity for expanding "contemplative-based grading methods," including self-reflection rubrics that build an inner structure for self-grading and empower students to honestly and responsibly self-evaluate (38).

Barbara Walvoord observes that "the assessment movement is exceptionally powerful because it has captured the accreditation process, which means the accreditors can make us do it" (2011, 336). The measurement of what she refers to as "the ineffable" is particularly germane to the assessment of interior dimensions and, as noted above, is often perceived as difficult if not impossible by those beholden to accreditors. Yet Walvoord reminds us that accreditors essentially require only three steps in the process, in spite of the many guidelines they publish: an articulation of the goals for student learning, a collection of information about how successful students are in achieving the goals, and dissemination of this information to inform decisions and future actions. She recommends locating a language that "plays at the edges" and that describes "ineffable" or "sublime" qualities as critical learning goals (336, 339, 340).

The introduction of contemplative and introspective practices into the college classroom offers many challenges but also important prospects. We as teachers are called to refine language, employ a deeper ethical awareness of our pedagogy, and develop a greater sensitivity toward and empathy for an institution making its way into the twenty-first century. However, the essential embedded in these challenges and opportunities is what Bush (2011b) calls "the question of academic value." She posits the following inquiries: "What value does mindful engagement offer to each discipline, both epistemologically and pedagogically? Does it enhance the creative process, deepen students' engagement with the material, or lead to specific insights that would otherwise be unavailable?" (195). These questions and challenges must be at the forefront when considering *all* teaching and learning methods. They must be continuously asked, answered, and refined and then asked again.

4 Contemplative Research

For all their power, the conventional methods of scientific research and critical scholarship need to be broadened. The reflective, contemplative and experiential methods developed within the contemplative traditions offer a complimentary [*sic*] set of research methods for exploring the mind and the world. When taken together with conventional methods, an enriched research methodology and pedagogy are available for opening up new pathways for deepening and enlarging perspectives which can lead to real and lasting solutions to the problems we confront.

—Art Zajonc, vision statement for the Association for Contemplative Mind in Higher Education

One of the things we learned from the work of the Carnegie Scholars is how hard it is for faculty, regardless of their own field and its rules of evidence, not to assume that credibility means a traditional social science model of inquiry. . . . [M]ost of the questions about human behavior we most want answered are not, in the end, "science" questions, ones that lend themselves to immutable general truth, but rather questions about phenomena as they occur in local, particular contexts (like classrooms!).

—Pat Hutchings and Lee Shulman, "The Scholarship of Teaching"

IN HIS DISCUSSION of the integration of contemplative pedagogies in higher education, Juan Mah y Busch (2014) asks how we might justify a pedagogy whose practices contest the goals of traditional assessment. The contemplative educator Art Zajonc and the SoTL leaders Pat Hutchings and Lee Shulman address this issue by suggesting that a new paradigm of research methods is needed, one that legitimizes multiple ways of knowing, examines new approaches to learning, and offers a wide range of methodological methods. However, SoTL and contemplative researchers have often struggled to locate this paradigm, relying instead on familiar research methods and positivistic models that evolve from their disciplinary traditions. While many traditional methods provide rich and productive venues for investigation and can be appropriate for some of the pedagogical questions raised, some are irrelevant. Consequently, a return to traditional methods has often failed to capture the nature and richness of innovative investigations and impeded the expansion of pedagogical understanding. The SoTL scholar Mary Taylor Huber comments on this tension by suggesting, "Doing the scholarship of teaching and learning sits, therefore, at the edge of most disciplines, calling on but also going beyond the normal knowledge of practices of most fields" (2006, 72).

Most recently, the SoTL practitioners Janice Miller-Young and Michelle Yeo (2015) argue that the interdisciplinary nature of SoTL has led to few research methods that specifically cohere in conceptualization and communication, a particular issue for new scholars. For example, Miller-Young and Yeo observe that within the SoTL community debates continue as to the use of theory and methodology and definitional questions around the constitution and purpose of SoTL. They call for a framework to demonstrate the "tacit links" between theory and methodology (2015, 37). Contemplative researchers echo these observations in pointing out the need to broaden outmoded definitions of higher education by developing new tools to assess such factors as emotional and social intelligence, contributors to life satisfaction, positive interpersonal engagement, ethics, and compassion. In many ways, SoTL and contemplative researchers have faced similar methodological challenges and barriers, many of which evolved from their multidisciplinary and transformative agenda. SoTL researchers have responded in some measure to these challenges in their advancement and broadening of methodological approaches to address their research questions and investigations. However, many of these same researchers continue to neglect interior dimensions with no systematic investigation of the integration of mind, body, and spirit. Although several of the investigative methods advanced by SoTL are slowly appearing in the contemplative practices research, there continues to be a remarkable scarcity of published studies supporting contemplative practices in the classroom. In their 2008 seminal review of research on the integration of contemplative practices into higher education, Shauna Shapiro, Kirk Brown, and John Astin (2008) called for a theory-driven empiricism that addresses such specific questions as: How do we integrate the contemplative into higher education? What outcome measures and methodologies best describe the multidimensional effects of contemplation? What are the underlying processes of various contemplative practices? These questions remain at the vanguard of contemplative research in education. As Grace Bullock (2015) noted, assessing multidisciplinary contemplative processes in terms of outcomes continues to be a point of consternation and struggle.

This chapter provides an overview of extant contemplative practice research as it intersects with teaching and learning. It seems axiomatic that some of the investigative methods used by contemplative researchers are those employed by SoTL since both contemplative and SoTL educators ground many of their methods in learning theory, curriculum development, and pedagogy. Qualitative approaches are examples of shared methodological approaches. However, as Peter Grossenbacher and Steven Parkin suggest, an "open awareness" differentiates contemplative approaches from other approaches to holistic education (2006, 2). The measurement of such dimensions as awareness, consciousness, and internality creates the need for additional types of approaches that have remained elusive for contemplative and SoTL researchers. As with all research, an array of limitations and challenges is associated with particular methods. These characteristics are particularly germane in the investigation of dimensions of learning seldom measured in educational research. The explicit challenge to the measurement of interiority and the implications of this challenge for a twenty-first-century research agenda in higher education are discussed in chapter 5.

Contemplative Practice Research: An Overview

Fran Grace posits that all contemplative investigation is fundamentally empirical in that contemplatives examine the veracity of an assertion through their own interior and experiential research. As she puts it, a "come and see" is the customary response to a "what is it" question (2011, 99). Grace's words are particularly relevant to research on contemplative practices in the classroom because they ask students to be present, attend, and explore their interiority. However, the validity of introspective methods continues to be a significant problem for all contemplative researchers regardless of their disciplinary perspectives. The issue is particularly relevant for educators, as reflected in the dearth of research on classroom practices centered in introspection.

Much of the current contemplative and mindfulness research is not focused on education and correlates of learning but rather on physiological and psychological well-being. Despite the significant report of Shapiro, Brown, and Astin in 2008 that demonstrated how contemplative approaches might be applied to education, empirical attention to the classroom context and processes of learning remains scant. The encouraging news is that contemplative research is burgeoning in the areas of physiological and psychological well-being. A PubMed search reveals that the number of peer-reviewed publications on mindfulness practices alone has increased significantly: fewer than 100 research studies were published in 1998 compared with 661 studies in 2014. Similarly, fewer than 10 studies were funded by the National Institutes of Health in 1998 but by 2014 this number had increased to 121. With few exceptions most of this research has looked at one practice, meditation, and its intersection with clinical populations. We now have impressive indicators, as reported in scientifically measurable ways, that meditative practices can influence physiological and mental changes. Studies in neuroplasticity (Begley 2007; Hölzel et al. 2011; Tang et al. 2012; Allen et al. 2012; Luders et al. 2013; Kurth, Cherbuin, and Luders 2015), psychoneuro-immunology (Davidson et al. 2003; Olivo 2009; Pace et al. 2009), neurogenesis (Lupien et al. 2009; McGowan et al. 2009), cognitive neuroscience (Zelazo and Lyons 2012; Dahl, Lutz, and Davidson 2015), and grounded cognition (Barsalou et al. 2003) support a new view of the mind-body association. These studies find that contemplative practices significantly promote health, alleviate symptomatology, reduce stress and anxiety, and increase longevity. However, Mirabai Bush (2011b, 184) suggests that, beyond such research, the classroom context advances thought-provoking questions regarding the potential of contemplative practices for cognitive transformation. The unambiguous inclusion of higher education in contemplative research is the important next wave.

Although a substantive body of evidence-based research on contemplative practices in higher education is still lacking, the above studies are propitious for contemplative educators. Tobin Hart (2004) claims that the effects of contemplation on physiology have significant implications for learning, specifically in terms of emotional response and cognition. He explains the mind-body changes as due to "physiological coherence," whereby the brain, body, and nervous system operate with efficient synchronization and balance, leading to enhanced cognitive performance (31). Richard Davidson and colleagues (2012) capture Hart's notion of coherence in their review of basic research on contemplative interventions. They strongly suggest there is a "synergistic collaboration" between the scientific assessment of contemplative practices and educational programs specifically intended to develop the cognitive, emotional, social, and ethical selves of students in the twenty-first century (148). This collaborative relationship between the scientific and educational communities has been observed most explicitly in the assessment of student mental health symptoms, such as levels of stress, anxiety, and depression (Roberts and Danoff-Burg 2010; Oman et al. 2008; Jain et al. 2007; Tang et al. 2007), and increases in psychological well-being, such as empathy and mood (Jain et al. 2007; Shapiro, Brown, and Biegel 2007). More recent approaches have concentrated on human development research that targets developmental changes in the brain that affect emotional and cognitive development (Davidson et al. 2012). While most of these studies have concentrated on elementary school children and adolescents, they do offer guidelines for higher education researchers, specifically in the areas of attention and executive function, self-representation and motivation, empathic concern, and prosocial behavior. Lisa Napora (2013) cites several of these developmental studies as being evidence that contemplative practices increase college students' levels of self-compassion and creativity. There is some empirical support for the influence of contemplative practice on undergraduate student performance. In their study of undergraduates receiving short-term contemplative training, Yi-Yuan Tang and colleagues (2007) found an enhancement of performance on executive functions in students exposed to contemplative training. However, Casey Helber, Nancy Zook, and Matthew Immergut (2012) argue that no reasons for such an occurrence have been identified. Nevertheless, studies such as that of Tang and colleagues (2007) offer support for contemplative practice benefiting executive functions in college students. Amishi Jha, Jason Krompinger, and Michael Baime (2007) found that mindfulness training in nursing and medical students is related to attentional subsystems by increasing orienting performance, a form of voluntary attention. As Rosemary Tannock (2008) points out, strong executive function is correlated with academic achievement, as are robust working memory and functioning attentional networks. Such findings suggest that contemplative practices may enable academic achievement.

The research of Sara Lazar and colleagues (2005) represents an important turn for the assessment of contemplative practices in higher education. Their body of research demonstrates that regions of the brain related to attention, interoception, and sensory processing were thicker in the frontal cortex for participants engaging in contemplative training compared with matched controls. Patricia Morgan (2015a) notes that research such as that of Lazar and colleagues and accompanying advancements in the neuroimaging of mindfulness, primarily the location of a neural substrate that strengthens the positive effects of contemplative practices, have wielded an impressive influence on contemplative education. Zoran Josipovic and Bernard Baars (2015) report that findings such as these suggest that mindfulness and contemplative practice have a beneficial impact on cognition, attentional networks, working memory, conflict monitoring, response inhibition, and activation of associated prefrontal areas.

Many contemplative educators are now turning to these findings as a springboard for both theory development and classroom practice evaluation. This junction in contemplative education has led to newly emerging, empirically oriented investigations of the usefulness of contemplative practices in higher education. Kristen Song and Glenn Muschert (2014) observe that such investigations primarily emphasize academic performance. In their summary of such studies, positive cognitive outcomes of mindfulness were correlated with attentional enhancement, stress reduction, better preparedness and information processing, and a reduction in mind wandering. However, David Borker argues that focusing on cognitive and content-directed features of mindfulness fails to integrate intellectual concepts with the dual character of mindfulness, or what he refers to as the "mindfulness of mind and body in harmony" (2013b, 43). Davidson and colleagues (2012) address these concerns in their call for a transdisciplinary research approach in which both the mind and the brain are studied when evaluating the usefulness of new models of learning and educational practices. Brendan Ozawa–de Silva captures the tenor of Borker's and Davidson's admonitions in his call for an approach to assessing contemplative practices that "takes seriously the importance of the body and the relationships between embodied cognitive states both synchronically and diachronically" (2014, 90). Drawing from the grounded cognition research of Lawrence Barsalou and colleagues (2003), Ozawa–de Silva notes that congruent embodied and cognitive states lead to smoother, quicker processing, and study of these states could show empirically how the alignment of body practices, thought, affect, and words produce formidable transformative experiences and shifts in subjectivity.

In their review of research on mental and socioemotional skills that are essential to the goals of education in the twenty-first century, Davidson and colleagues (2012) posit that contemplative practices offer the possibility to strengthen emotion regulation, executive function, attentional control, self-representation, academic motivation and learning, self-awareness, empathic concern, and prosocial behavior. According to these researchers, substantial empirical evidence supports the use of contemplative practices as important and necessary interventions for American education for two fundamental reasons. Contemplative practices entail repetition and practice to develop increased positive habits of the mind associated with complex cognitive function. Contemplative practices also heighten professional development by supporting the desirable qualities in teachers that in turn support compassionate and nurturing classrooms.

One of the most promising bodies of research on contemplative practices in higher education is the current work of Willoughby Britton and her colleagues at Brown University. For the past several years Britton has been assessing the effects of first-person pedagogy courses combined with mindfulness training labs on a group of students who are compared with a control group of students in third-person pedagogy courses who have not had such training. Results thus far suggest increases in attention capacities among the first-person pedagogy students with contemplative practice training. However, Britton also found (purportedly a surprise to her) that mindfulness training correlated with improvements in body awareness, reduction in anxiety and depression, and an increase in compassion for self and others (cited in Roth 2014, 112). Britton's research is among the first to demonstrate the integration of intellectual conceptions with the dual quality of mindfulness in a college student population.

Research Methods, Limitations, and Challenges

The introduction of contemplative modes of learning into the classroom requires an integrity of practice that has as its core a carefully articulated intention and rationale and evidence-based outcomes that support it. Although contemplative practices seem to have the potential to address many of the most pressing questions in higher education and are being integrated in college classrooms by ethical contemplative educators across the country, there remains too little empirical support for these practices. My review of *Mindfulness Research Monthly*, an overview of monthly research updates sponsored by the American Mindfulness Research Association, from its inauguration in 2010 through February 2016, found no published studies on mindfulness as it directly intersects with learning in higher education. Very few studies were based in higher education and focused on students. The few studies that do exist focus on the outcomes of anxiety and stress, sleep quality, and self-regulatory self-efficacy (albeit each of these outcomes can be critical to learning processes). For the most part, contemplative educators currently integrating contemplative dimensions into the secular classroom do such work in silence and with little sense of a collegial commons. If higher education is to be persuaded by contemplative practices for learning, a clear assessment agenda and published evidence-based outcomes are imperative. However, research on contemplative practices introduces unique challenges given the practices' distinctive features and history. The assessment of attention and awareness in the college classroom, dimensions that undergird all contemplative practices and fundamentally differentiate them from all other transformative approaches, has little precedence in research on teaching and learning. There is an irony in this deficiency. Zajonc points out that attention is fundamental to learning, and "while few would deny this, conventional pedagogy makes little effort to develop the student's native capacity for attention directly" (2008, 9). Perhaps the most salient explanation for this lack is that such dimensions are located in the present moment and first-person experience, which are seldom emphasized in the classroom and involve subtle changes that are difficult to quantify. An understanding of these subtle changes entails a radically different approach to assessment and one that might better capture the transformative nature of learning offered by such practices.

The following methods offer possibilities for contemplative and SoTL researchers committed to an assessment of interiority. Some contemplative scholars employ these methods. For many, however, the assessment of contemplative dimensions in the classroom remains unfamiliar and dilemmatic. Consequently, educators either avoid assessment of contemplative practices out of trepidation or integrate the practices with little confirmation that they are effective. SoTL scholars have been among the first researchers in higher education to call for and validate a diverse set of methods that assess multiple ways of knowing. For example, Harry Hubball and Anthony Clarke (2010) underscore methodological approaches derived from SoTL inquiries in higher education that include action research and implementation analysis, experimental design, phenomenological study, quasi-experimental strategies, and narrative case study inquiry. These might be considered quantitative, qualitative, or both, as in a mixed-methods approach. Other methods, such as ethnography and grounded theory, are also used by many SoTL researchers. Although many of these methods are typically used by contemplative researchers, some are not. Correspondingly, those used by contemplative researchers, such as intuitive inquiry and embodied cognitive logics, have not been considered by SoTL researchers in systematic ways. In my own research as a Carnegie scholar in 2000, I found few approaches for capturing significant interior dimensions critical for affective development. Both contemplative and SoTL methods could offer promising models of investigation for one another to consider as we advance the research of interior dimensions in teaching and learning. Contemplative educators conceptualize interior practices as a springboard to learning. As Olen Gunnlaugson states, contemplative knowing is a careful attention to one's thoughts for accessing "a more unconditioned awareness . . . [and, therefore,] a more clear, wise, and compassionate source of knowing that is always already present" (2011, 5). In this way we interrupt our habitual and conditioned thinking processes. SoTL practitioners more often begin with reflective and critical ways of thinking directed toward exterior practices as a venue for accessing interior space. How might we balance these two perspectives, learn from them, and develop new methods that dance together?

Phenomenology

As an assessment method, phenomenology is considered qualitative, focusing on meanings and interpretation and conceptualizing knowledge as coconstructed. Amedeo Giorgi (1997), a pioneer in the early use of phenomenology and qualitative research, describes three characteristics of all phenomenological methods: reduction, description, and the examination of essences. As Tone Saevi (2014) suggests, the phenomenological approach to educational research emphasizes the first-person, "lived concrete, situated experience" of individuals. A fundamental question asked by phenomenologists and one critical to contemplative research is how to maintain and investigate the unspoken and wordless qualities of the classroom (Saevi 2014). Many contemplative researchers seeking to assess classroom practices would agree that phenomenology is an important approach to the understanding of contemplative reflection and reflexivity. Robert McInerney points out that phenomenological methods are "not mediated by scientific constructs, axiomatic presupposition, common sense, or experimentation" (2013, 33), and therefore he rejects cognitivism and cognitive constructs. As he notes, phenomenology will have little to say about learning if we cling to the notion that knowledge is passively constructed by the learner. However, if mindfulness is the intended outcome of contemplative practice (and contemplative scholars believe it is), phenomenological inquiry might be one important and appropriate approach to the central questions around classroom contemplative practice. As Alberto Chiesa (2013) observes, the root for mindfulness is *Sati*, a Sanskrit term that means clear awareness of what is arising in the phenomenological field. The Canadian professor emeritus of education Max Van Manen, like contemplative researchers, sees phenomenology as a "poetizing project . . . [in which] the phenomenologist directs the gaze toward the regions where meaning originates, wells up, percolates through the porous membranes of past sedimentation . . . infuses us, permeates us, infects us, touches us, stirs us, exercises a formative affect" (2007, 12). Given this definition, there is a seemingly comfortable relationship between contemplative and phenomenological perspectives.

Disagreement about how to do phenomenological research in actual practice and what actually counts as phenomenology continues to haunt the field (Finlay 2009). The Western tradition of phenomenology adds to this disagreement with its numerous types of phenomenological research, such as interpretative, hermeneutic, and existential. A discussion of the distinguishing features of each is beyond the scope of this section. However, most contemplative scholars draw on a phenomenological approach that is intersubjective in terms of the relationship between the researcher and participant; interdisciplinary, centered on careful attention to rhetoric and texts, writing and rewriting; and directed toward rich narrative descriptions of experience (Kafle 2011). All are grounded in reflection, clarification, and listening, critical elements in contemplative practices.

A common method in phenomenological research is the semistructured interview, which is typically audio recorded, transcribed, and interpreted and has themes developed based on the data. For example, Pooja Hermanth and Paul Fisher (2015) explored the experience and effect of mindfulness on clinical psychology students through interpretive phenomenological analyses to assess each student's experience of mindfulness training. They point out that in this approach the researcher is the primary instrument for analysis and that the researcher's assumptions are not treated as predispositions or partialities to be excluded but rather as requirements for understanding the student's experience. Through semistructured, individual interviews, two recurring themes emerged: an increased comfort with mindfulness over time and confidence in incorporating mindfulness-based interventions in their self-care, a particularly important dimension for students preparing to serve others.

Michael Strawser (2009), who does not identify as a contemplative researcher or as one steeped in contemplative practice, describes his SoTL project, which applies hermeneutic phenomenology to the assessment of mindful reading assignments. In his introduction to philosophy classes, Strawser requires four such assignments and prompts students to identify a passage and explain its significance. As he explains, the goal of the assignment is not to establish knowledge about content or reasoning but rather to show how the text engages each student's self and transforms the student through his or her interpretation of the text. Strawser categorizes student responses using six themes (defined by Sharon Solloway and Nancy Brooks [2004]): "new energy/excitement for learning, new visions of how they want to enact teaching and learning, new ways of being in the world, new wisdom about themselves, new experience of learning, [and] concrete horizons" (Strawser 2009, 62). According to Strawser, this phenomenological assessment of the mindful reading assignments indicates important pedagogical benefits, which he describes as

> allow[ing] students to determine which passages they find significant rather than the ones I (and the tradition I am following) find significant, and when these passages become the focus of our discussion and analysis, or when the students' reflections provide new questions for their own research papers (which I suspect will happen), it broadens the horizons of us all. (63)

The limitations of phenomenological research include biased recall by participants, small sample size, and lack of a control group, which restricts the generalizability of findings. However, the aim of all qualitative research is to spawn concepts for research as opposed to generalizing outcomes. Linda Finlay (2009) also observes that phenomenology researchers must ask about the extent of interpretation in the basic descriptive project, how to handle researcher subjectivity, and whether researchers are pursuing normative or idiographic understanding. However, in spite of these challenges, Sebastian Sauer and colleagues (2013) emphasize that phenomenological methods provide valuable sources of information for three reasons. When compared with quantitative approaches qualitative data allow a more nuanced inquiry of subjective phenomena, potentially identify various types of mindfulness in a more in-depth manner, and may complement quantitative data in that their essence are explorative rather than confirmatory. For Sauer and colleagues, qualitative approaches such as phenomenology are crucial because they increase the researcher's response to intricate research questions and provide a venue for eliminating simplistic cause-effect models.

Brent Robbins (2013) observes that we are standing on a new frontier of affective neuroscience in which phenomenology has a distinct opportunity for relevance in education. One of the phenomenological methods considered central to this new frontier and the assessment of contemplative practices is neurophenomenology. It is a hybrid of phenomenology and experimental cognitive science and aims to understand first-person experience, the nature of consciousness, and the relationship of consciousness to the brain and body (E. Thompson 2006). Like Robbins, Ozawa–de Silva contends that the use of contemplative practices in education may bear even greater fruit in the field of education than in their current health-related arenas by promoting cognitive, affective, and behavioral changes, or what he refers to as "embodied cognitive logics" (2014, 92); all of these changes are situated in neurophenomenology. This embodied cognition view challenges the brain-computer model posited by many cognitive scientists and neuroscientists. It is grounded in the work of such theorists as Francisco Valera, who suggested that consciousness research is incomplete and called on the research community to arm itself with new methodological tools based in human experience itself (1996, 330). Valera's strategy of including neurophenomenology emphasizes first-person accounts as "a valid domain of phenomena." Valera states,

> To the long-standing tradition of objectivist science this sounds anathema, and it is. But this is not a betrayal of science: it is a necessary extension and complement. Science and experience constrain and modify each other as in a dance. This is where the potential for transformation lies. It is also the key for the difficulties this position has found within the scientific community. It requires us to leave behind a certain image of how science is done, and to question a style of training in science which is part of the very fabric of our cultural identity. (347)

Similarly, Evan Thompson (2006) suggests that first-person reports that are the product of mental training can facilitate recognition and understanding of physiological processes relevant to consciousness. In their study of brain dynamics using first-person data, Lutz and colleagues (2002) found that first-person data were appropriate for detecting and interpreting neural processes, specifically readiness or unreadiness for a perceptual assignment. However, their method has limitations as a research method for classroom practices in that it assumes an experience with phenomenological methods by research participants. In an attempt to address this, Claire Petitmengin (2006) found that interview techniques can assist untrained participants in accurately describing their subjective experience. Patricia Morgan (2015a) argues that these studies lend credibility to the effect of contemplation on learning and thus are significant for higher education. McInerney describes his use of the "neurophenomenological portfolio assessment" in his classroom, or data gathering consisting of the student's description of learning, teacher's ethnographic accounts, and third-person corroborative inquiries "front-loaded into an experimental design using third person methods"

(2013, 49). He argues that phenomenological findings and neuroscience evidence facilitates curricular design and assessment.

Two major criticisms haunt neurophenomenological methods: (1) a reductionist assumption that all explanations of consciousness and cognition can be reduced to physiological descriptions, which inherently rejects first-person experiences, and (2) the explanatory gap between consciousness and physiological events. However, Patricia Bockelman, Lauren Reinerman-Jones, and Shaun Gallagher argue for a science that can expand its approaches so as to embrace "phenomenological practices that capture, investigate, and explain what may be irreducible to strictly neural processes (2013, 3). They posit two significant ways for addressing these challenges. First, neurophenomenology requires rethinking traditional scientific processes and improving communication among researchers to more clearly articulate the methods and goals of neurophenomenology. Second, rigorous scientific practices, such as control, reliability, generalizability, and replication, must be woven into neurophenomenological approaches.

Ethnography

Ethnography, like phenomenology and grounded theory, is considered one of the most influential qualitative research methods. Ethnography is grounded firmly in anthropology, developing out of field research of groups and cultures. However, in more recent years it has also become associated with sociology, social psychology, health, and education. It is an interpretive research process and method with the goal of "thick description" and "webs of meaning" relevant to daily life and practice (Geertz 1973). Nonparticipant observation is the traditional central method used to collect data, although interviews, documentary information, diaries, journals, and so on, strengthen what is observed. Carol Nichols, Lisa Mills, and Mehul Kotecha (2014) observe that while ethnographic observation in applied research is underused, it offers much potential, particularly in research foci that encompass complex interactions that challenge description and subconscious behaviors difficult to access or convey in words. In this respect ethnography offers an important tool for capturing contemplative and transformative practices. Contemplative and SoTL researchers tend to draw on the anthropological practice of reflexive ethnography, whereby the personal experience of the researcher is central to the inquiry and revelatory of the cultural context under study (Ellis and Bochner 2000). Michael Burawoy articulates two basic dilemmas inherent in reflexive ethnography: "(1) There is a world outside ourselves (realist moment), but ethnographers can only know it through their relation to it (constructivist moment); and (2) ethnographers are part of that world (internal moment), but *only* part of it (external moment)" (2003, 668).

The professor of management Fernanda Duarte used autoethnography, a style of reflexive ethnography and genre of writing, to study and reflect on her participation in a professional development project and its impact on her scholarship of teaching and learning. Through a thick descriptive narrative of her experiences over a twelve-month period, followed by reflective analyses of these experiences, she became what she calls "a neophyte pedagogue on a journey of discovery about SoTL" (2007, 2). In using a reflexive ethnographic process, Duarte became the research phenomenon, one that illuminated her constructed narrative and resulted in challenges inherent in the redesign of her courses and the clarification of important institutional issues that emerged from her process. She describes the experience as a metamorphosis that allowed her to view her teaching practice through another lens, which transformed her into a learner. Duarte writes, "I became 'the other,' which in turn prompted me to appraise my experience more critically from the other side of the mirror" (9).

In fieldwork with undergraduate students in communication studies, Christine Davis and Deborah Breede (2015), employed a holistic ethnography to explore communicative and cultural practices of enslaved Africans at the end of life. They argue that holistic ethnography is comparable to an embodied meditation practice in which the researcher focuses attention on physical sensations, contemplation, emotions, and discourse for deep meaning-making and critical investigation. Davis and Breede describe each step in this process, beginning with their cultivation of embodied knowledge through instructing their students to attend and attune to sensory details. They invited their students to transform their field notes into narrative, access their emotions related to their experiences using exercises of mindful attention, and share their experiences with one another to facilitate the potential for new connections and meaning. For these instructors, holistic ethnography offers the type of understanding that is critical for many research approaches, especially those that occur within and outside the classroom. They used this holistic approach not only in this undergraduate end-of-life communication class but also in graduate courses in research methods.

The anthropologist Alicia DeNicola constructs her undergraduate economic anthropology course around an inquiry-based pedagogy that in some important and interesting ways uses reflexivity and participant observation as critical essentials. The understanding of the inquiry element is measured progressively by DeNicola, beginning with participant observation in which "the *observational* mode of experience intrinsic to the role of researcher is hybridized with the more *participatory* experiential mode of the research subject" (Galle et al. 2014, 134–135; emphasis in original). As she attended more deeply to the arc of students' thought and their self-exploration of key questions in the course, she observed that they came to "a kind of crisis" that promoted a more profound level of questioning (135). Using Grant Wiggins and Jay McTighe's (2005) rubric for six facets of understanding as her assessment method, DeNicola was particularly interested in those facets labeled perspective, empathy, and self-knowledge. Through students' papers and their midterm feedback she found that students moved from the bottom of this rubric to the middle section. DeNicola, admittedly not a contemplative researcher in the traditional sense, told me, "I love that you are talking about ethnography as a contemplative practice. . . . Anthropology is very much about not just studying other cultures but thinking about what studying other cultures means. You can't *do* ethnography without this key ethical contemplation" (2016). This ethical contemplation is firmly rooted in the attention processes that frame contemplative studies.

Performance ethnography, a method used by teachers and researchers working within and outside contemplative studies, also relies on reflexivity as central to assessment. The "research field" is based in scripted performances drawn from such contexts and venues as field notes and interviews, documentaries, digital storytelling, and photography. Judith Hamera sees performance ethnography as critical to student learning and moral meaning-making and calls on researchers and teachers to "interpret, and represent what can, must, cannot and will not be said in our research sites" (2011, 327). Carol Oberg (2008) discusses the use of performance ethnography in the college classroom, suggesting that students might be directed toward the field or research site so as to consider a social issue or injustice in the community. In this context they might make observations and do interviews, collect narratives, and reenact in the classroom. According to Oberg, this type of method, or catalyst to thinking and reflection, has significant applications to SoTL. Jessica Lester and Rachael Gabriel describe their integration of a performance ethnography, a written play, into their research methods and education courses. They argue that the introduction of "alternative, arts-based approaches to data representation" (2016, 125) yields significant pedagogical potential. As a methodological perspective, students become participants, observers, and creators:

> It continually strikes us how direct engagement with performative texts links to the emotional, with students moving to laughter, tears, and anger during and after their engagement in ways we do not typically associate with the reading of traditionally presented findings in journal articles or even the engagement with other forms of qualitative research. (129)

As Victoria Foster suggests, theater as one venue for performance ethnography has always been a repository for reflecting on, examining, and interpreting potentially altering dimensions of the human condition. Thus, it continues its tradition as a contemplative art form. Performance ethnography embraces dimensions that are significant to all contemplative practices, "a listening with our eyes [and] an attention to nuances, silences, and embodied feeling" (Foster 2016, 6).

As most ethnographers point out, ethnography is interpretive, subjective, and incomplete, and these features are both its strength and its weakness. In a response to the criticism of the interpretive dimension, Nathalie Depraz, Francisco Varela, and Pierre Vermersch note, "No methodological approach to experience is neutral; they all inevitably interpret their phenomenal data. The hermeneutical dimension of the process is inescapable: every examination is an interpretation, and all interpretation reveals and conceals at the same time" (2003, 9). Central to other criticisms is the sampling and generalizability issue and the accompanying notion that ethnography is context specific and cannot produce a generalizable knowledge that is relevant to other contexts (Taber 2010). Lack of methodological clarity and problems of reliability and validity are also challenges for ethnographers and remain as significant criticisms. An ongoing debate particularly germane to the college classroom is the research-practice relationship that amplifies the questions: How does a pedagogical method such as ethnography translate into progressive practices and influences? How do the observational, contemplative, and activist fieldwork dimensions of ethnography result in knowledge production made *with* people in a manner that is reciprocal and mutually beneficial? Certainly, these are questions asked of social justice and service learning researchers also, and they beg our attention and mindful intention toward professional and personal responsibility whether in or out of the classroom context.

Grounded Theory

Individuals in the tradition of Barney Glasser and Anselm Strauss (1967) argue that the advancement of grounded theory was seminal to the acceptance of qualitative approaches as viable research methods. A grounded approach is often considered an empirical, data-driven, flexible, and systematic method for collecting and analyzing qualitative data when constructing theories. Therefore, theory is grounded in the distilled data. While situated in an interpretative tradition similar to phenomenology, case studies, and ethnography, grounded theory's primary objective is to build substantive theory (in contrast with formal or grand theory) out of the lived experiences and real-world situations encountered by research participants. This objective determines the way the research process is conducted and analyzed. Ruth Fassinger (2005) holds that grounded theory is a methodological prototype of the researcher-practitioner model. Interviews and observations are the more typical data sources. However, as Glasser and Strauss point out, there are other potential sources such as documentary materials, literature, and prior research. Data are analyzed in terms of groupings, properties, and hypotheses and on elucidating relationships among these.

Kathy Charmaz (2011) suggests that two recent developments in measurement offer new and significant paths for grounded theory: mixed-methods research and social justice inquiry. In recent years some critical theorists' work has been faulted for its failure to increase social justice. In response to this critique Gaile Cannella and Yvonna Lincoln (2009) urge us to consider how we adopt research methods for social justice purposes, disseminate critical studies into the broader civic conversation, and interrupt the politics of evidence-based research and knowledge production. Contemplative researchers raise similar admonitions. Grounded theory methods afford an approach that is particularly fitting for social justice and contemplative researchers given that they both attend to thoughts about being human, the construction of benevolent societies, and the exploration of "tensions between complicity and consciousness, choice and constraint, indifference and compassion, inclusion and exclusion, poverty and privilege, and barriers and opportunities" (Charmaz 2014, 326). Charmaz posits that grounded theory's emphasis on empirical examination and methodical precision creates a distinctive and thick critique of how social and economic conditions operate in given situations. The process of grounded theory not only contributes to knowledge production but also highlights the policies and practices that social justice researchers desire to transform. For contemplative researchers, grounded theory methods illuminate an intentional attention to self, others, and the contexts in which they are situated and also offer the potential for addressing one of the central questions in contemplative studies.

Barbara Patterson and colleagues (2015) applied grounded theory methods in a religion and ecology course to assess transformative learning outcomes. The undergraduate course investigated the relationship of the individual to nature by imagining questions around the experiences of place, living systems, and ethical activism. Using data from more than eighty student portfolios over several iterations of the course, they report outcomes strongly suggesting that grounded theory provides the necessary tools for representing the range of complex results resulting from generative transformative pedagogies. They further contend that this type of analytic is particularly well situated for pedagogies that center on inquiry-motivated, experiential, and transformative learning in that they systematically review data and track changes in learning. The authors' attention to and blending of transformative learning theory with contemplative pedagogy through grounded theory is noteworthy and represents an exemplar of a thick, interpretative model of contemplative educational research.

Although the method of grounded theory has notable strengths, particularly for contemplative and critical and social justice researchers, it also has limitations and cautions. The labor-intensive processes inherent in grounded theory, conceptual skills and training required of the investigator, explicit acknowledgment of the investigator's bias, and difficulty in reporting outcomes succinctly because of large amounts of data are all prohibitive and sometimes intimidating for many educational researchers (Fassinger 2005). Some vociferously argue that grounded theory as an inductive method continues to be used by teachers, researchers, and scholars in the field in spite of a deeply rooted belief of the fallaciousness of induction held primarily by those who adopt the hypothetico-deductive method (Pratt 2012). However, psychological research suggests that all human sensibilities are derived from both inductive and deductive reasoning and that learning is contingent on inductive and deductive cycles of analyses (Gasson 2004). Some of the criticisms emanate from confusion arising from a variety of versions of grounded theory and the ontological compatibility or incompatibility of various perspectives. Antony Bryant responds that researchers should be less concerned about the quality of the process and more focused on the research product, noting that "the key issue becomes the extent to which their substantive research produces conceptual innovations and theoretical insights that prove useful. . . . [T]he ultimate criterion for good research is that it makes a difference" (2009, 32).

Intuitive and Narrative Inquiry

Intuitive inquiry, established in the constructivist paradigm, refers to a transpersonal and hermeneutical research method that systematically balances both objective and subjective knowledge through an interpretive process. Rosemarie Anderson (2004, 2011) explains that intuitive researchers pursue a description of what is and imagine new opportunities for the future via a deep reflection process embedded in five iterative cycles. She observes that the method of intuitive inquiry is a way of knowing associated with scientific insight and points to accounts from prominent scientists who have demonstrated the importance of intuitive inquiry to their scientific discoveries. Central to intuitive inquiry is the validation of multiple ways of knowing and meaning rooted in human experience.

In her master's thesis Virginia May (2005) describes the process of artistic practice via the intuitive inquiry methods of questioning, stream-of-consciousness writing and drawing, and mindfulness. She argues that the application of these methods captures the complexity, subtlety, and nuances of the creative process. May observes that intuitive inquiry and the creative process are equivalent undertakings. She asks, "But how have I changed?" and answers,

> I have changed by engaging with my world through intuitive creative processing. Just as in my painting practice I add a new piece of paper to accommodate new visions, I am looking beyond what I already know into unknowingness. Prior to this study I practiced my art in private, often disengaged from my audience, intuitively developing tools and methods for personal exploration. Now through the rigorous process of studying my artistic practice as demanded by the research, I am beginning to see the larger implications of my work as an artist and a researcher. (73)

Dorit Netzer and Nancy Rowe also describe their application of intuitive inquiry for an online course on creativity in which their students integrated the academic theory of the course with personal experience through readings, discussions, transpersonal inquiry, and creative activities. The course was rooted in current scholarship yet encouraged extemporaneous discovery. The instructors encouraged their students to approach their work "in an intuitive, multimodal fashion, as they bridged theory and practice in embodied and deeply conscious ways" (2010, 125). Assessment for these instructors involved anecdotal records in which students offered rich descriptions of how they expanded their understanding of the scholarly literature while experiencing significant inner shifts. According to Netzer and Rowe, their students understood creativity from the "outside in" and from the "inside out" (142) within the structure of the five intuitive inquiry cycles.

While intuitive inquirers argue that validity for this method is formed through consensus building between participants and listeners and centers on meaning, researchers consistently voice several limitations. The current lack of standards for data analysis makes for too few limits on the actual procedures. Some critics argue that while creative freedom can introduce a positive dimension into research, it also has the possibility for researcher irresponsibility and undeveloped research (Frick 1990). Finally, as in the case with all the methods discussed above, the emphasis on subjectivity and personal experience can augment the researcher's bias. However, in reflecting on their use of heuristic methodologies, Ivana Djuraskovic and Nancy Arthur note that inherent in this approach is the paradox that "structure can be found in a highly subjective research method" (2010, 1585).

Self-Report Methods

Self-report outcomes assessing contemplative practices in the college classroom have focused primarily on mindfulness and meditation training. Methods such as questionnaires that require students to provide accounts of their experiences, structured course evaluations, and pre- and postcourse responses via inventories tend to be the most common. Studies relying on self-report methods to describe the effect of contemplative practices on learning are primarily inferential. For example, Doug Oman and colleagues (2008) evaluated stress on college students by gathering data from pre- and post-tests and self-report measures. They found that meditation-based stress-management practices decreased anxiety among college undergraduates. They point out that this type of stress reduction has been linked to improved academic performance, concentration, perceptual sensitivity, reaction time, memory, and self-control, all critical to learning. In their review of evidence-based research of meditative practices in higher education Shapiro, Brown, and Astin (2011) summarize studies on mindfulness-based training as they relate to self-reported decreases in stress and negative emotion and enhancement of positive psychological states in college students. Like Oman and colleagues, they suggest that these studies have important ramifications for the classroom context since positive emotions and stress reduction have been shown to increase ability to process and retain new information, thought patterns that are malleable and creative, and abstract and long-term thinking.

Bullock (2015) holds that while each of these methods can be acceptable evaluative tools, they do have their limitations. She observes that often questionnaires do not explain the mechanisms through which contemplative practices lead to change and do not articulate how and why the change occurs. Similarly, pre- and postsurvey approaches often fail to describe the breadth of student and teacher experience and the processes inherent in these experiences. Many of the published studies associated with self-report measures of mindfulness, such as the Mindfulness Attention Awareness Scale, the Kentucky Inventory of Mindfulness Skills, and the Toronto Mindfulness Scale, have one of two goals: (1) reviews of the development and psychometric properties of the instruments or (2) reports on health-related effects in clinical populations. While there is evidence that self-report measures of mindfulness indicate some validity in clinical populations, there is little support for the generalizability of these effects to other populations and dimensions such as college students and mechanisms of learning. The advantages to these psychometric scales are notably their convenience and familiar methodology. However, in their systematic review of instruments measuring self-reported mindfulness, Taehwan Park, Maryanne Reilly-Spong, and Cynthia Gross (2013) argue that current mindfulness scales have significant conceptual differences, absence of qualitative methods, and questionable construct validity. A major criticism is the lack of a well-articulated definition of mindfulness from which these scales derive. Sauer and colleagues (2013) opine that some of the mindfulness scales operationalize the construct as unidimensional, while others suggest that it has two or more dimensions. Further criticisms of self-report methods are directly related to assessment in education, specifically in the evaluation of learning. Among these is the concern that students inaccurately report their experiences, and memory research strongly supports this apprehension. Another, related concern is a social desirability bias, whereby students overreport positive information and underreport less desirable information (Porter 2012). In his overview of empirical explorations of mindfulness, Richard Davidson (2010) observes that a fundamental and unresolved question is whether research participants can dependably report on the features and magnitude of their mindfulness. Davidson also raises the concern that self-report approaches may alter introspective ability. Claudia Bergomi, Wolfgang Tschacher, and Zeno Kupper (2013) argue that there are three major open issues with self-report measures of mindfulness: (1) questionnaire coverage of the facets of mindfulness to be measured, (2) the quality of the relationships among these facets, and (3) the validity of mindfulness measures using self-report. Harold Roth, however, argues *on behalf of* those subjective experiences captured in self-reports when they are accompanied by rigorous training in and development of "attentional stability and vividness of focus" (2014, 102), critical sources for the analysis and interpretation of subjective experience. For Roth, this type of observation and impartial use of subjectivity is the foundation of contemplative study. From this perspective, self-report assessments potentially offer a stunning understanding of contemplative dimensions in the classroom.

Mary Wright and Joseph Howard (2015) agree that legitimate criticisms surround student self-reports for assessment, but in the case of surveys and scales, prior validation can significantly increase confidence in the resultant data. In their investigation of models assessing quantitative reasoning, they argue that survey-based self-report measurements of student learning might offer the most feasible, resource-efficient, and cost-effective approach. In his investigation of the use of self-report in research focused on the relationship between college students' experience and learning outcomes, Gary Pike argues for the use of construct validity to assess the acceptability and appropriateness of self-report data. He faults much of the research on self-reports, stating,

Too many studies have failed to consider how self-report data are to be interpreted and used. Many of these studies are also atheoretical; they examine the presence or absence of empirical relationships without first developing evaluation criteria rooted in theories of the constructs that the self-reports are intended to represent. (2011, 54)

Contemplative researchers raise similar questions about investigations that lack a theoretical foundation. Shaun Harper and George Kuh hold that little evidence suggests that self-reported data, when competently gathered, are any less reliable than data gathered via other methods. In fact, they argue that "accountability for the accurate representation of voice and sense making is actually more possible" (2007, 9). Likewise, Sauer and colleagues (2013) suggest that the shortcomings of self-report questionnaires sometimes call for alternative ways to measure mindfulness—namely, interview-based methods. For these researchers, interview data may, in specific cases, be a more appropriate choice, particularly when research questions are intricate and when an explorative rather than a confirmative method is more suitable to the investigation.

Cognitive and Attentional Tasks

Research has consistently demonstrated that the capacity to sustain attention is related to academic performance (Shapiro et al. 2006; Treadway and Lazar 2009; Lutz et al. 2009) and that mindfulness training enhances those specific features of attention associated with alertness, focus, and information processing (Tang et al. 2007; Jha, Krompinger, and Baime 2007). Intentionally paying attention to present-moment experiences without responsivity is central to mindfulness and cognition. As Daniel Siegel suggests, "Where we focus our attention channels our cognitive resources" (2011, 85). As in the research emanating from self-report measures, many investigators are turning to cognitive and attentional tasks to make inferences about mindfulness practices as they inform learning (Davidson and Kaszniak 2015). For example, Alexander Morrison and colleagues (2013) assessed the effects of mindfulness training on attention processes in university students. Results revealed mindfulness training advantages in performance on the sustained attention to response task. They suggest that mindfulness training may help diminish the type of mind wandering that negatively affects learning and that is implicated in mood disturbances. Morrison and colleagues suggest that "when developing strategies for improving classroom learning, it may be especially effective to target both attention and mood" (2013, 897). Likewise, Fadel Zeiden and colleagues (2010) employed the Attention Network Test to assess the relationship between mindfulness practices, mood, and cognition in undergraduates. They found that short-term mindfulness training promoted benefits on a variety of cognitive tasks, improving mood, visuospatial processing, working memory, meta-awareness, and executive functioning. The Stroop test, an attentional task measure widely used in psychological and educational research, is increasingly used to assess the relationship between mindfulness and attentional control and flexibility. Elisa Kozasa and colleagues (2012) applied the Stroop test to assess the impact of mindfulness training on brain efficiency in an attentional task. They concluded that mindfulness training increases sustained attention, attentional performance, and impulse control. These measures are also widely used by SoTL researchers, specifically in research pertaining to second-language acquisition (Tomlin and Villa 1994; Thomas, Hameed, and Perkins 2015), working memory and the ability to control attention (Redick and Engle 2006), prediction of academic performance (Kyndt et al. 2015), and attention deficit hyperactivity disorder (Lansbergen, Kenemans, and van Engeland 2007).

Research centered on cognitive and attentional task methods is interesting and promising, and it adheres to a more traditional, familiar paradigm of research that can be significant in encouraging institutional support for contemplative practices. However, as is true with many of the other methods discussed above, cognitive and attentional tasks fail to address several important issues in contemplative research. Chief among these is the inability to determine the length and intensity required to produce any effect on learning. As Alfred Kaszniak (2014) points out, what kinds of educationally advantageous changes in attention necessitate a longer training period are not known. A second major issue and one that Kaszniak among others addresses is whether brief mindfulness training can result in lasting change since so few studies concentrate on follow-up assessment.

Mixed Methods

Each of the lines of research discussed above is introduced as a single method, and the qualitative versus quantitative debate continues. But the qualitative-quantitative bifurcation is significantly decreasing. Many researchers, including contemplative and SoTL educators, are choosing mixed methods and blended approaches that best lend themselves to a more nuanced and rich description of the lived experience of humans. In recent years a mixed-methods approach (or what some researchers label integrative or blended research) has been considered the gold standard for rich, imaginative, balanced, and practical research. It is generally recognized as the third major research prototype, along with quantitative and qualitative methods, in which both perspectives, with their data collection, analyses, and inference practices, are employed for their breadth, depth, comprehension, and corroboration (Johnson, Onwuegbuzie, and Turner 2007). Because of these specific characteristics, many SoTL and contemplative researchers draw on mixed-methods paradigms as the most appropriate response to the inquiries pursued in their multidisciplinary contexts and studies of complex teaching and learning processes. Sharon Solloway and William Fisher (2007) point out that the time has never been better for researchers to nimbly move between qualitative and quantitative measures. In their study of mindfulness in measurement they found that qualitative evidence from student journals supported the existence of measurable mindfulness properties. These researchers concluded that the hermeneutic integration of qualitative and quantitative methods evidenced contemplative practice as measureable, teachable, and learnable and as a object of empirical research. Their study further suggests that the derived qualitative data substantiated by quantitative data support the value of mindfulness practices as assignments in the university classroom.

David Sable (2014) combined a SoTL and a contemplative investigation of critical thinking. He argued that there is a disparity in the literature between traditional models of critical thinking and students' descriptions and explanations of their critical thinking experience. He asked how classroom-based contemplative practices (mindfulness meditation, reflective inquiry, reflective journal writing, dialogue, and facilitated class discussions) augment the essential dispositions for critical thinking in undergraduate courses. Sable applied a mixed-methods approach to develop a response to his research question. His grounded theory approach (transcripts from audio recordings of interviews) allowed him to construct theory from his students' experiences "rather than preconceiving theory to confirm or disprove" (2014, 9). These experiences were dependent variables in the quantitative stage of the research. Sable summarizes his findings as supporting the positive impact of contemplative practices on the reflective dispositions for critical thinking.

The director of the Contemplative Studies Initiative at Brown University, Harold Roth (2014), describes the contemplative pedagogy research that has been developing among more than four hundred students at Brown. He points to the substantive correlation between quantitative and qualitative results. Roth notes that the qualitative dimensions of students' self-reported increase in their ability to concentrate on present tasks along with a decreased attachment to the static idea of a judgmental self leads to less fluctuation in emotionality. He also found that students demonstrated the capability to tolerate negative feelings. For Roth, such results confirm two major goals of contemplative practices in the classroom: experiential knowledge with course material and a broader and deeper understanding of this material. The research results demonstrate a strong positive outcome of teaching contemplative practices within an academic and classroom context.

Laura Rendon's (2009) study of college and university faculty members does not rely on a mixture of quantitative and qualitative methods. Rather, she chose blended methods, viewpoints, and dialogues grounded primarily in heuristic research and transpersonal methods. She describes her process as merging traditional methods with imaginative tools, which engage the dynamic quality of teaching and learning. Rendon interviewed college and university teachers (as well as some of their students) who adopted an integrative method to teaching and learning and "who understood, at least intuitively, that educating for heart was as important as fostering intellectual development" (2009, 154). Her work culminated in the description of a model of "integrative, consonant pedagogy," which she calls *sentipensante* pedagogy. This model has been an important contribution to the academic fields of service learning and social justice and to classroom practices that value subjectivity, emotion, intuition, and personal experience (Rice and Horn 2014; Saltmarsh 2010; Saltmarsh, Hartley, and Clayton 2009).

The mixed-methods approach has some drawbacks. For example, Louise Doyle, Anne-Marie Brady, and Gobnait Byrne (2009) discuss the incompatibility idea, that qualitative and quantitative methods cannot be combined in one study because of their differing ontological and epistemological origins, a type of dichotomy between positivist and postpositivist positions. However, some respond that mixed methods provide an opportunity for researchers to disable this erroneous dichotomy. R. Burke Johnson and Anthony Onwuegbuzie (2004) observe that mixed methods are time consuming and often expensive. Charles Teddlie and Abbas Tashakkori suggest that one remedy to some of these criticisms would be to provide greater in-depth experiences at the doctoral level, where students might have recourse to mixed-methods mentors and "methodological connoisseurs" (2011, 296). Some critics of mixed methods point to the tendency of mixed-methods researchers' claim of greater validity of results than warranted. These same critics call for an appropriate use and interpretation of "quantitized coding from qualitative data" and appropriate generalization given the choice of the sample and the methods used (Bazeley 2004). While the mixed-methods paradigm is now seen as a viable research approach, strategies to guarantee the rigor of the methods are still being established. R. Burke Johnson, Anthony Onwuegbuzie, and Lisa Turner (2007) observe that some disagreement remains regarding the stages of the research progression in which mixing can or should occur and what the effective strategies are for integration in the various stages. They also question whether equal use of qualitative and quantitative designs and epistemologies is even possible. Kate Fitzpatrick asserts that every stage of the research design should align with the rigor each method mandates, with the primary question being, "Would the design of this portion of the study be able to stand alone were it not part of a mixed methods study?" (2014, 219).

Broader Research Challenges

The methods described above are those most frequently chosen by contemplative scholars. Many SoTL scholars also, unsurprisingly, draw on these same methods because contemplative and SoTL researchers have foundations that share several important characteristics. Virtually all contemplative educators and many SoTL scholars honor first-person practices that rely on personal reflection and ways to enrich these reflective processes. An emphasis is placed on the documentation of teaching and learning effectiveness in ways that often cannot be captured in the experimental strategies of traditional research. They expand the definition of *science* from its emphasis on hypotheses, measurement, experimentation, and prediction to include deeper methods of understanding and experiential knowledge. Each privileges the important question raised by the SoTL scholar Randy Bass "How can students 'learn to be,' through both the formal and the experiential curriculum?" (Bass 2012). Both assume that their classroom practices are the research itself. Contemplative teachers see their research as a venue for "being aware of [their] own assumptions and biases, openness to 'not knowing,' valuing questions as much as answers, a willingness to be surprised" (Bush 2015, 339). Correspondingly, SoTL teachers define their research as an examination of practice, an "ethic of inquiry" and the actual character of SoTL (Hutchings 2000, 9). Clearly, SoTL research has been directed toward a comprehension and interrogation of the complexities integral in teaching and learning and the legitimization of innovative questions. Contemplative researchers see their goal as the creation of learning and research environments that look deeply into personal experience and meaning in the service of a more just and compassionate society. While most of the methods used by these two groups of researchers are similar, if not the same in many cases, the *intent* driving selected methods can be fundamentally dissimilar.

Broad and substantive issues remain. Chief among them is definitional properties. Like SoTL researchers and their struggle with defining the qualitative dimensions of its model and research approaches, contemplative researchers have yet to articulate and fully refine the construct of mindfulness, the core of contemplative practices. Richard Davidson and Alfred Kaszniak (2015) note that contemplative scholars fail to agree on a meaning of *mindfulness*, resulting in little evidence that the practices associated with the term are similar and yield the same outcomes. Similarly, John Dunne discusses the ramifications of undefined fundamental terms by arguing that "it's easier to ignore inconsistencies in meditative practices, personal bias in research, the potential for negative side effects, and doubt when there isn't one agreed-upon definition" (quoted in Bogle 2012, 16). Patrick Comstock (2015) observes that there are seemingly two very different vocabularies in defining *mindfulness*: (1) an existential, phenomenological lexis that refers to the experience of mindfulness from a first-person perspective and (2) a scientific language that operationalizes and reduces the content and effects of mindfulness to empirically verifiable terms. A related and critical factor contributing to an ambiguous definition is the tension between definitions of mindfulness grounded in Eastern wisdom traditions and modern definitions conceptualized within Western psychology. Inherent in the modern Western psychology perspective is the debate over mindfulness as a unitary versus multifaceted trait. Chiesa (2013) observes that while the modern perspectives are easier to understand, they nevertheless fail to answer significant questions, such as Do mindfulness levels increase following participation in mindfulness-based practices? Are these increases specific to the contemplative or mindfulness practice or are they due to other effects? Is it possible to generate an unambiguous operational definition? Is it conceivable that no behaviors or physiological markers are specific to mindfulness? Josipovic and Baars (2015) continue the conversation in suggesting that science alone may not be able to adequately respond to ontological and metaphysical questions about the quality of consciousness embedded in contemplative practices. They observe that one of the most thought-provoking issues for mindfulness practices is the few indexes of individual experience during the actual practice other than self-reports. Lutz and colleagues (2015) hold that while these different perspectives, questions, and approaches to research on mindfulness add an important diversity for enhancing our exploration and understanding, they also create unresolved tensions among subdisciplines such as cognitive psychology, developmental psychology, psychiatry, preventive medicine, and education.

A second major concern is related to the goal of measurement. Song and Muschert (2014) point out that the majority of empirical studies measuring the utility of mindfulness in academic performance are concentrated on outcomes that tend to minimize processes that generate outcomes. Therefore, a focus on learning as a process may highlight and best capture the value of depth and breadth afforded by contemplative practice in the classroom. As seductive as outcomes might be to those who identify as empiricists, most of the classroom contemplative practices stress present-moment awareness and the value of experience in contrast to secondary outcomes as reflected in improved grades or behavior. The benefits of calmness of mind and deep awareness, while difficult to quantify, are nevertheless fundamental to learning (Hart 2004). SoTL scholars have also urged educators to attend to process as a crucial contribution to the field of higher education. SoTL's legitimization of research that seeks to understand teaching and learning processes has led to a new paradigm that lends credibility to alternative ways of assessment. This contribution can offer support to contemplative educators at a time when the evaluation of contemplative methods continues to be located in neuroimaging and physiological measures with little attention to classroom practices in higher education.

In their excellent review of conceptual and methodological issues in research on mindfulness, Davidson and Kaszniak (2015) conclude that while progress has been made over the past decade with more sophisticated designs, mindfulness and contemplative research is still in its infancy with many questions remaining. They point to significant conceptual and methodological difficulties. For example, interventions and practices still lack "rich description . . . and [an articulation of] how and by whom [they are] being taught" (2015, 590). Instructor qualifications, training, and preparation to guide mindfulness practices remains a quintessential and worrisome issue among contemplative scholars. Davidson and Kaszniak also point to control groups as a problem for researchers, in that double-blind, placebo-controlled trials are not possible for mindfulness research. Other contemplative scholars raise concerns around the integrity and the amount of practice. As Madhav Goyal and colleagues (2014) note, various types of mindfulness practice may produce a differential effect on outcomes. Lutz and colleagues raise a concern not yet investigated and yet critical to mindfulness practices: "Regardless of the domains targeted by any specific instruction, what do individuals actually do when they engage in any contemplative practice?" (2015, 652).

They suggest that contemplative research lacks a nuanced first-person method that illustrates how individuals engage contemplative instructions and that describes the context of their practice, both of which are critical to the demonstration of outcomes if, in fact, outcomes are seen as critical to the integrity of the research.

Several other issues plague contemplative research. In her research on contemplative pedagogy with college students, Joanne Bagshaw (2014) found that many instructors and researchers continue to implement contemplative practices in the classroom on the sole basis of evidence from former studies of clinical populations or stress-reduction programs. Reliance on these studies may or may not lend support to studies in the college classroom. Bagshaw and others argue that most mindfulness studies have a small number of self-selected research participants, have inadequate control groups, and lack diversity. Replication and generalizability are significantly limited. Davidson and colleagues (2012) also see little specificity about age-appropriate contemplative interventions and culturally appropriate adaptations. For example, much current discussion is about developmental changes in brain structure, function, and cognitive development. This issue becomes particularly salient for those who teach undergraduates, many of whom are in the transition from late adolescence to early adulthood. It is possible (and perhaps probable) that certain classroom practices might be more appropriate for traditional-age undergraduates than for graduate students and older adults returning to college. Davidson and colleagues (2012) remark that the language used in mindfulness-based practices might be acceptable or unacceptable to ethnic groups.

Many of these concerns deal primarily with the risk of oversimplification and lack of precision related to the mindfulness construct. Thus, they significantly hamper research in the emerging field of contemplative studies (Harrington and Dunne 2015). The implications for higher education might be even more significant. Of course, definition per se and the approaches to and gathering of evidence are concerns all pedagogues experience as they introduce nascent methods and theories. In Max Van Manen's eloquent and encouraging words,

> Human research is rigorous when it is "strong" or "hard" in a moral and spirited sense. A strong and rigorous human science text distinguishes itself by its courage and resolve to stand up for the uniqueness and significance of the notion to which it has dedicated itself. . . . [A] rigorous human science is prepared to be "soft," "soulful," "subtle," and "sensitive" in its effort to bring the range of meanings of life's phenomena to our reflective awareness. (1997, 18)

Nevertheless, the methodological issues that haunt contemplative practices must be confronted in deliberate and serious ways for the future of contemplative practices in higher education and for the development of a much-needed portico into what Phyllis Robinson describes as the "deeper dimensions of learning" (2004, 107).

5 The Contemplative Mind

A Vision of Higher Education for the Twenty-First Century

The greatest educational challenge today is not downloading more, better, sophisticated knowledge and skills into students but helping them to cultivate the unity of heart and mind (and let's not forget the *embodied* nature of this cultivation) through the work of awareness, and bring this unity fully into all contexts of their personal, communal, academic, and professional lives. . . . Can our schools, from kindergarten to university, be institutions of wisdom?

—Heesoon Bai et al., "A Call for Wisdom in Higher Education"

THE CALL OF Heesoon Bai and colleagues in 2014 for an academy of wisdom continues unanswered by most universities in 2017. For Robert Thurman wisdom is the "engine of liberation" and the "ultimate cause of awakening" (2006, 1770, 1769). At the Mindfulness, MOOCs, and Money in Higher Education Conference, John Pryor (2016), senior researcher with Gallup, presented his assessment of well-being in college graduates. Only 11 percent of college students were thriving in all five of the indexes measuring well-being. David Germano (2016), University of Virginia's founding director of its Contemplative Sciences Center, expands Pryor's finding by suggesting that failures in universities are manifested by (1) student suffering (stress, anxiety, sleep difficulties, depression, and relationship difficulties, among many others), (2) fragmentary knowledge that fails to include an attention to the heart and an ontology of care, (3) hidden knowledge, whereby much of what is produced has no rewards or venues, (4) disrupted knowledge as evidenced in an explosion of data with little ability to handle it, and (5) inert classrooms where the skills needed in the world are undeveloped. As Lisa Napora (2011) argues, these issues are situated in a world of increasing complexity and turmoil and a fluctuating, international, and information-grounded economy. Many of the competencies now required bear little resemblance to those necessary in past decades. Given these serious concerns, a university positioned in wisdom might appear inaccessible and yet be never more needed.

Embedded within the crises of higher education are important inquiries that offer great potential and promise. The call for a modern skill set signifies an expansion of higher education's goals beyond the procurement of information. These newly articulated skill sets afford an opportunity for the reimagination of the university's purpose and practice, one centered in an ethical and compassionate vision for the twenty-first century. Contemplative methods are requisites for the creation of a new type of academy that best meets the needs of students, staff, faculty, administrators, and communities beyond the campus gates.

This chapter envisages such an academy and the components critical to its sustainability, health, growth, and integrity. The integration of the contemplative mind into teaching and learning is a vital support to these components and to the maturation of the modern university. This chapter explores how the contemplative vision might be better articulated, interrogated, strengthened, and systematically assimilated into teaching and learning in higher education, thereby contributing to the wisdom development required for this new century. The contemplative turn in education offers an attention to those aspects of our being long forgotten by the university but essential today if we as learners, teachers, and citizens of the world are to thrive and build a saner and more considerate twenty-first century. As Thurman (2006) argues, if liberal education is to realize its mission and its responsibility, the teaching of contemplative skills is not a luxury but an obligation.

A Reconciliation of the Definition Mandate

One of the most enduring challenges to contemplative pedagogy is the lack of a clear definition. Many contemplative educators explain the mindfulness construct in a variety of ways: a single or multifaceted trait or state, a specific type of mental process, a method for fostering any or all of these categories, or an independent variable. Paul Grossman (2008) observes that this multidimensionality of the construct has led to a conceptual pluralism that is problematic, particularly in assessment. For Oren Ergas (2013) the lack of definitional resolution further complicates the meaning of contemplative pedagogy and contributes to its marginalization in Western higher education. However, Sebastian Sauer and colleagues (2013) argue that pluralism is not necessarily a weakness but may be a strength. They point out that mindfulness can be conceptualized as a universal psychological experience that is situated in context and culture. From this perspective, multiple definitions are not necessarily contradictory but rather add to the exploratory nature critical in understanding the many dimensions of mindfulness and contemplation. One of the most pervasive tensions in contemplative pedagogy is whether practices writ large, including many pedagogical approaches, reduce contemplative pedagogy to an anything-goes approach that is harmful to student and faculty development and further development of the field of contemplative studies (Sarath 2014). While few of us would endorse an anything-goes approach in contemplative classrooms, casting a wide net of contemplative practices seems critical to integrating them into higher education and into teaching and learning. If contemplation and mindfulness cohere around three major features—awareness, presence, and acceptance—and most contemplative scholars agree that they do, might we not introduce a variety of practices into classrooms that honor these features without compromising the integrity of contemplative pedagogy? As we introduce a contemplative practice into our classroom, one steeped in integrity, salient questions to direct our energy toward are: Why introduce contemplation and this particular practice? Do we fully understand the practice and are we sufficiently trained and prepared for its introduction? Is the practice developmentally and culturally appropriate? Do we fully appreciate its contextual strengths and its potential weaknesses and dangers? Are we prepared to devote the time necessary to understand a practice effect? How might we evaluate this effectiveness? These questions and their accompanying responses seem far more critical to the growth of contemplative pedagogy in the secular university than a fluid and elegant definition that is operationalized solely for outcome-based research (albeit such research will be necessary). In the struggle to interrogate and understand the importance of these questions and respond to them, we probably will move closer to the refinement of terms and definitions. As we move forward into the twenty-first century, in spite of the progress and development made so far in the field of contemplative studies, agreement on a single definition of mindfulness and contemplation is unlikely. An agreement might be reductionist and contribute to more serious problems relevant to the field. What we might agree on, however, is the need to judiciously qualify the method used as we conceptualize and introduce contemplative practices.

A Contemplative Research Initiative

Definitional properties are, of course, critical to measurement. If we are to find legitimacy as contemplative educators in the academy, a research initiative is an imperative. Contemplative practices in the classroom abound with ambiguous effects. Alfred Kaszniak (2014) suggests that it is difficult to differentiate the effects of contemplative practices from other practices in the classroom. He admits that while he is encouraged by the use of contemplative practices in his own classroom, his research does not suggest an unambiguous interpretation. Much of the momentum of contemplative educational research comes from several concerns.

Contemplative researchers often rely on traditional, well-known empirical methods that have approval and credibility in the university. However, many of these methods are outcome centered and not well suited for the questions asked by contemplative educators. The complex questions regarding internal experiences voiced by contemplative researchers cannot be addressed by the relatively simple cause-and-effect model. Thus, assessment of contemplative practices necessitates an openness to and intentional use of explorative, mixed methods that include cognitive, affective, and interpersonal assessment tools that are based in first-person (subjective), second-person (peer or teacher report), and third-person (behaviors or observations) reports. Richard

Davidson and colleagues (2012) hold that a complete understanding of the influence of these practices is multilayered and requires assessment methods from neuroscience, behavioral measures of cognition and attention, measures of physical health outcomes and academic performance, and reports by and interviews with students, teachers, and parents regarding behavior and experience. While seeking acceptance for contemplative practices in the academy through empirical verification, it behooves us to remember that the measurement of these practices calls for care, caution, and a substantive reimagining of the traditional research paradigm. As Evan Thompson (2006) points out, some cognitive scientists are beginning to accept the idea that there cannot be a complete science of the mind without understanding subjectivity, consciousness, and first-person reports of experiences. One major task for contemplative educators is to demonstrate a method for decoding subjective experiences and first-person accounts and translating them into shared and replicated research findings. Qualitative methods are nuanced and may provide one of the most robust approaches to assessing contemplative experiences. However, other methods also offer promise, such as neurophenomenology, action research and implementation analysis, quasi-experimental strategies, intuitive inquiry, grounded theory, and cognitive and attentional tasks. These methods not only advance the field of contemplative studies in higher education but also demonstrate a response to those research questions that center on phenomenological states, experience, transformation, and interiority, particularly as each interacts with and informs teaching and learning.

Contemplative scholars Daniel Barbezat and Allison Pingree (2012) appropriately turn to SoTL as a guide for contemplative researchers. They point out that evaluative research of contemplative practices is currently underdeveloped and call on teaching and learning centers and SoTL scholars for much-needed direction in studying them. SoTL scholars have been among the first educational researchers to broaden understanding of assessment in higher education and subsequently introduce innovative methods of measurement. A review of the work of Carnegie scholars alone clearly demonstrates advancement not only in the conceptualization of teaching and learning but also in approaches to research questions. The senior Carnegie scholar Pat Hutchings (2000) posits a taxonomy for questions asked in SoTL research: What works? (questions of evidence), What is? (questions of description rather than evaluation), What are visions of the possible? (questions related to goals), and How to build theory? (questions constructed to build theoretical frameworks). These questions are particularly relevant and appropriate for contemplative researchers in that they both include and expand traditional assessment models. They serve as important prototypes for contemplative research questions. Once again, the potential reciprocity and collaboration between SoTL and contemplative educators offers assurance, particularly in the area of assessment development.

A closely related issue for contemplative researchers is the primacy placed on data collection rather than the actual creation of contemplative practices in the classroom.

David Borker (2013a) observes that practices in the classroom should drive data collection rather than the reverse and argues that the prospects for empirical research of contemplative practices will depend initially on the judicious use of these practices in the classroom. Similarly, the educational researcher Nadine Dolby holds that research questions cannot lead but only follow: "Researchers cannot begin to ask questions and unravel problems about things that we cannot see nor understand" (2016, 3). As contemplative researchers, we cannot ask questions and hypothesize about classroom practices until we consider and analyze what is fully present in the context of our own classrooms, a fundament of SoTL research. As a classroom community, we must be willing to be present with, or attend to, our practices and thoughtfully consider how they might deepen teaching and learning, as well as personal growth. Of course, critical to this consideration are student voices and the insights students bring to the discussion of classroom practices. Kirsten Song and Glenn Muschert's (2014) research points to the importance of asking how students comprehend contemplative practices in the classroom and how they assess the efficacy of these practices in their learning. This process prepares us for the study of best practices, the questions we might ask for the development of a research initiative, and for the longitudinal studies sorely needed in contemplative practice research in higher education.

The significance of theoretically guided investigations is another concern to contemplative studies and too often absent in contemplative practice research. Hutchings (2000) also emphasizes the importance of theoretical inquiries in SoTL research. As early as 2008 Shauna Shapiro, Kirk Brown, and Alexander Astin voiced concern regarding the dearth of studies available in contemplative higher education. They recommended the use of theory-based models "to make logical predictions about behavior, to explain it, and to apply research-derived principles of behavior to real-world settings" (2008, 24). Too few studies of contemplative practices have heeded this call despite models grounded in empirical support and applicable to the study of contemplative practices being indeed available. As discussed in the introduction and also by Shapiro, Brown, and Astin (2008), models of attention, metacognition, transformative learning, and emotional intelligence have the potential for providing a theoretical basis and one starting point for investigations, further theory development, and more precise questions. However, it is also critically important to include theoretical diversity that allows indigenous explanations advanced by individuals in traditions unfamiliar to many in the teaching and learning communities. In contemplative and SoTL research, indigenous perspectives are more often than not absent. As Rendon argues, we must "push and expand theoretical paradigms regarding knowledge construction, production, and use . . . [through] a multiperspectival approach" (2009, 44).

Collaboration and synergy among scientists, educational researchers, and contemplatives from wisdom traditions is growing, but much more is needed. The substantive research done by cognitive and developmental scientists and neuroscientists on contemplative interventions is disconnected from classroom practices. While this research is compelling and has important inferential ramifications for college and university classrooms, much of it has been done in laboratory settings and on clinical or other special populations. Research approaches such as neuroimaging and other physiological measures are typically inaccessible for classroom research, and generalizations from studies using such measures and applied to classroom practices provide questionable support.

Madhav Goyal and colleagues (2014) observe that the scarcity of methodological controls adds to the limitations in contemplative research and possibly inflates the size of benefits. Richard Davidson and Alfred Kaszniak (2015) point out that studies lacking control groups for comparison do not provide credible evidence for the efficacy of such interventions. They argue that the most reasonable approach is to use a comparison treatment condition that corresponds to the mindfulness intervention in all of the rudimentary elements. Few studies of classroom practices use control groups, which would make their results more robust. However, nonrandomized control groups are possible, particularly in the case of two classes that are equally matched, with the exception of the contemplative intervention. While Davidson and Kaszniak's discussion primarily refers to clinical populations, some of their recommendations are worth consideration as we deliberate the use of control and comparison groups in assessment of classroom practices. Structural matching of groups is essential. Classes should be comparable in length, requirements, and expertise and confidence of the teachers. Data on the faithfulness of the practice implementation should be regularly collected for analysis. As they point out, such recommendations "constitute a high bar" but are requisites if we are to address these methodological limitations (2015, 589).

An issue allied to methodological controls is the training and qualifications of classroom teachers who implement classroom practices. Many instructors have little to no training in contemplative perspectives, whereas others bring a fully developed and well-practiced understanding of mindfulness into the classroom. The differential of teacher experience has seldom been controlled for in research on contemplative practices, particularly in higher education classrooms, often resulting in either an inflation or deflation of research findings. Many scholars hold that teacher expertise in mindfulness practices is essential if teachers are to guide students in the practice and report on their experiences (Shapiro, Brown, and Astin 2008). Researchers should assess teacher experience in the measurement of practices and also consider how this experience affects the practice. A venue for the development of these understandings is often inaccessible or absent primarily because of the lack of teacher training models in contemplative higher education. Interestingly, teacher training models in contemplative methods are in the K–12 literature, creating possibilities for research initiatives and prototypes for higher education research. A collaboration among primary, secondary, and higher education teachers and researchers could yield greater insight into the assessment of contemplative practices at all classroom levels. SoTL researchers have modeled this collaboration effectively. For example, SoTL scholars often acknowledge the ways action research, primarily associated with K–12 assessment, can illuminate and corroborate SoTL research at the university level. In reflecting on the transformation of his teaching practice through action research, SoTL researcher Kalpana Goel observes that "the scholarship of teaching and learning is all about sharing, demonstrating, implementing, evaluating and learning from experience—a cycle of action research . . . [yielding] an evidence-based grounding" (2012, 3). Collaborative efforts among all researchers are critical if we are to provide practices that are respectful of the contemplative tradition and that allow appropriate assessment.

Another issue that continues to haunt contemplative researchers is an unclear understanding of the amount of time and intensity of practice required for certain outcomes and benefits. A one-minute mindfulness meditation for sixteen weeks in class might produce very different results from mindfulness exercises woven through each daily classroom experience. Although there is support for the hypothesis that mindfulness practices are associated with enhanced attention and emotional regulation, additional research is needed to determine the length of practice that will produce the desired changes in these dimensions. Associated with a discussion of the time variable are questions regarding stability versus momentary effects of the practices. Future studies need to look specifically at these variables through well-crafted longitudinal assessment.

Finally, we have little understanding of individual differences as they intersect with classroom contemplative practices. Are some students more likely to benefit from these practices than others, and are some students more vulnerable to the practices in comparison to others? Some students enter classrooms from homes where mindfulness and meditation are central to their daily lives. These students tend to embrace such practices, find comfort in them, and see them as deepening learning. Other students feel their religious identities are threatened, which may interfere with learning and a sense of safety in the classroom. Thomas Plante and Adi Raz (2010) emphasize the importance of culture, socioeconomic status, and religion of origin in the investigation of contemplative practices in the classroom and call for examining the effectiveness of contemplative practices with certain populations of students and the role that belief in these practices plays in obtaining the desired effect. Well-trained contemplative instructors can address these issues with acumen and clarity. Nevertheless, such issues and questions are serious and require far more studies than what we currently have available.

A future research agenda must address these issues in a systematic and rigorous manner. Research initiatives have the power to inform education policy by centering on variables emphasized by the Association of American Colleges and Universities and promoted in the majority of college and university mission statements: social and emotional well-being, academic development (specifically metacognition and attention processes), self-regulatory skills, prosocial dispositions, and ethical maturation. Robert Roeser and colleagues state that researchers should thoughtfully and carefully attend to "contexts of reception or rejection" that will, respectively, facilitate or hinder the introduction of contemplative classrooms and programs (2012, 171). In this respect we might ask: What changes are occurring in higher education that yield opportunities for the introduction of contemplative practices into the classroom? What does the university need, and how might a contemplative curriculum respond to this need? Answering these questions offers concrete ways to move a research agenda forward. Each suggests an opportunity for building a viable contemplative classroom, curriculum, and academy.

Ethical Discernment for a Transcultural and Global World

The state of humanity globally and transculturally in the initial years of the twenty-first century requires first and foremost a conversation on ethics. Brendan Ozawa–de Silva and colleagues contend that "an analysis of the most pressing problems facing humanity, whether they are political, economic, social or environmental, shows that their causes lie fundamentally in human choices, and those choices are largely shaped by values" (2012, 147). Jing Lin (2013) particularizes this conversation in calling for a new value system in education that rejects the emphasis on competition, individualism, ego-centeredness, and anthropocentricism that has dominated the paradigm of higher education and is no longer relevant in a new world order. A wisdom-based education that instrumentalizes the learning of unselfishness, service, and cooperation is a requisite for the twenty-first century. Each of these has a fundamental relationship to how individuals relate to one another with respect to happiness and suffering and ethical and compassionate responsiveness.

The contemplative practices of concentrated awareness, the extension of this awareness to other beings, and the accompanying sense of connectivity with these beings are gateways to the development of compassion and the moral, ethical imagination. As I have noted often in this book, awareness and attention to the present moment are the common denominators for virtually all other contemplative practices in the classroom. Therefore, the contemplative classroom, imbued with an emphasis on deep awareness, attention, and appreciation of a shared world, provides a critical context in which students might explore their moral imaginations and ethical dilemmas. Scott Rogers and Jan Jacobowitz (2015) draw on recent research to suggest that contemplative training is strongly associated with improvements in moral reasoning and moral action. Similarly, research by the neuroscientists Richard Davidson and Antoine Lutz (2008) on neuroplasticity found that compassion training affects regions of the brain associated with greater sensitivity and empathy toward others. In the vision statement of the Association for Contemplative Mind in Higher Education, Art Zajonc (n.d.) writes that a contemplatively oriented college or university can provide a context and community for the practice of "an ethics of genuine compassion." The educational researcher Encarnacion Soriano (2015) connects the ethical stance to a reinvention of education in the global world, arguing that one of the major challenges confronting education is the development of student values that will contribute to their citizenship in a democratic world. Students, as participants in and constructors of the twenty-first century, are called on to coproduce "a universal and transcultural moral" centered on social justice, human rights, and a resistance to major ethical offenses (2015, 53). Contemplative methods offer the foundation for an ethical consciousness, compassion, and a moral attitude. They address what Parker Palmer describes as the "ethical gap" between those who are educated and their subsequent behavior (2014, vii).

The task for contemplative educators is to demonstrate clearly how a pedagogy of ethics and compassion serves as a critical response to the urgent issues of a global world. We are obliged to teach in a way that moves our students past ideas of boundaries and tribalism and toward a compassionate understanding of the self in relationship with the noble community of nations. This is not easy for a multiplicity of reasons. As Martha Nussbaum argues, "It is relatively easy to construct a gentleman's education for a homogeneous elite. It is far more difficult to prepare people of highly diverse backgrounds for complex world citizenship. Curricula aiming at these ideals fit no general mold" (1997, 295). Her words are prophetic for the twenty-first century and particularly germane to the discourse on complex worldwide and societal issues as reflected in higher education. However, contemplative educators might take issue with Nussbaum's position that there is no curricular prototype for addressing such complex issues in education. The curriculum espoused by contemplative educators does, in fact, provide a mold and a guide, and it is up to contemplative teachers to advance the specific classroom practices known to be effective for the cultivation of compassion and an ethical position. We must be deliberate, transparent, and tenacious in defining this type of curriculum in classrooms and in the broader university. This means structuring classrooms around an ontology of care and respect with an emphasis on interdependence, universal responsibility, and the creation of a just society. Thus, the epistemology of monoculturalism would no longer dominate what is taught or how it is taught and indigenous ways of knowing would be included in classroom discourse. The rhetoric of service, diversity, ethical sensitivity, and spiritual and moral development, so often embedded in college and university mission statements, would not only exist on the institutional website but also translate into actual practices in the classroom. This may mean a different type of faculty acculturation and training is needed and perhaps a different type of faculty. It will necessitate contemplative educators' collaboration with many others in the higher education community who also care deeply about intercultural and global education and the advancement of such an education in the context of an ontology of care. It will mean that all voices are heard at the table of teaching and learning, not just those that emanate from structures that are familiar, vociferous, and privileged with power. Higher education requires a certain type of education that is becoming increasingly more difficult to a larger number of students.

Laura Rendon (2016) points to projections that by 2044 people of color will be in the majority and notes that this will have major implications for higher education in the United States. She argues that marginalized groups, specifically people of color, low-income populations, and nontraditional students must be at the center of educators' work. Educators' responsibility is to connect with those populations and ways of knowing that have not been included in the priorities of higher education. In so doing all students are invited into their own agency and welcomed for their much-needed diversity of viewpoints, particularly those that have not adapted to privileged norms, ethnicities, and paradigms of power.

The reimagination of our curriculum in no way supplants the narrative of our disciplines but rather changes the discourse around these narratives. A curriculum of care and compassion is not new but has existed throughout the ages. As Mirabai Bush (2016) points out, contemplative practices are human practices existing in every tradition throughout time. They are the core of human beings and, therefore, have an innate integrity. Perhaps there has never been a time in American education more in need of such practices than now. Contemplative practices can address the critical issues facing higher education in this century by returning us to our interior selves, the initial source of all knowing and wisdom. Addressing these issues in this way restores our position as citizens of the world capable of kindheartedness and ethical discernment. Contemplative practices offer great promise for a reenvisioned academy of honor, veracity, and relevance for the twenty-first century.

The Conundrum of Technology

As I write this book on contemplative approaches, I am keenly aware of the two large monitors that stare at me, sitting in front of my PC, with a laptop to my left, an iPad to my right, and an iPhone within easy reach for an immediate response to texts and e-mails. Virtually all of these are in use for most of the day, emitting sounds, displaying words, and flashing fluctuating colors, and all have been my intimate writing partners for the past year. I have convinced myself that each is a requisite for the expeditious writing of this manuscript, and, eerily, they give me comfort. I am a contemplative, and I am wired! My conundrum appears not unlike that of my colleagues, students, and other contemplative scholars who are mindful of the stress, distraction, and urgency produced by these technogadgets and yet dependent on them. We are traversing a tension between our internal and external worlds and attempting to locate breath, meaning, and our own humanity in a world that is dominated by technological wizardry. This dilemma has been a familiar one through the ages and is not particular to the twenty-first century. Hartmut Rosa cites the work of the historian Reinhart Koselleck, who observed that the "high speed society" has existed since the eighteenth century (Rosa 2003, 3). Although digital screens are very recent, we are not in unexplored territory. William Powers (2010) also observes that for thousands of years individuals have been connecting with one another over space and time through mechanisms that produce many of the same challenges as we witness today: information overload and the accompanying stress and anxiety. He draws from the works of the "Seven Philosophers of Screens": Plato, Seneca, Gutenberg, Shakespeare, Franklin, Thoreau, and McLuhan. Each dealt with the same human questions that we find today in our personal and professional lives: "What do you do when your life has become too outward and crowd-driven?" and "How to quiet the busy mind?" (5–6).

Throughout history we have been confronted with cultural debates and paradoxes emerging from technology. For example, many current scholars convincingly argue that the digital environment has ushered in a widespread loss of attention and reflection capacities, while others hold that technologies will actually enhance these same capacities (Levy 2014). However, the debate is far more complex than this simple bifurcation of positions. Information technology has provided us with tools that ease the labor of life as well as contribute to and exacerbate this labor. It has allowed greater connection to others and the global world and at the same time produced a disconnection from the self and one another. The digital world has facilitated greater ownership of student learning by potentially shifting the learner from a passive to active position in the classroom. Yet research clearly demonstrates that this shift does not guarantee an improvement in learning. It has enhanced our scholarship and academic lives as well as interfered with them. For example, David Levy (2007) notes that technological tools yield extraordinary venues for the expeditious development of research and scholarship. He makes the compelling argument that the human genome could not have been deciphered without technology. However, he also ponders the loss of time for thought and contemplation at the very point when this advanced technology widens our world for investigation.

The conversation around the use of digital tools in higher education requires a response from educators that is not a rumination on the ills brought by the tools. Rather, educators should offer concrete approaches to the thoughtful use of technology in the classroom. Jon Kabat-Zinn argues that the externality of the digital world mandates "a robust counterbalance of the inner world, one that calms and tunes the nervous system and puts it in the service of living wisely, both for ourselves and others" (2005, 155–156). In this respect, contemplative educators are particularly poised for the task of counterbalance. As we consider the place of technology in the classroom, several questions are critical.

What practices address Kabat-Zinn's counterbalance? Attention and mindful awareness have the potential to interrupt technologies of distraction. At the heart of all contemplative practices is a quieting of the mind in the service of deep concentration, reflection, and insight, cardinal processes in learning. Recent research finds that these practices disrupt habitual patterns of inattention so often associated with text messaging, e-mailing, viewing slides in presentation software, and even note-taking on iPads and laptops. If and when we use such technologies in our classrooms, it might be well to offset these with periodic practices of quiet, attention, and awareness. Marc Weiser and John Brown refer to these practices as "calm technologies" that facilitate reflection and rest and are contextual essentials for a digital classroom (1995, 1). Evidence strongly suggests that even a few moments of silence and contemplation better prepare students for knowledge production and meaning-making. Structured silence or a simple pause in the classroom also appears to be a productive response to the omnipresent exhaustion of students, much of which is related to technological overload. Many educators, whether they come from a contemplative perspective or not, recognize the need to integrate the slow technologies into their digital classrooms. In their new book *The Slow Professor*, Maggie Berg and Barbara Seeber contest "the culture of speed" in the academy. They claim that technology is a major contributor and that the introduction of "slow ideals" fosters "emotional and intellectual resilience" (2016, 90), requisites for combatting the effects of technology and the associated corporatization of the academy.

Kendra Bryant introduces a type of slow technology in her contemplative reading and writing classes. Drawing from the work of Robert Altobello to exemplify how blogging, particularly if it is supported by the contemplative practice of freewriting, provides students with the tools and space to find their own voice. This approach results in a holistic student "who doesn't fragment her mind through technology use, but is able to focus and deepen her mind with it" (Bryant 2014, 81). Bryant also integrates use of WordPress, which she calls an "online social networking community" and which essentially consists of writing portfolios. She argues that WordPress and blogging engage her students and elevate their consciousness about their audience and selves as writers. She observes that introducing this type of technology in learning is critical given that the twenty-first century is so technologically absorbed.

While the computer technology of presentation software has failed to show improvements in learning, grades, classroom performance, or short- and long-term memory, it continues to be used in the classroom. Evidence does suggest that students unequivocally prefer presentation software over the traditional lecture. Some instructors have turned to software that is similar to and yet substantively different from Microsoft PowerPoint. PechaKucha, which means "the sound of conversation" in Japanese, holds great potential for the contemplative classroom. Designed by Tokyo architects Astrid Klein and Mark Dytham to encourage organized, time-efficient presentations, PechaKucha presents twenty slides, each in view for twenty seconds to be narrated by the speaker before the next slide appears. The narrator cannot stop the slides or return to the previous slide and, thus, must devote practice to the presentation before it and concentration during it. While the format might initially appear contradictory to contemplative approaches, it focuses on contemplative dimensions in compelling ways. PechaKucha is about storytelling that when done well by the presenter engages others emotionally and imaginatively. It delivers ideas through imagery rather than words and requires creativity in that deliverance. My students often use their own photographs for images that add greater depth to their presentations primarily because of their investment in these images. Students must consider the suitability and effects of words chosen given how few words they can use in the allotted time. PechaKucha encourages the simplification of complicated topics, requiring a return to the essential dimensions of the topic. Devotees of this software point to the intimacy of this presentation style in that it calls for a conversation with the audience on a topic about which one is passionate or that is personally anecdotal. I have used PechaKucha in my own classes, and in spite of what appears to be an emphasis on rapidity at its very core, I see the potential of a slow technology, one based in mindful awareness and attention, allowing an appreciation of the aesthetics of imagery, meaningful concentration, and quiet pondering that are crucial to the contemplative classroom. In many ways PechaKucha interrogates PowerPoint and its accompanying criticisms and offers an important alternative that is contemplative based.

How might we guide our students in contemplative critiques of using e-mail, text messaging, and other such technologies? Levy (2014) describes a contemplative assignment focused on mindful technology, a first-person exploration and journaling of e-mail habits and practices. His students found that they used these technologies when they were anxious or bored, an illuminating discovery for them. They also found that e-mailing did not decrease their anxiety. I also explore mindful e-mailing and texting with my students but in a somewhat different manner from Levy. I became more conscious of the need for mindful e-mailing when a student of mine was deeply hurt by an e-mail I sent and responded with volatility. Both of us had sent e-mails to one another without a pause to contemplate and construct an appropriate and heart-based response. The result was one of shame, embarrassment, and sadness on both our parts, which could have been easily avoided had we taken a moment to breathe, consider the personhood of the other, and choose a response in the service of kindness rather than expediency and retaliation. I have shared this story with my students, what I learned from it, and why in our classroom I adopt the approach of Wendy Kuhn (2015): (1) Breathe deeply, and take time to collect your thoughts before you reply. (2) Visualize the person who will receive the e-mail. (3) Clarify the purpose of the e-mail by asking if it is true, necessary, kind, and the best way to deliver the message. We talk at length about this approach throughout the semester and interrogate why it is so difficult for us. While I have not empirically investigated the impact of this classroom manifesto on e-mailing and texting, I do see changes in the tenor of my e-mails and those of my students. We seem to feed on one another in a way much more productive than the regrettable incident with my student. More often than not, I now find that e-mails from my students have become more of a joy than a task to be encountered, and I hope that, in return, my e-mails to them honor their spirits, hearts, and minds.

In what ways can we use digital tools in our classrooms that reaffirm an interconnected world? Soriano (2015) holds that immigration and technology create worldwide relationships that offer students an opportunity to reflect on the myriad points of view on the planet and the issues and dilemmas that result from them. Such reflection makes a contemplative lens possible. As Phillip Thompson (2012) suggests, a contemplative discernment applied to these global and communal relationships is a necessity. He urges the development of a lens of civic and communal responsibility and a reprioritizing of individual and collective interests. While Aharon Aviram (2010, 2015) does not identify his work as contemplative, he nevertheless emphasizes what he sees as the current crisis of meaning in the lives of our students that leaves them inadequately prepared for the global world. For Aviram two branches of computer science, artificial intelligence and virtual reality, potentially develop students' expanded ability to reflect in ways that enhance their personal and cultural maturation in postmodern democracies. He refers to these as "technological revolutions" that deconstruct "lococentrism," and says that the related "hierarchical, centralist, and synchronic organizations . . . require that all concerned with their activities be present at the same time and in the same place" (2010, 6). Aviram argues for holistic approaches to the way education is conceptualized and linked to social justice and calls on the academy to orient itself toward "individual autonomy, morality, and dialogical belonging" (2010, xii).

How do we respond to and create contemplative online learning environments that are accessible to a wide array of students? The controversy surrounding online education continues among faculty and administrators and dominates much of the conversation on learning with digital media. There is excitement over the potential of MOOCs (massive open online courses) and their cost efficiency, accessibility to nontraditional students, and flexibility, but there is also concern, particularly around the potential weakening of on-campus education and the teacher-student relationship. Regardless of our predilections, online courses appear here to stay. When carefully used they afford new opportunities for students, their teachers, and the future of higher education. A fundamental and perhaps paradoxical dimension of these opportunities, and one that is central to the contemplative stance, is the focus on the individual student. For example, students can move at a speed that suits each because, as Bobbie Hawkins writes, "everyone online is given the chance to learn within a personal time frame" (2004, 21). Likewise, John Davis (2004) points out that online courses give instructors the ability to respond to individual learning, regulation, and communication styles. Karen Willcox, Sanjay Sarma, and Philip Lippel (2016) argue that online education is a catalyst for and critical facilitator in higher education reforms. For them, online courses encourage a student-centered approach to teaching and learning, in that teachers can "sense the student experience" and customize content for each. Christian Dalsgaard and Klaus Thestrup (2015) emphasize the sociocultural aspects of online education and the position of the student in relationship to the culture and the broader society. The element of openness in online education opens up existing but also developing educational practices that work with society. They suggest that MOOCs present pedagogical opportunities for openness in the academy related to transparency between students and teachers, communication between students and the outside world, and joint engagement in the world. Laura Douglass (2007) addresses the interactivity factor of online education when discussing websites and online forums such as MySpace and YouTube, streaming videos, and instant messages, all potentially communities of practice. She notes that knowledge is a social construct grounded in the presence of communities. Proponents of online education such as Willcox, Sarma, and Lippel, Dalsgaard and Thestrup, and Douglass underscore online dimensions that are also mirrored in contemplative education: social interactivity, inclusivity, relationship, connection, reflection, collaboration, and the significance of each these in the construction of knowledge. As Douglass suggests, mindful inquiry might be used to assist us in a careful examination of how we use online education and shape our relationship with the digital world.

Naropa University (n.d., "Distance"), recognized for its innovation in integrating contemplative practices in its online, or distance-learning, courses, suggests that such courses can not only meet students where they are but also promise the same emphases as on-campus courses. Richard Brown, a professor of education at Naropa, speaks of the "five qualities of contemplative education" as a model for online communication: openness, resourcefulness, clarity, communication, and effective action (2004, 10). Each of these represents a practice for student and teacher and is incorporated in all online courses just as they are in on-campus courses.

In his consideration of critical thinking, experiential education, and contemplative education online, Davis (2004), also a Naropa faculty member in psychology, points to several major advantages of an online, contemplative education. For him the depth of discussion is more substantive in online courses, suggesting that this may be due to the time available online. He also notes that teachers are more able to cast a wider net with their online courses in terms of collecting information, theories, conversations, and opinions. Davis also observes that the requirement of writing down responses online calls for greater consideration and clarity as opposed to just speaking, sometimes carelessly, in a classroom. He notes that the quiet or slower-processing student is under less pressure to speak immediately online and yet must speak at some point. Davis relates that one student said, "I used to sit quietly in the back row of class, but online, there is no back row" (2004, 28).

We are all submerged in a digital age. Technical gadgets will remain in classrooms. Many teachers will be asked to teach an online course in the near future (if this has not already occurred). One answer to the technology conundrum is not to do away with the use of these technologies in the classroom or reject online education but to assume a judicious, contemplative manner that offers Kabat-Zinn's counterbalance. Evolving technology will make it possible for students to attain many of the skills critical for survival in our complex and technologically based economies. It offers a multiplicity of ways for teachers to partner with and guide a variety of learners. When properly used, digital tools enhance relationships between student and teacher, student and student, and the classroom community and those communities beyond the academic walls. Carl McColman (2013) reminds us that technology is ultimately utilitarian and that contemplation emphasizes meaning and relationships. A contemplative approach to a digital technology does not ask, "Will it work?" but rather, "Is it good?" and "Is it just?" Modern technology partnered with contemplative methods can transform higher education. The digital world is fundamental for the twenty-first century, and it is incumbent on educators, specifically those with a contemplative lens, to work with this technology in a manner that honors teaching and learning processes and the humanity of students.

Programmatic Implementation of the Contemplative Perspective

Among its many contributions to teaching and learning, SoTL has been particularly adept at programmatic implementation. SoTL has consistently called for including the various voices of the academic community in the service of advancing teaching and learning principles. These voices disseminated SoTL research and scholarship and also integrated SoTL into key academic structures. In important and illuminating ways SoTL provides a road map for integrating contemplative perspectives into colleges and universities. Contemplative dimensions, however, offer programmatic challenges, addressed below.

Just as SoTL carefully crafted and translated definitions and concepts of language and needs of its stakeholders (administrators, researchers, teaching faculty, and policy makers), so might the discourse around contemplative practices be shaped. However, one particular issue in this translation for contemplative educators is the risk of what Oren Ergas refers to as "instrumental mindfulness-based curricular interventions" (2015a, 203) that are grounded in "scientification, secularization, commercialization and commodification" (217). For many contemplative educators this translation potentially diminishes and distances the practices from their wisdom traditions. At the same time, as Ergas also points out, science can be an important venue for explaining contemplative practices in a manner more easily engaged by others, particularly administrators who are negotiating accountability pressures from their constituents outside the institutional gates. Cognitive science, neuroplasticity, neurogenesis, and psychoneuroimmunology research has been critical in understanding the mind-body connection and is increasingly being welcomed into teaching and learning discourse. In fact, recent scientific evidence suggests that the increase in the teaching of ethics and values in the university seems to have lessened the concern and fear around the place of moral principles in the classroom (Ozawa–de Silva 2014). Loyalty to the contemplative tradition should not lead to a rigidity that precludes a respectful access of contemplative practices.

Secular contemplative practices are a practical and ingenious embodiment of most college and university mission statements. Many of these same institutions are currently under fire for not honoring this rhetoric in actual classroom practices. The language of contemplative practices, if articulated in a manner that responds to the institution's struggle to teach to the whole student, not only includes the contemplative tradition in higher education but offers much-needed assistance and support to the institution. As is the case with mission statements, the institution's strategic plan can serve as another wise venue for programmatic implementation of contemplative practices and contemplative language. Most teachers and administrators in higher education have been or are developing a new strategic plan for their institutions. Even a cursory glance at these plans provides fertile ground for programmatic connections between contemplative practices and those common phrases of strategic plans, such as "innovative teaching," "student centered," "public service," "character development," "global connections," "celebration of diversity." Contemplative practices practically address the goals of these plans, and contemplative educators can assume leadership in the facilitation of these connections. The introduction of a resonant, contemplative language to stakeholders may not necessarily be the first step toward garnering support for contemplative studies, but most certainly it is a pivotal one. Without the support of key individuals, particularly deans, department chairs, and committee chairs who are entrusted with funding sources, there will be little of the financial investment necessary to build contemplative courses and programs.

Faculty development programs enjoy a unique opportunity for providing financial subsidies to faculty members. Therefore, they are critical to the advancement of contemplative practices and contemplative teachers, particularly those new to the field. Chief among the needs of new contemplative teachers is training. While there is some debate as to the quantity and quality of training necessary for contemplative teachers, what appears certain is that training is necessary. As discussed in chapter 3, there is little teacher training in contemplative pedagogy, other than preservice and in-service teacher education, and this is limited. The Association for Contemplative Mind in Higher Education, Mind and Life Institute, Garrison Institute, and the Omega Institute for Holistic Studies routinely offer workshops, symposia, conferences, and weeklong training sessions specifically for higher education teachers. Colleges and universities with a contemplative lens, such as Brown University, Smith College, Amherst College, Naropa University, and the University of Virginia, regularly offer support through residency programs, webinars, and workshops. These institutions provide structured opportunities to examine the contemplative perspective in teaching and learning and, therefore, better understand how this perspective is applicable to the daily interaction with students and colleagues and in teachers' respective disciplines.

Just as funding is a requisite for teacher training in contemplative practices, so is it necessary for contemplative course development, evidence gathering, conference presentation, and publication, all required for teacher tenure and promotion. Although SoTL's actual place in tenure and promotion guidelines typically depends on individual college and university climate, it has nevertheless been extraordinarily effective in validating specific types of scholarship. A review of contemplative pedagogy consistently demonstrates the considerable amount of creativity, reflection, preparation, and commitment by teachers employing the paradigm shift of contemplative practices. A financial investment in contemplative pedagogical development and scholarship and the inclusion of these in tenure and promotion guidelines ensure their sustainability and raise consciousness about the significance of contemplative approaches in teaching and learning. Likewise, it demonstrates the institution's commitment to what it says it honors in virtually all its narratives.

While funding is crucial to advancing contemplative studies, individuals might also take steps. Workshops, reading and discussion groups, new-faculty orientation meetings, and even brief but consistent conversations about contemplative dimensions in faculty and department meetings offer fundamental places from which to begin. While teaching and learning centers typically receive programmatic funding, their faculty members are mostly not funded for their contributions but nevertheless are committed to the advancement of teaching and learning. Teaching and learning centers can be places of welcome for teachers seeking support for innovative work and for those who generously mentor and advocate. Contemplative pedagogues should find a home in such places, a legitimacy for their work, and an encouragement to move their work forward.

It will take commitment by contemplative teachers to bring their work into the discourse of the institution and the wider academy. However, contemplative novitiates, particularly junior academicians, need assurance that contemplative practices, methods, and epistemology are firmly grounded in effective teaching and learning and are evidence based. They also require an atlas of concrete ways and sites for integrating contemplative approaches into their classes, disciplines, and scholarship. Teaching and learning centers are poised to address many of these issues. However, one major concern hovering over contemplative methods scholarship is limited accessibility to conferences and publication venues that welcome and integrate the contemplative into the wider teaching and learning narrative. Currently, very few articles appearing in SoTL journals and even fewer chapters in SoTL books clearly address contemplative practices and provide openings for contemplative scholarship. This calls to contemplative educators for disseminating their work beyond the parochial boundaries of contemplative journals and conferences. SoTL must also be willing to engage contemplative scholarship in its journals, conferences, and publications. The growth of contemplative studies and its place in higher education will necessitate this type of inclusion and transparency by those whose goal is to transform higher education.

The implementation of contemplative practices in interdisciplinary courses provides a powerful approach to familiarizing others with the practices and their applicability. Contemplative courses such as those also identified as writing intensive, service learning, inquiry, and travel abroad are particularly influential prototypes for demonstrating how contemplative dimensions can be woven into traditional courses to enhance and deepen these courses.

Many contemplative courses already exist on campuses, although their titles may be disassociated from traditional disciplines. Paradoxically, they are among the oldest disciplinary traditions. Mind-body classes such as yoga, tai chi, and qigong can be models and springboards for instructors considering contemplative approaches in their courses and be opportunity for collaboration with colleagues whose work seems unrelated to contemplative approaches.

The contemplative college or university asks for a shift in understanding of authority and expertise. A contemplative academy can never be defined solely by its practices in the classroom. Many contemplative scholars would argue that such is true for most academic institutions regardless of the lack or presence of a contemplative identity. Randy Bass (2012) argues that "bounded, self-contained courses" and the curriculum at large may no longer be the center of academic experience and the single place where the most important learning occurs. Just as many programs on campus are supported and even led by many who are not classroom teachers, so is the case for contemplative studies. In many ways, campus life professionals and staff have always done contemplative work. They are critical guides and resources for building a contemplative campus. They know how to listen carefully, nurture and soothe broken spirits, develop communities, collaborate, organize around and serve in the spirit of social justice, and wisely navigate the sometimes tense relationship between the curricular and cocurricular worlds. Cocurricular programs provide important connections whose absence diminishes and impedes formalizing a contemplative program. The cultivation of relationships with those devoted to contemplative work beyond the classroom can also diffuse the sense of isolation so often reported by contemplative teachers.

Spaces created on campus for contemplation, most often developed by those outside the classroom walls, can enhance these relationships by bringing mindfulness to the central stage of the campus. A labyrinth, meditative garden, or even a chapel that can accommodate a pluralistic and contemplative perspective are examples of programmatic implementation of the contemplative. Colgate's Chapel House, Skidmore's Gazebo, DePauw's Reflection Center, Stanford's Contemplative Center, Colorado College's Labyrinth, Carnegie Mellon's Mindfulness Room, Temple's Healing Garden, and Mount Holyoke's Japanese Teahouse and Meditation Garden are just a few such contemplative spaces. In my own institution, Oxford College of Emory University, founded by the Methodist Church, the chapel serves as a place for meditation groups, centering supplications, chanting, pondering, and quiet. When such spaces are valued, sustained, and allowed to flourish the seeds for a contemplative campus are planted.

Most contemplative practices are typically conceived of as a pedagogical method rather than an academic field or program and are located across disciplines and departments. However, some universities are beginning to offer degree programs and concentrations in contemplative studies. Among them are Brown University, the University of Michigan, Burlington College, Naropa University, Rice University, and Lesley University. These programs signal encouragement about the future of contemplative studies and are exemplars for a systemic presence of the contemplative on campuses. However, it is crucial to remember that such programs are the result of a tenaciousness by faculty members and a substantive financial commitment from administrators and other stakeholders.

The integration of contemplative practices in both the curriculum and the institution will necessitate intentional and comprehensive programmatic approaches as outlined above. These approaches are not new or revolutionary. Yet programmatic development for the integration of contemplative methods continues to lack appropriate and adequate attention in most academic institutions. Contemplative methods, while grounded in traditions of long ago, are relatively new in today's academy and will require vigilance and persistence from those committed to contemplative dimensions. These voices must be central to the processes of programmatic development and the conversations around funds committed to these developments. It is teachers' responsibility, as ones committed to contemplative teaching and learning, to envision and forward innovative proposals for programmatic changes and additions, articulate a thoughtful and intelligent rationale for these proposals, ask questions about programmatic expenditures, and guide the stewards who are entrusted with funding these programs.

Coda

I END THIS book as we grapple with a vitriolic political campaign, increases in poverty and the resulting wage gaps between socioeconomic classes, and a vulnerable health care system, in a world negotiating terror and its aftermath and sustained tribalism and resistance to embracing difference. Not surprisingly, our educational system reflects this turmoil in what many see as its brokenness and insurmountable crises.

I also end this book with great optimism about the future, particularly the future of higher education and the place of the contemplative in higher education, the scholarship of teaching and learning, and the world. Much is dying and much is being born in higher education, and in these transitions are unparalleled opportunities and hope. Although I have devotedly carried the SoTL banner for over twenty years, I was a contemplative novitiate when I began this manuscript. With that initial mind-set I saw little evidence of connections between SoTL and contemplative education, and my first draft to the editors reflected this narrowness in vision. The language and praxis seemed substantively different with little room for interconnections. However, as I traversed the literature and research, read and reread, listened carefully to SoTL and contemplative educators at conferences, symposia and workshops, educational retreat centers, and campuses around this country, I found a compelling complementarity and connection between contemplative perspectives in SoTL and SoTL methods in the contemplative orientation. I have tried to adequately capture this and demonstrate the evidence in this book.

For the first time in modern higher education, we are defining indexes of success and accomplishment that honor the importance of our humaneness rather than what can be merely performed and measured. A new vocabulary is evolving in teaching and learning conversations that is dramatically different from what many of us have known. Words such as *awareness, mindful, compassion, embodiment, care, justice, morality* and *ethics*, and even *love* no longer seem to be closeted, or at least relegated to discourses outside the classroom walls. As has always been, valiant educators committed to far-reaching transformation in the academy and subsequently in the world are leading the way. These educators inhabit both the SoTL and contemplative communities. Although arguably they may be in the minority, they are our front-line warriors carving out portals for educators to enter.

In spite of what many of us have been led to believe, we have great power. Teachers can change the fabric of the world. Never has the call to assume this agency been more immediate and crucial than now. We are standing on the hallowed ground of the academy at a privileged moment in time. We are called to assume this power and authority in the service of our students, one another, and the planet. Of course, we must summon a radical bravery, a willingness to step beyond the comfortable boundaries of traditions that no longer sustain us, and embrace the traditions of wisdom that have been so marginalized by an academy of the past. As Albert Einstein so eloquently said, "The significant problems we face cannot be solved at the same level of thinking we were at when we created them." The planet's cry for judiciousness, integrity, insight, compassion, harmony, goodwill, and deep thoughtfulness is palpable. This cry is no longer met and subdued by tools of the past. The response should, and indeed must, be led by those of us entrusted with guiding future generations. Might all of us as SoTL and contemplative scholars, committed to deep and far-reaching change in the academy and outside its gates, step up and heed the call? In the contemplative tradition of every classroom at Naropa University, might we sit up straight, bow slowly to one another, and respectfully yet resolutely greet the day, engaging the work we were always meant to do. It is our time, and it is our great privilege.

References

Adelman, M. 2014. "Kindred Spirits in Teaching Contemplative Practice." In *Contemplative Learning and Inquiry across Disciplines*, edited by O. Gunnlaugson, E. W. Sarath, C. Scott, and H. Bai, 51–67. Albany: State University of New York Press.

Allen, M., M. Dietz, K. S. Blair, M. van Beek, G. Rees, P. Vestergaard-Poulsen, A. Lutz, and A. Roepstorff. 2012. "Cognitive-Affective Neural Plasticity following Active-Controlled Mindfulness Intervention." *Journal of Neuroscience* 32 (44): 15601–15610.

Anderson, H. 1952. "Needed Research in Listening." *Elementary English* 29 (4): 215–224.

Anderson, R. 2004. "Intuitive Inquiry: An Epistemology of the Heart for Scientific Inquiry." *Humanistic Psychologist* 32 (4): 307–341.

———. 2011. "Intuitive Inquiry: Exploring the Mirroring Discourse of a Disease." In *Five Ways of Doing Qualitative Analysis: Phenomenological Psychology, Grounded Theory, Discourse Analysis, Narrative Research and Intuitive Inquiry*, edited by F. J. Wertz, K. Charmaz, L. M. McMullen, R. Josselson, R. Anderson, and E. McSpadden, 243–276. New York: Guildford Press.

Association of American Colleges and Universities. 2007. "College Learning for the New Global Century." https://www.aacu.org/sites/default/files/files/LEAP/GlobalCentury _final.pdf.

Astin, A. W., H. S. Astin, and J. A. Lindholm. 2011. *Cultivating the Spirit: How College Can Enhance Students' Inner Lives*. San Francisco: Jossey-Bass.

Aviram, A. 2010. *Navigating through the Storm: Reinventing Education for Postmodern Democracies*. Rotterdam, Netherlands: Sense.

———. 2015. "ICT in the Service of Humanism: An Optimistic Vision for the Future of Education in Postmodern Democratic Societies." In *Rethinking Education for a Global, Transcultural World*, edited by E. Soriano, 3–39. Charlotte, NC: Information Age.

Bach, D., and J. Alexander. 2015. "Contemplative Approaches to Reading and Writing: Cultivating Choice, Connectedness, and Wholeheartedness in the Critical Humanities." *Journal of Contemplative Inquiry* 2 (1): 17–36.

Bagshaw, J. L. 2014. "Contemplative Pedagogy and Student Success in Community College Students: A Mixed Methods Research Study." Ph.D. diss., Capella University.

Bai, H., A. Cohen, T. Culham, S. Park, R. Shahar, C. Scott, and S. Tait. 2014. "A Call for Wisdom in Higher Education: Contemplative Voices from the *Dao*-Field." In *Contemplative Learning and Inquiry across Disciplines*, edited by O. Gunnlaugson, E. W. Sarath, C. Scott, and H. Bai, 287–302. Albany: State University of New York Press.

Bain, K. 2004. *What the Best College Students Do*. Cambridge, MA: Harvard University Press.

Bao, D. 2015. "The Japanese Perception of Silence in the Australian Educational Context." In *Asia as Method in Education Studies: A Defiant Research Imagination*, edited by H. Zhang, P. Chan, and J. Kenway, 50–65. New York: Routledge.

Barbezat, D. P. 2015. "Contemplative Practices and 21st Century Skills." Center for Contemplative Mind in Society, June 4. http://www.contemplativemind.org/archives/3641.

Barbezat, D. P., and M. Bush. 2014. *Contemplative Practices in Higher Education*. San Francisco: Jossey-Bass.

Barbezat, D., and A. Pingree. 2012. "Contemplative Pedagogy: The Special Role of Teaching and Learning Centers." In *To Improve the Academy*, vol. 31, edited by James E. Groccia and L. Cruz, 177–191. San Francisco: Jossey-Bass.

Barsalou, L. W., P. M. Niedenthal, A. K. Barbey, and J. A. Ruppert. 2003. "Social Embodiment." *Psychology of Learning and Motivation* 43:43–92.

Bass, R. 2012. "Disrupting Ourselves: The Problem of Learning in Higher Education." *EDUCAUSE Review* 47 (2). http://er.educause.edu/articles/2012/3/disrupting-ourselves-the-problem-of-learning-in-higher-education.

Baugher, J. 2014a. "Contemplating Uncomfortable Emotions: Creating Transformative Spaces for Learning in Higher Education." In *Contemplative Learning and Inquiry across Disciplines*, edited by O. Gunnlaugson, E. Sarath, C. Scott, and H. Bai, 233–252. Albany: State University of New York Press.

———. 2014b. "Reflection and Contemplative Pedagogy." Post to Center for Contemplative Mind in Society mailing list, November 15. "ACMHE_discussion" forum. http://lists.contemplativemind.org/private.cgi/acmhe_discussion-contemplativemind.org/2014-November/000217.html.

Baumgartner, L. M. 2012. "Mezirow's Theory of Transformative Learning from 1975 to Present." In *Handbook of Transformative Learning*, edited by E. W. Taylor and P. Cranton, 99–115. San Francisco: Jossey-Bass.

Bazeley, P. 2004. "Issues in Mixing Qualitative and Quantitative Approaches to Research." In *Applying Qualitative Methods to Marketing Management Research*, edited by R. Buber, J. Gadner, and L. Richards, 141–156. New York: Palgrave Macmillan.

Begley, S. 2007. *Train Your Mind, Change Your Brain*. New York: Ballantine.

Belanoff, P. 2001. "Silence: Reflection, Literacy, Learning and Teaching." *College Composition and Communication* 52 (3): 399–428.

Belenky, M. F., B. V. Clinchy, N. R. Goldberger, and J. M. Tarule. 1986. *Women's Ways of Knowing: The Development of Self, Voice, and Mind*. New York: Basic Books.

Berg, M., and B. K. Seeber. 2016. *The Slow Professor: Challenging the Culture of Speed in the Academy*. Toronto: University of Toronto Press.

Bergomi, C., W. Tschacher, and Z. Kupper. 2013. "The Assessment of Mindfulness with Self-Report Measures: Existing Scales and Open Issues." *Mindfulness* 4 (3): 191–202.

Berila, B. 2014. "Contemplating the Effects of Oppression: Integrating Mindfulness into Diversity Classrooms." *Journal of Contemplative Inquiry* 1:55–69.

Bernstein, J. L. 2012. "Defending Our Life: The Scholarship of Teaching and Learning in an Academy under Siege." *International Journal for the Scholarship of Teaching and Learning* 6 (1). http://digitalcommons.georgiasouthern.edu/cgi/viewcontent.cgi?article=1310&context=ij-sotl.

Bockelman, P., L. Reinerman-Jones, and S. Gallagher. 2013. "Methodological Lessons in Neurophenomenology: Review of a Baseline Study and Recommendations for Research Approaches." *Frontiers in Human Neuroscience* 7:1–9.

Bodie, G. D., and M. Fitch-Hauser. 2010. "Quantitative Research in Listening: Explication and Overview." In *Listening and Human Communication in the 21st Century*, edited by A. Wolvin, 46–94. Chichester, UK: Blackwell.

Bogle, A. L. 2012. "Magical Thinking." *Emory Magazine*, Summer, pp. 16–17.

Borker, D. 2013a. "Mindfulness Practices and Learning Economics." *American Journal of Business Education* 6 (5): 495–504.

———. 2013b. "Mindfulness Practices for Accounting and Business Education: A New Perspective." *American Journal of Business Education* 6 (1): 41–56.

Boyer, E. L. 1990. *Scholarship Reconsidered: Priorities of the Professoriate*. New York: Jossey-Bass.

———. 1997. *Selected Speeches, 1979–1995*. Princeton, NJ: Carnegie Foundation for the Advancement of Teaching.

Bradshaw, C. P., A. Goldweber, D. Fishbein, and M. T. Greenberg. 2012. "Infusing Developmental Neuroscience into School-Based Preventive Interventions: Implications and Future Directions." *Journal of Adolescent Health* 51 (2): 41–47.

Braman, S. 2007. "When Nightingales Break the Law: Silence and the Construction of Reality." *Ethics and Information Technology* 9:281–295.

Briggs, S. 2015. "Be. Still. Move: Creative Contemplative Movement." *Vimeo*, March 25. https://vimeo.com/124032865.

Bringle, R. G., and J. A. Hatcher. 1999. "Reflection in Service Learning: Making Meaning or Experience." *Educational Horizons*, Summer, pp. 179–185.

Brody, J. 2016. "Contemplating Infinity." Paper presented at the 2016 Joint Mathematics Meetings, January, Seattle, WA.

Brown, R. C. 2004. "The Five Qualities in Online Discussion." In *Best Practices in Online Contemplative Education: Naropa Online Faculty Panel Discussions*, edited by J. Hladiš, 10–14. Boulder, CO: Naropa University. http://www.naropa.edu/documents/depart ments/ extended-studies/distance-learning/best-practices-online-contemplative-educa tion.pdf.

———. 2011. "The Mindful Teacher as the Foundation of Contemplative Pedagogy." In *Meditation and the Classroom*, edited by J. Simmer-Brown and F. Grace, 75–83. Albany: State University of New York Press.

———. 2014. "Transitions: Teaching from the Spaces Between." In *Contemplative Learning and Inquiry across Disciplines*, edited by O. Gunnlaugson, E. W. Sarath, C. Scott, and H. Bai, 271–286. Albany: State University of New York Press.

Bruneau, T. J. 1973. "Communicative Silences: Forms and Functions." *Journal of Communication* 23 (1): 17–46.

Bryant, A. 2009. "Grounded Theory and Pragmatism: The Curious Case of Anselm Strauss." *Forum: Qualitative Social Research* 10 (3): 1–38.

Bryant, K. N. 2014. "Composing Online: Integrating Blogging into a Contemplative Classroom." In *Exploring Technology for Writing and Writing Instruction*, edited by K. E. Pytash and R. E. Ferdig, 77–99. Hershey, PA: Information Science Reference.

Buell, F. 1999. "A Report on the Contemplative Practice Fellowship Program." http://www .contemplativemind.org/admin/wp-content/uploads/2012/07/99academicreport.pdf.

Bueno, V. F., E. H. Kozasa, M. Aparecida da Silva, T. M. Alves, M. R. Louzã, and S. Pompéia. 2015. "Mindfulness Meditation Improves Mood, Quality of Life, and Attention in Adults with Attention Deficit Hyperactivity Disorder." *BioMed Research International* 2015. https://www.hindawi.com/journals/bmri/2015/962857.

Bullock, B. G. 2015. "Re: Higher Education Classroom Pre and Post-test Surveys?" Post to Center for Contemplative Mind in Society mailing list, December 10. "ACMHE_discussion" forum. http://lists.contemplativemind.org/private.cgi/acmhe_discussion-contemplative mind.org/2015-December/000153.html.

Burack, C. 2014. "Responding to the Challenges of a Contemplative Curriculum." *Journal of Contemplative Inquiry* 1:35–52.

Burawoy, M. 2003. "Revisits: An Outline of a Theory of Reflexive Ethnography." *American Sociological Review* 68:645–678.

Burggraf, S. 2011. "Contemplative Higher Education: A Case Study of Naropa University." In *Contemplation Nation: How Ancient Practices Are Changing the Way We Live*, edited by M. Bush, 237–245. Kalamazoo, MI: Fetzer Institute.

Burggraf, S., and P. Grossenbacher. 2007. "Contemplative Modes of Inquiry in Liberal Arts Education." *Liberal Arts Online*, June, pp. 1–9.

Burtt, E. A. 1954. *The Metaphysical Foundations of Modern Science*. New York: Doubleday.

Bush, M. 2010. "Contemplative Higher Education in Contemporary America." https://mindfulcampus.files.wordpress.com/2012/03/mbush-contemplativehighereducation.pdf.

———. 2011a. "Contemplative Higher Education in Contemporary Life." In *Contemplation Nation: How Ancient Practices Are Changing the Way We Live*, edited by M. Bush, 221–236. Kalamazoo, MI: Fetzer Institute.

———. 2011b. "Mindfulness in Higher Education." *Contemporary Buddhism* 12 (1): 183–197.

———. 2015. "Awakening at Work: Introducing Mindfulness into Organizations." In *Mindfulness in Organizations: Foundations, Research, and Applications*, edited by R. Reb and P. Atkins, 333–354. Cambridge: Cambridge University Press.

———. 2016. "Unpacking the Crisis in Higher Education Today." Panel presentation at the Mindfulness, MOOCs, and Money in Higher Education Conference, Naropa University, Boulder, CO, March.

Cambridge, B. L. 2000. "Fostering the Scholarship of Teaching and Learning: Communities of Practice." In *To Improve the Academy*, vol. 19, edited by D. Lieberman and C. Wehlburg, 3–16. Bolton, MA: Anker.

Cannella, G. S., and Y. S. Lincoln. 2009. "Deploying Qualitative Methods for Critical Social Purposes." In *Qualitative Inquiry and Social Justice*, edited by N. L. Denzin and M. D. Giardina, 53–72. Walnut Creek, CA: Left Coast Press.

Caranfa, A. 2004. "Silence as the Foundation of Learning." *Educational Theory* 54 (2): 211–230.

Catalano, G. 2012. "Listening to the Quiet Voices: Unlocking the Heart of Engineering Grand Challenges." *International Journal of Engineering, Social Justice, and Peace* 1 (2): 152–159.

Center for Contemplative Mind in Society. n.d. "Contemplative Practice Fellowships." http://www.contemplativemind.org/archives/fellowships#ninety7 (accessed March 24, 2017).

———. n.d. "Deep Listening." http://www.contemplativemind.org/practices/tree/deep-listen ing (accessed March 23, 2017).

———. 2002. "Inviting the World to Transform: Nourishing Social Justice Work with Contemplative Practice." http://www.contemplativemind.org/admin/wp-content/uploads/2012/09/inviting.pdf.

———. 2012. "Ritual and Reflection: A Workplace Table of Inspiration." http://www.contem plativemind.org/archives/socialjustice/ritual.

Charmaz, K. 2011. "Grounded Theory Methods in Social Justice Research." In *The SAGE Handbook of Qualitative Research*, 4th ed., edited by N. K. Denzin and Y. S. Lincoln, 359–360. Thousand Oaks, CA: Sage.

———. 2014. *Constructing Grounded Theory*. 2nd ed. London: Sage.

Chiesa, A. 2013. "The Difficulty of Defining Mindfulness: Current Thoughts and Critical Issues." *Mindfulness* 4:255–268.

Christie, D. 2013. *The Blue Sapphire of the Mind: Notes for a Contemplative Ecology*. New York: Oxford University Press.

Claxton, G. 2006. "Thinking at the Edge: Developing Soft Creativity." *Cambridge Journal of Education* 36 (3): 351–362.

Coles, R. 1990. *The Spiritual Life of Children*. Boston: Houghton Mifflin.

Comstock, P. W. 2015. "The Retrieval of Contemplation: Mindfulness, Meditation, and Education." Ph.D. diss., Columbia University.

Dahl, C. J., A. Lutz, and R. J. Davidson. 2015. "Reconstructing and Deconstructing the Self: Cognitive Mechanisms in Meditation Practice." *Trends in Cognitive Sciences* 19 (9): 515–523.

Dalke, A. F. 2002. *Teaching to Learn, Learning to Teach: Meditations on the Classroom*. New York: Peter Lang.

Dalsgaard, C., and K. Thestrup. 2015. "Dimensions of Openness: Beyond the Course as an Open Format in Online Education." *International Review of Research in Open and Distributed Learning* 16 (6): 78–96.

Davidson, R. J. 2010. "Empirical Explorations of Mindfulness: Conceptual and Methodological Conundrums." *Emotion* 20 (1): 8–11.

Davidson, R. J., J. Dunne, J. S. Eccles, A. Engle, M. Greenberg, P. Jennings, A. Jha, et al. 2012. "Contemplative Practices and Mental Training: Prospects for American Education." *Child Development Perspectives* 6 (2): 146–153.

Davidson, R. J., J. Kabat-Zinn, J. Schumacher, M. Rosenkranz, D. Muller, S. F. Santorelli, F. Urbanowski, et al. 2003. "Alterations in Brain and Immune Function Produced by Mindfulness Meditation." *Psychosomatic Medicine* 65:564–570.

Davidson, R. J., and A. W. Kaszniak. 2015. "Conceptual and Methodological Issues in Research on Mindfulness and Meditation." *American Psychologist* 70 (7): 581–592.

Davidson, R., and A. Lutz. 2008. "Buddha's Brain: Neuroplasticity and Meditation." *IEEE Signal Process Magazine* 25 (1): 174–176.

Davis, C. S., and D. C. Breede. 2015. "Holistic Ethnography: Embodiment, Emotion, Contemplation, and Dialogue in Ethnographic Fieldwork." *Journal of Contemplative Inquiry* 2 (1): 77–100.

Davis, E. 2015. "Standardization." Post to Center for Contemplative Mind in Society mailing list, August 13. "ACMHE_discussion" forum. http://lists.contemplativemind.org/private .cgi/acmhe_discussion-contemplativemind.org/2015-August/000075.html.

Davis, J. 2004. "Critical Thinking, Experiential Education, and Contemplative Education Online." In *Best Practices in Online Contemplative Education: Naropa Online Faculty Panel Discussions*, edited by J. Hladiš, 26–32. Boulder, CO: Naropa University. http:// www.naropa.edu/documents/departments/extended-studies/distance-learning/best -practices-online-contemplative-education.pdf.

Deng, F., D. Chen, C. Tsai, and C. S. Chai. 2011. "Students' Views of the Nature of Science: A Critical Review of Research." *Science Education* 95 (6): 961–999.

DeNicola, A. O. 2016. Personal communication, February 27.

Depraz, N., F. J. Varela, and P. Vermersch. 2003. *On Becoming Aware: A Pragmatics of Experiencing*. Philadelphia: John Benjamins.

Dewey, J. 1984. "The Copernican Revolution." In *The Later Works of John Dewey, 1925–1953*. Vol. 4, *1929: The Quest for Certainty*, edited by J. A. Boydston, 229–250. Carbondale: Southern Illinois University.

Dilley, B. 2014. "Continuous Present: An Excerpt; Summer of 1975." *Naropa Magazine*, Spring. http://magazine.naropa.edu/2014-spring/features/continuous-present-excerpt.php.

Dirkx, J. M. 1998. "Transformative Learning Theory in the Practice of Adult Education: An Overview." *PAACE Journal of Lifelong Learning* 7:1–14.

Djuraskovic, I., and N. Arthur. 2010. "Heuristic Inquiry: A Personal Journey of Acculturation and Identity Reconstruction." *Qualitative Report* 15 (6): 1569–1593.

Dolby, N. 2016. "Seeing the World Anew: The Lessons of Qualitative Research." *Teachers College Record*, February 15, pp. 1–4.

Douglass, L. S. 2007. "Contemplative Online Learning Environments." *Journal of Online Education*. http://www.nyu.edu/classes/keefer/waoe/douglass.htm.

Doyle, L., A. Brady, and G. Byrne. 2009. "An Overview of Mixed Methods Research." *Journal of Research in Nursing* 14 (2): 175–185.

Duarte, F. P. 2007. "Using Autoethnography in the Scholarship of Teaching and Learning: Reflective Practice from 'the Other Side of the Mirror.'" *International Journal for the Scholarship of Teaching and Learning* 1 (2): 1–11.

Duerr, M. 2002. "Inviting the World to Transform: Nourishing Social Justice Work with Contemplative Practice." http://www.contemplativemind.org/admin/wp-content/uploads/2012/09/inviting.pdf.

———. 2004. *A Powerful Silence: The Role of Meditation and Other Contemplative Practices on American Life and Work*. Northampton, MA: Center for Contemplative Mind in Society. http://www.contemplativemind.org/admin/wp-content/uploads/2012/09/APS.pdf.

———. 2011. "Assessing the State of Contemplative Practices in the United States." In *Contemplation Nation: How Ancient Practices Are Changing the Way We Live*, edited by M. Bush, 9–34. Kalamazoo, MI: Fetzer Institute.

Duerr, M., A. Zajonc, and D. Dana. 2003. "Survey of Transformative and Spiritual Dimensions of Higher Education." *Journal of Transformative Education* 1 (3): 177–211.

Dunn, D. 2014. "Bearing Witness: Seeing as a Form of Service." *Liberal Education* 100 (2): 36–41.

Elbow, P. 1998. *Writing without Teachers*. New York: Oxford University Press.

Ellis, C., and A. Bochner. 2000. "Autoethnography, Personal Narrative, Reflexivity: Researcher as Subject." In *The Sage Handbook of Qualitative Research*, 2nd ed., edited by N. Denzin and Y. Lincoln, 733–768. Thousand Oaks, CA: Sage.

Ergas, O. 2013. "Descartes in a 'Headstand': Introducing 'Body-Oriented Pedagogy.'" *Paideusis* 21 (1): 4–12.

———. 2015a. "The Deeper Teachings of Mindfulness-Based Curricular Interventions as a Reconstruction of 'Education.'" *Journal of Philosophy of Education* 49 (2): 203–220.

———. 2015b. "Mindfulness for Faculty." Post to Center for Contemplative Mind in Society mailing list, August 9. "ACMHE_discussion" forum. http://lists.contemplativemind.org/private.cgi/acmhe_discussion-contemplativemind.org/2015-August/thread.html.

Erikson, E. 1950. *Childhood and Society*. New York: W. W. Norton.

Evergreen State College. n.d. "The Writing Center." http://evergreen.edu/writingcenter/about (accessed June 8, 2017).

Fassinger, R. E. 2005. "Paradigms, Praxis, Problems, and Promise: Grounded Theory in Counseling Psychology Research." *Journal of Counseling Psychology* 52 (2): 156–166.

Felten, P. 2013. "Principles of Good Practice in SoTL." *Teaching and Learning Inquiry: The ISSOTL Journal* 1 (1): 121–125.

Finlay, L. 2009. "Debating Phenomenological Research Methods." *Phenomenology and Practice* 3 (1): 6–25.

Fischer, N. 2003. *Taking Our Places.* San Francisco: Harper Collins.

Fitzpatrick, K. R. 2014. "Mixed Methods Research in Music Education." In *The Oxford Handbook of Qualitative Research in American Music Education*, edited by C. M. Conway, 209–226. Oxford: Oxford University Press.

Foster, V. 2016. *Collaborative Arts-Based Research for Social Justice.* New York: Routledge.

Francl, M. n.d. "Contemplative Practices in the Sciences." http://tinyurl.com/contemplative science (accessed March 24, 2017).

Franklin, M. 2014. "Self-Reflection Assessment Tools for Teaching Evaluation of Artwork and Participation." Presentation at Sixth Annual ACMHE Conference, University of Washington, Seattle, October 10–12.

Freire, P. 1970. *Pedagogy of the Oppressed.* Translated by M. R. Ramos. New York: Herder and Herder.

———. 1973. *Education for Critical Consciousness.* New York: Continuum.

———. 1990. "Conflicts Are the Midwife of Consciousness." In *We Make the Road by Walking: Conversations on Education and Social Change*, edited by Brenda Bell, John Gaventa, and John Peters, 180–198. Philadelphia: Temple University Press.

Frick, W. B. 1990. "The Symbolic Growth Experience: A Chronicle of Heuristic Inquiry and a Quest for Synthesis." *Journal of Humanistic Psychology* 30:64–80.

Friedel, S., S. L. Whittle, N. Vijayakumar, J. G. Simmons, M. L. Byrne, O. S. Schwartz, and N. B. Allen. 2015. "Dispositional Mindfulness Is Predicted by Structural Development of the Insula during Late Adolescence." *Development Cognitive Neuroscience* 14:62–70.

Freud, S. 1955. *The Interpretation of Dreams.* Edited by James Strachey. New York: Basic Books.

Fuhrmann, B. S., and A. F. Grasha. 1983. "The Past, Present, and Future in College Teaching: Where Does Your Teaching Fit?" In *A Practical Handbook for College Teachers*, edited by B. S. Fuhrmann and A. F. Grasha, 5–19. New York: Little, Brown.

Furco, A. 2011. Foreword to *Problematizing Service Learning: Critical Reflections for Development and Action*, edited by T. Stewart and N. Webster, ix–xi. Charlotte, NC: Information Age.

Gale, R. 2009. "Asking Questions That Matter . . . Asking Questions of Value." *International Journal for the Scholarship of Teaching and Learning* 3 (2). http://digitalcommons.georgia southern.edu/cgi/viewcontent.cgi?article=1169&context=ij-sotl.

Galle, J., B. Harmon, A. DeNicola, and B. Gunnels. 2014. "The Distinctiveness of the Oxford College General Education Program." In *Inquiry-Based Learning for Faculty and Institutional Development: A Conceptual and Practical Resource for Educators*, edited by P. Blessinger and J. Carfora, 121–146. Bingley, UK: Emerald.

Gardener, E., P. E. Calderwood, and R. Torosyan. 2007. "Dangerous Pedagogy." *Journal of the Assembly for Expanded Perspectives on Learning* 13:13–21.

Gasson, S. 2004. "Rigor in Grounded Theory Research: An Interpretive Perspective on Generating Theory from Qualitative Field Studies." In *Handbook for Information Systems Research*, edited by M. E. Whitman and A. B. Woszcynski, 97–102. Hershey, PA: Idea Group.

Geertz, C. 1973. *The Interpretation of Cultures: Selected Essays.* New York: Basic Books.

Germano, D. 2016. "Cultivating Student Resiliency and Well-Being in a Contemplative University." Presentation at the Mindfulness, MOOCs, and Money in Higher Education Conference, Naropa University, Boulder, CO, March.

Gilead, T. 2012. "Education and the Logic of Economic Progress." *Journal of Philosophy of Education* 46 (1): 113–131.

Gilligan, C. 1982. *In a Different Voice: Psychological Theory and Women's Development.* Cambridge, MA: Harvard University Press.

Giorgi, A. 1997. "The Theory, Practice, and Evaluation of the Phenomenological Method as a Qualitative Research Procedure." *Journal of Phenomenological Psychology* 28 (2): 235–260.

Giroux, H. 1992. *Border Crossings: Cultural Workers and the Politics of Education.* New York: Routledge.

Glasser, B. G., and A. L. Strauss. 1967. *The Discovery of Grounded Theory.* Chicago: Aldine.

Glenn, C. 2004. *Unspoken: A Rhetoric of Silence.* Carbondale: Southern Illinois University Press.

Goel, K. 2012. "Personal Reflection: Transforming Teaching Practice through Action Research: The Role of the Scholarship of Teaching and Learning." *International Journal for the Scholarship of Teaching and Learning* 6 (2): 1–4.

Goleman, D. 1995. *Emotional Intelligence.* New York: Bantam Books.

Goyal, M., S. Singh, E. M. S. Sibinga, N. F. Gould, A. Rowland-Seymour, R. Sharma, A. Berger, et al. 2014. "Meditation Programs for Psychological Stress and Well-Being: A Systematic Review and Meta-analysis." *JAMA Internal Medicine* 174:357–368.

Grace, F. 2011. "Learning as a Path, Not a Goal: Contemplative Pedagogy—Its Principles and Practices." *Teaching Theology and Religion* 14 (2): 99–124.

Gravois, J. 2005. "Meditate on It." *Chronicle of Higher Education* 52 (9): A10.

Grossenbacher, P. G., and S. S. Parkin. 2006. "Joining Hearts and Minds: A Contemplative Approach to Holistic Education in Psychology." *Journal of College and Character* 7 (6): 1–13.

Grossenbacher, P. G., and A. J. Rossi. 2014. "A Contemplative Approach to Teaching Observation Skills." *Journal of Contemplative Inquiry* 1:23–34.

Grossman, P. 2008. "On Measuring Mindfulness in Psychosomatic and Psychological Research." *Journal of Psychosomatic Research* 64 (4): 405–408.

Gunnlaugson, O. 2011. "Advancing a Second-Person Contemplative Approach for Collective Wisdom and Leadership Development." *Journal of Transformative Education* 9 (1): 3–20.

Gunnlaugson, O., E. W. Sarath, C. Scott, and H. Bai. 2014. "An Introduction to Contemplative Learning and Inquiry across Disciplines." In *Contemplative Learning and Inquiry across Disciplines,* edited by Gunnlaugson, Sarath, Scott, and Bai, 1–12. Albany: State University of New York Press.

Hall, M., and O. Archibald. 2008. "Investigating Contemplative Practice in Creative Writing and Education Classes: A Play (or Practice and Theory) in Three Acts." *International Journal for the Scholarship of Teaching and Learning* 2 (1): 1–18.

Hamera, J. 2011. "Performance Ethnography." In *The SAGE Handbook of Qualitative Research,* edited by N. K. Denzin and Y. S. Lincoln, 317–329. Thousand Oaks, CA: Sage.

Hargreaves, J. 2004. "So How Do You Feel about That? Assessing Reflective Practice." *Nurse Education Today* 4 (3): 196–201.

Harkavy, I. 2006. "The Role of Universities in Advancing Citizenship and Social Justice in the 21st Century." *Education, Citizenship, and Social Justice* 1 (1): 5–37.

Harper, S. R., and G. D. Kuh. 2007. "Myths and Misconceptions about Using Qualitative Methods in Assessment." *Using Qualitative Methods in Institutional Assessment*, no. 136: 5–14.

Harrington, A., and J. Dunne. 2015. "When Mindfulness Is Therapy: Ethical Qualms, Historical Perspectives." *American Psychologist* 70 (7): 621–631.

Hart, T. 2004. "Opening the Contemplative Mind in the Classroom." *Journal of Transformative Education* 2 (1): 28–46.

———. 2009. *From Information to Transformation: Education for the Evolution of Consciousness.* New York: Peter Lang.

———. 2010. "The Inner Liberal Arts." Presentation at the second annual conference of the Association for Contemplative Mind in Higher Education, Amherst College, September 24–26.

———. 2012. "Survey of Transformative and Spiritual Dimensions of Higher Education." http://www.contemplativemind.org/admin/wp-content/uploads/2012/09/fetzer_report.pdf.

Hawkins, B. L. 2004. "Teaching on Campus and Online: Same or Different?" In *Best Practices in Online Contemplative Education: Naropa Online Faculty Panel Discussions*, edited by J. Hladiš, 20–23. Boulder, CO: Naropa University. http://www.naropa.edu/documents/departments/extended-studies/distance-learning/best-practices-online-contemplative-education.pdf.

Helber, C., N. A. Zook, and M. Immergut. 2012. "Meditation in Higher Education: Does It Enhance Cognition?" *Innovative Higher Education* 37 (5): 349–358.

Heller, M. 2009. "Case Studies: Transformative and Spiritual Practices in the Classroom." http://www.contemplativemind.org/admin/wp-content/uploads/2012/09/case_studies.pdf.

Hermanth, P., and P. Fisher. 2015. "Clinical Psychology Trainees' Experiences of Mindfulness: An Interpretive Phenomenological Analysis." *Mindfulness* 6 (5): 1143–1152.

Hill, R. 2014. "Honor the Negative Space." *Journal for Contemplative Inquiry* 1 (1): 135–140.

Hjeltnes, A., P. Binder, C. Moltu, and I. Dundas. 2015. "Facing the Fear of Failure: An Explorative Qualitative Study of Client Experiences in a Mindfulness-Based Stress Reduction Program for University Students with Academic Evaluation Anxiety." *International Journal of Qualitative Studies on Health and Well-Being* 10. https://www.ncbi.nlm.nih.gov/pmc/articles/PMC4545197.

Hobson, J., and A. Morrison-Saunders. 2013. "Reframing Teaching Relationships: From Student-Centered to Subject-Centered." *Teaching in Higher Education* 18 (7): 773–783.

Holland, D. 2006. "Contemplative Education in Unexpected Places: Teaching Mindfulness in Arkansas and Austria." *Teachers College Record* 108 (9): 1842–1861.

Holton, G. 1998. *The Scientific Imagination.* New York: Cambridge University Press.

Hölzel, B. K., J. Carmody, M. Vangel, C. Congleton, S. M. Yerramsetti, T. Gard, and S. W. Lazar. 2011. "Mindfulness Practice Leads to Increases in Regional Brain Gray Matter Density." *Psychiatry Research: Neuroimaging* 191:36–43.

hooks, b. 1989. *Talking Back: Thinking Feminist, Thinking Black.* Cambridge, MA: South End Press.

———. 1994. *Teaching to Transgress.* New York: Routledge.

Horney, K. 1950. *Neurosis and Human Growth: The Struggle toward Self-Realization.* New York: W. W. Norton.

Hubball, H., and A. Clarke. 2010. "Diverse Methodological Approaches and Considerations for SoTL in Higher Education." *Canadian Journal for the Scholarship of Teaching and Learning* 1 (1): 1–11.

Huber, M. T. 2006. "Disciplines, Pedagogy, and Inquiry-Based Learning about Teaching." In "Exploring Research-Based Teaching." Special issue, *New Directions for Teaching and Learning* 107:63–72.

———. 2013. Foreword to *The Scholarship of Teaching and Learning In and Across the Disciplines*, edited by K. McKinney, ix–xiv. Bloomington: Indiana University Press.

Huber, M. T., and P. Hutchings. 2005. *The Advancement of Learning: Building the Teaching Commons*. San Francisco: Jossey-Bass.

Hutchings, P. 2000. *Opening Lines: Approaches to the Scholarship of Teaching and Learning*. Menlo Park, CA: Carnegie Foundation for the Advancement of Teaching.

Hutchings, P., and L. S. Shulman. 1999. "The Scholarship of Teaching: New Elaborations, New Developments." *Change* 31 (5): 10–15.

Hyland, T. 2016. "The Limits of Mindfulness: Emerging Issues for Education." *British Journal of Educational Studies* 64 (1): 97–117.

Indiana University–Purdue University Indianapolis. n.d. "The University Writing Center: About." https://theden.iupui.edu/organization/writingcenter/about (accessed June 8, 2017).

Jain, S., S. L. Shapiro, S. Swanick, S. Roesch, P. Mills, I. Bell, and G. Schwartz. 2007. "A Randomized Controlled Trial of Mindfulness Meditation versus Relaxation Training: Effects on Distress, Positive States of Mind, Rumination, and Distraction." *Annals of Behavioral Medicine* 33:11–21.

James, W. 1890. *Principles of Psychology*. Vol. 1. New York: Henry Holt.

Jha, A. P., J. Krompinger, and M. J. Baime. 2007. "Mindfulness Training Modifies Subsystems of Attention." *Cognitive, Affective and Behavioral Neuroscience* 7 (2): 109–119.

Johnson, R. B., and A. J. Onwuegbuzie. 2004. "Mixed Methods Research: A Research Paradigm Whose Time Has Come." *Educational Researcher* 33 (7): 14–26.

Johnson, R. B., A. J. Onwuegbuzie, and L. A. Turner. 2007. "Toward a Definition of Mixed Methods Research." *Journal of Mixed Methods Research* 1 (1): 112–133.

Josipovic, Z., B. J. Baars. 2015. "Editorial: What Can Neuroscience Learn from Contemplative Practices?" *Frontiers in Psychology*, November 10. http://journal.frontiersin.org/article/10.3389/fpsyg.2015.01731/full.

Kabat-Zinn, J. 1994. *Wherever You Go, There You Are*. New York: Hyperion.

———. 2003. Mindfulness-Based Interventions in Context: Past, Present, and Future." *Clinical Psychology: Science and Practice* 10 (2): 144–156.

———. 2005. *Coming to Our Senses: Healing Ourselves and the World through Mindfulness*. New York: Hyperion.

Kafle, N. P. 2011. "Hermeneutic Phenomenological Research Method Simplified." *Bodhi: An Interdisciplinary Journal* 5:181–200.

Kahane, D. 2014. "Learning about Obligation, Compassion, and Global Justice: The Place of Contemplative Pedagogy." In *Contemplative Learning and Inquiry across Disciplines*, edited by P. Gunnlaugson, E. Sarath, C. Scott, and H. Bai, 119–132. Albany: State University of New York Press.

Kalamaras, G. 1994. *Reclaiming the Tacit Dimension: Symbolic Form in the Rhetoric of Silence*. Albany: State University of New York Press.

Kaleem, J. 2014. "Contemplative Studies Grow at Brown University—and Beyond." *Huffington Post*, November 10. http://www.huffingtonpost.com/2014/11/10/contemplative-studies -brown_n_6124030.html.

Kanagala, V., and L. I. Rendon. 2013. "Birthing Internal Images: Employing the *Cajita* Project as a Contemplative Activity in a College Classroom." *New Directions for Teaching and Learning*, no. 134: 41–51.

Kaszniak, A. W. 2014. "Contemplative Pedagogy: Perspectives from Cognitive and Affective Science." In *Contemplative Learning and Inquiry across Disciplines*, edited by O. Gunnlaugson, E. W. Sarath, C. Scott, and H. Bai, 197–211. Albany: State University of New York Press.

Kegan, R. 1982. *The Evolving Self*. Cambridge, MA: Harvard University Press.

———. 1994. *In Over Our Heads: The Mental Demands of Modern Life*. Cambridge, MA: Harvard University Press.

Keller, E. F. 1983. *A Feeling for the Organism: The Life and Work of Barbara McClintock*. New York: W. H. Freeman.

Kirsch, G. E. 2009. "Creating Spaces for Listening, Learning, and Sustaining the Inner Lives of Students." *Journal of the Assembly for Expanded Perspectives on Learning* 14:56–67.

Klein, A. C., and A. Gleig. 2011. "Contemplative Inquiry: Beyond the Disembodied Subject." In *Meditation and the Classroom*, edited by J. Simmer-Brown and F. Grace, 187–193. Albany: State University of New York Press.

Kolb, A. Y., and D. A. Kolb. 2005. "Learning Styles and Learning Spaces: Enhancing Experiential Learning in Higher Education." *Academy of Management Learning and Education* 4 (2): 193–212.

Kolb, D. A. 1984. *Experiential Learning: Experience as the Source of Learning and Development*. Upper Saddle River, NJ: Prentice-Hall.

Komjathy, L. 2011. "Field Notes from a Daoist Professor." In *Meditation and the Classroom: Contemplative Pedagogy for Religious Studies*, edited by J. Simmer-Brown and F. Grace, 95–103. Albany: State University of New York Press.

Kozasa, E. H., J. R. Sato, S. S. Lacerda, M. A. Barreiros, J. Radvany, T. A. Russell, L. G. Sanches, et al. 2012. "Meditation Training Increases Brain Efficiency in an Attention Task." *NeuroImage* 59 (1): 745–749.

Kreber, C. 2006. "Developing the Scholarship of Teaching through Transformative Learning. *Journal of Scholarship of Teaching and Learning* 6 (1): 88–109.

Kuhn, W. F. 2015. "5 Steps to Be More Mindful with Email." *Mindbodygreen*, March 18. https:// www.mindbodygreen.com/0-17887/5-steps-to-be-more-mindful-with-email.html.

Kurth, F., N. Cherbuin, and E. Luders. 2015. "Reduced Age-Related Degeneration of the Hippocampal Subiculum in Long-Term Meditators." *Psychiatry Research* 232:214–218.

Kyndt, E., M. Musso, E. Cascallar, and F. Dochy. 2015. "Predicting Academic Performance: The Role of Cognition, Motivation and Learning Approaches. A Neural Network Analysis." In *Methodological Challenges in Research on Student Learning*, edited by V. Donoche, S. DeMayer, D. Gijbels, and H. van den Bergh, 55–76. Antwerp, Belgium: Garant.

Lakoff, R. 1973. "Language and Women's Place." *Language in Society* 2 (1): 45–80.

Langer, E. J. 1997. *The Power of Mindful Learning*. Cambridge, MA: Perseus.

Lansbergen, M. M., J. L. Kenemans, and H. van Engeland. 2007. "Stroop Interference and Attention-Deficit/Hyperactivity Disorder: A Review and Meta-analysis." *Neuropsychology* 21 (2): 251–262.

Lazar, S., C. Kerr, R. Wasserman, J. Gray, D. Greve, M. Treadway, M. McGarvey, et al. 2005. "Meditation Experience Is Associated with Increased Cortical Thickness." *NeuroReport* 16 (17): 1893–1897.

Ledoux, A. O. 1998. "Teaching Meditation to Classes in Philosophy." Paper presented to the 20th World Congress of Philosophy, Boston, August 10–16. https://www.bu.edu/wcp/Papers/Teac/TeacLedo.htm.

Lee, V. S. 2004. *Teaching and Learning through Inquiry: A Guidebook for Institutions and Instructors.* Sterling, VA: Stylus.

Lester, J. N., and R. Gabriel. 2016. "Engaging in Performance Ethnography in Research Methods." *Qualitative Inquiry* 22 (2): 125–131.

Levy, D. M. 2007. "No Time to Think: Reflections on Information Technology and Contemplative Scholarship." *Ethics and Information Technology* 9 (4): 237–249.

———. 2014. "Information and Contemplation: Exploring Contemplative Approaches to Information Technology." In *Contemplative Learning and Inquiry across Disciplines*, edited by O. Gunnlaugson, E. W. Sarath, C. Scott, and H. Bai, 183–195. Albany: State University of New York Press.

———. 2016. *Mindful Tech.* New Haven, CT: Yale University Press.

Levy, D. M., J. Wobbrock, A. Kaszniak, M. Ostergren. 2012. "The Effects of Mindfulness Meditation Training on Multitasking in a High-Stress Information Environment." In *Proceedings of Graphics Interface*, 45–52. Toronto: Canadian Information Processing Society.

Lewis, H. R. 2006. *Excellence without a Soul.* Cambridge, MA: Perseus.

Lin, J. 2013. "Education for Transformation and an Expanded Self: Paradigm Shift for Wisdom Education." In *Re-envisioning Higher Education: Embodied Pathways to Wisdom and Social Transformation*, edited by J. Lin, R. L. Oxford, and E. J. Brantmeier, 23–32. Charlotte, NC: Information Age.

Loeb, P. 1999. *Soul of a Citizen: Living with Conviction in Challenging Times.* New York: St. Martin's Press.

———. 2004. *The Impossible Will Take a Little While.* New York: Basic Books.

Lucas, C. J. 1994. *American Higher Education: A History.* New York: St. Martin's.

Luders, E., F. Kurth, A. W. Toga, K. L. Narr, and C. Gaser. 2013. "Meditation Effects within the Hippocampal Complex Revealed by Voxel-Based Morphometric and Cytoarchitectonic Probabilistic Mapping." *Frontiers in Psychology* 4:398.

Lupien, S. J., B. S. McEwen, M. R. Gunnar, and C. Heim. 2009. "Effects of Stress throughout the Lifespan on the Brain, Behaviour and Cognition." *Nature Reviews Neuroscience* 10 (6): 434–445.

Lutz, A., L. L. Greischar, N. B. Rawlings, M. Ricard, and R. J. Davidson. 2004. "Long-Term Meditators Self-Induce High-Amplitude Gamma Synchrony during Mental Practice." *Proceedings of the National Academy of Science* 101 (46): 16369–16373.

Lutz, A., A. P. Jha, J. D. Dunne, and C. D. Saron. 2015. "Investigating the Phenomenological Matrix of Mindfulness-Related Practices from a Neurocognitive Perspective." *American Psychologist* 70 (7): 632–658.

Lutz, A., J. Lachaux, J. Martinerie, and F. J. Varela. 2002. "Guiding the Study of Brain Dynamics by Using First-Person Data: Synchrony Patterns Correlate with Ongoing Conscious States during a Simple Visual Task." *Proceedings of the National Academy of Sciences* 99 (3): 1586–1591.

Lutz, A., H. Slagter, N. Rawlings, A. Francis, L. Greischar, and R. J. Davidson. 2009. "Mental Training Enhances Attentional Stability: Neural and Behavioral Evidence." *Journal of Neuroscience* 29 (42): 13418–13427.

Magee, R. V. 2016. "The Way of ColorInsight: Understanding Race and Law Effectively through Mindfulness-Based ColorInsight Practices." *Georgetown Law Journal of Modern Critical Race Perspectives*, January. https://papers.ssrn.com/sol3/papers.cfm?abstract_id=2638511.

Mah y Busch, J. D. 2014. "A Pedagogical Heartbeat: The Integration of Critical and Contemplative Pedagogies for Transformative Education." *Journal of Contemplative Inquiry* 1:113–134.

Mann, H. (1840) 1989. *On the Art of Teaching* Bedford, MA: Applewood Books.

Maslow, A. (1962) 2014. *Toward a Psychology of Being.* Floyd, VA: Sublime Books.

May, V. 2005. "Intuitive Inquiry and Creative Process: A Case Study of an Artistic Practice." Master's thesis, Queensland University of Technology. http://eprints.qut.edu.au/16038/1/Virginia_May_Thesis.pdf.

McColman, C. 2013. "Would Thomas Merton Use an iPad? Contemplation, Technology and Discernment." *Huffington Post*, January 3. http://www.huffingtonpost.com/carl-mccolman/would-thomas-merton-use-an-ipad-contemplation-technology-and-discernment_b_2376428.html.

McGowan, P. O., A. Sasaki, A. C. D'Alessio, S. Dymov, B. Labonte, M. Szyf, G. Turecki, and M. J. Meaney. 2009. "Epigenetic Regulation of the Glucorticoid Receptor in Human Brain Associates with Childhood Abuse." *Nature Neuroscience* 12 (3): 342–348.

McInerney, R. G. 2013. "Neurophenomenological Praxis: Its Applications to Learning and Pedagogy." In *Neurophenomenology and Its Applications to Psychology*, edited by S. Gordon, 25–60. New York: Springer Science and Business Media.

Meixner, C. 2013. "Locating Self by Serving Others." In *Re-envisioning Higher Education: Embodied Pathways to Wisdom and Social Transformation*, edited by J. Lin, R. L. Oxford, and E. J. Brantmeier, 317–334. Charlotte, NC: Information Age.

Mezirow, J. 1981. "A Critical Theory of Adult Learning and Education." *Adult Education Quarterly* 32 (3): 3–24.

———. 1985. "A Critical Theory of Self-Directed Learning." In *Self-Directed Learning: From Theory to Practice*, edited by S. Brookfield, 17–30. San Francisco: Jossey-Bass.

———. 2000. *Learning as Transformation: Critical Perspectives on a Theory in Progress.* San Francisco: Jossey-Bass.

Michigan State University. n.d. "Our Philosophy: The Writing Center's Vision Statement." http://writing.msu.edu/about/our-philosophy (accessed June 8, 2017).

Middleton, D. 2014. "Reflection and Contemplative Pedagogy." Post to Center for Contemplative Mind in Society mailing list, November 15. "ACMHE_discussion" forum. http://lists.contemplativemind.org/private.cgi/acmhe_discussion-contemplativemind.org/2014-November/thread.html.

Miller, J. P. 1994. "Contemplative Practice in Higher Education: An Experiment in Teacher Development." *Journal of Humanistic Psychology* 34 (4). http://journals.sagepub.com/doi/abs/10.1177/00221678940344005.

Miller-Young, J., and M. Yeo. 2015. "Conceptualizing and Communicating SoTL: A Framework for the Field." *Teaching and Learning Inquiry* 3 (2): 37–53.

Mitchell, T. F., D. Richard, R. Battistoni, C. Rost-Banik, R. Netz, and C. Zakoske. 2015. "Reflective Practice That Persists: Connections between Reflection in Service-Learning

Programs and in Current Life." *Michigan Journal of Community Service Learning* 21 (2): 49–63.

Montessori, M. 1967. *Discovery of the Child*. New York: Random House.

Morgan, P. F. 2015a. "A Brief History of the Current Reemergence of Contemplative Education." *Journal of Transformative Education* 3 (3): 197–218.

———. 2015b. "Standardization." Post to Center for Contemplative Mind in Society mailing list, August 11. "ACMHE discussion" forum. http://lists.contemplativemind.org/private .cgi/acmhe_discussion-contemplativemind.org/2015-August/thread.html#75.

Morrison, A. B., M. Goolsarran, S. L. Rogers, and A. P. Jha. 2013. "Taming a Wandering Attention: Short-Form Mindfulness Training in Student Cohorts." *Frontiers in Human Neuroscience* 7. https://www.ncbi.nlm.nih.gov/pmc/articles/PMC3880932.

Murphy, A., S. Donovan, and E. Taylor. 1997. *The Physical and Psychological Effects of Meditation: A Review of Contemporary Research, 1991–1996*. 2nd ed. Petaluma, CA: Institute of Noetic Sciences.

Murray, P. 2006. "Center for the Contemplative Mind in Society Contemplative Practice in Arts Education Meeting." http://www.contemplativemind.org/admin/wp-content /uploads/2012/09/boulderarts_report.pdf.

———. 2008. "Meeting on Contemplative Pedagogy in the Disciplines: Philosophy, Religious Studies, Psychology." http://www.contemplativemind.org/admin/wp-content/uploads /2012/09/08_Disciplinary_Report.pdf.

Musolino, G. M., and E. Mostrom. 2005. "Reflection and the Scholarship of Teaching, Learning, and Assessment." *Journal of Physical Therapy Education* 19 (3): 52–66.

Napora, L. 2011. "Meditation in Higher Education: The Question of Change, a Current Problem, and Evidence toward a Solution." *Biofeedback* 39 (2): 64–66.

———. 2013. "The Impact of Classroom-Based Meditation Practice on Cognitive Engagement, Mindfulness and Academic Performance of Undergraduate College Students." Ph.D. diss., University at Buffalo, State University of New York. http://pqdtopen.proquest.com /doc/1459751586.html?FMT=AI.

Naropa University. n.d. "Distance Learning." https://www.naropa.edu/academics/distance -learning (accessed June 8, 2017).

———. n.d. "Transpersonal Service Learning." http://www.naropa.edu/academics/masters/eco psychology/about/transpersonal-service-learning.php (accessed June 8, 2017).

———. n.d. "What Is Contemplative Education?" https://www.naropa.edu/the-naropa-experi ence/contemplative-education (accessed March 24, 2017).

National Survey of Student Engagement. 2014. "Bringing the Institution into Focus: Annual Results 2014." http://nsse.indiana.edu/NSSE_2014_Results/pdf/NSSE_2014_Annual _Results.pdf.

Nelson, M. 2001. "Aborigine in the Citadel." *Hudson Review* 53 (4): 543–553.

Netzer, D., and N. M. Rowe. 2010. "Inquiry into Creative and Innovative Processes: An Experiential, Whole-Person Approach to Teaching Creativity." *Journal of Transformative Education* 8 (2): 124–145.

Nichols, C. M., L. Mills, and M. Kotcha. 2014. "Observation." In *Qualitative Research Practice: A Guide for Social Science Students and Researchers*, 2nd ed., edited by J. Richie, J. Lewis, Carol M. Nicolls, and R. Ormston, 243–268. Los Angeles: Sage.

Nussbaum, M. S. 1997. *Cultivating Humanity: A Classical Defense of Reform in Liberal Education*. Boston: Harvard University Press.

Oberg, C. M. 2008. "Performance Ethnography: Scholarly Inquiry in the Here and Now." *Transformative Dialogues: Teaching and Learning Journal* 2 (1): 1–4.

Oberski, I. 2014. "Reflection and Contemplative Pedagogy." Post to Center for Contemplative Mind in Society mailing list, November 15. "ACMHE_discussion" forum. http://lists .contemplativemind.org/private.cgi/acmhe_discussion-contemplativemind.org/2014 -November/thread.html.

Ohiyesa [Charles Alexander Eastman]. 2001. "The Power of Silence." In *The Soul of an Indian and Other Writings from Ohiyesa*, edited by K. Nerburn, 7–8. Novato, CA: New World Library.

Olivo, E. L. 2009. "Protection through the Lifespan: The Psychoneuroimmunological Impact of Indo-Tibetan Meditative and Yoga Practices." *Annals of the New York Academy of Sciences* 1172:163–171.

Ollin, R. 2008. "Silent Pedagogy and Rethinking Classroom Practice: Structuring Teaching through Silence rather than Talk." *Cambridge Journal of Education* 38 (2): 265–280.

Oman, D., S. L. Shapiro, C. E. Thoresen, T. G. Plante, and T. Flinders. 2008. "Meditation Lowers Stress and Supports Forgiveness among College Students: A Randomized Controlled Trial." *Journal of College American College Health* 56:569–578.

O'Reilley, M. R. 1998. *Radical Presence*. Portsmouth, NH: Boynton-Cook.

O'Sullivan, E. 2003. "Case Study 1: In the Classroom." In "Survey of Transformative and Spiritual Dimensions of Higher Education," edited by M. Duerr, A. Zajonc, and D. Dana. Special issue, *Journal of Transformative Education* 1 (3): 188–190.

Owen-Smith, P. 2004. "What Is Cognitive-Affective Learning (CAL)?" *Journal of Cognitive Affective Learning* 1:11.

———. 2016. "Constructing a Social Justice Pedagogy through Contemplative Service-Learning." In *Teaching, Pedagogy, and Learning: Fertile Ground for Campus and Community Innovations*, edited by J. Galle and R. Harrison, 117–142. Washington, DC: Rowman and Littlefield.

Ozawa–de Silva, B. R. 2014. "Secular Ethics, Embodied Cognitive Logics, and Education." *Journal of Contemplative Inquiry* 1:89–109.

Ozawa–de Silva, B. R., B. Dodson-Lavelle, C. L. Raison, and L. T. Negi. 2012. "Compassion and Ethics: Scientific and Practical Approaches to the Cultivation of Compassion as a Foundation for Ethical Subjectivity and Well-Being." *Journal of Healthcare, Science and the Humanities* 11 (2): 145–161.

Pace, T. W., L. T. Negi, D. D. Adame, S. P. Cole, T. I. Sivilli, T. D. Brown, M. L. Issa, and C. L. Raison. 2009. "Effect of Compassion Meditation on Neuroendocrine, Innate Immune and Behavioral Responses to Psychosocial Stress." *Psychoneuroendocrinology* 34 (1): 87–98.

Palmer. P. J. 2014. Foreword to *Contemplative Practices in Higher Education*, edited by D. P. Barbezat and M. Bush, vii–ix. San Francisco: Jossey-Bass.

Palmer, P. J., and A. Zajonc. 2010. *The Heart of Higher Education*. San Francisco: Jossey-Bass.

Park, T., M. Reilly-Spong, and C. R. Gross. 2013. "Mindfulness: A Systematic Review of Instruments to Measure an Emergent Patient Reported Outcome." *Quality of Life Research* 22 (10): 2639–2659.

Patterson, A. B., L. Munoz, L. Abrams, and C. Bass. 2015. "Transformative Learning: A Case for Using Grounded Theory as an Assessment Analytic." *Teaching Theology and Religion* 18 (4): 303–325.

Patterson, B. 2011. "Sustaining Life: Contemplative Pedagogies in a Religion and Ecology Course." In *Meditation and the Classroom*, edited by J. S. Brown and F. Grace, 155–161. Albany: State University of New York Press.

Perry, W. G. 1970. *Forms of Intellectual and Ethical Development in the College Years: A Scheme*. New York: Holt, Rinehart, and Winston.

———. 1985. "Perry's Perplex: Issues Unresolved and Irresolvable; Notes to Participants in the Project Match Conference, Davidson College, North Carolina." Published in *Perry Newsletter*, Fall, pp. 1–5.

Petitmengin, C. 2006. "Describing One's Subjective Experience in the Second Person: An Interview Method for the Science of Consciousness." *Phenomenology and the Cognitive Sciences* 5 (3): 229–269.

Piaget, J. 1977. *The Equilibration of Cognitive Structures*. Chicago: University of Chicago Press.

Pike, G. R. 2011. "Using College Students' Self-Reported Learning Outcomes in Scholarly Research." *New Directions for Institutional Research* 2011 (150): 41–58.

Pink, D. H. 2005. *A Whole New Mind*. New York: Penguin.

Plante, T. G., and A. Raz. 2010. "Contemplative Practices in Action: Now What?" In *Contemplative Practices in Action: Spirituality, Meditation, and Health*, edited by T. G. Plante, 243–246. Santa Barbara, CA: Praeger.

Porter, S. R. 2012. "Using Student Learning as a Measure of Quality in Higher Education." http://www.hcmstrategists.com/contextforsuccess/papers/PORTER_PAPER.pdf.

Powers, W. 2010. *Hamlet's Blackberry*. New York: Harper Collins.

Pratt, J. 2012. "The Problem of Grounded Theory." Working paper, University of East London. http://roar.uel.ac.uk/1433/1/GroundedTheory.pdf.

Prochnik, G. 2011. *In Pursuit of Silence: Listening for Meaning in a World of Noise*. New York: Anchor.

Pryor, J. H. 2016. "Redefining Success in Higher Education." Presentation at the Mindfulness, MOOCs, and Money in Higher Education Conference, Naropa University, Boulder, CO, March.

Redick, T. S., and R. W. Engle. 2006. "Working Memory Capacity and Attention Network Test Performance." *Applied Cognitive Psychology* 20 (5): 713–721.

Reetz, D. R., B. Krylowicz, and B. Mistler. 2014. "The Association for University and College Counseling Center Directors Annual Survey: Reporting Period September 1, 2013 through August 31, 2014." http://campusmentalhealth.ca/wp-content/uploads/2015/05/2014-aucccd-monograph-public1.pdf.

Rendon, L. I. 2009. *Sentipensante Pedagogy*. Sterling, VA: Stylus.

———. 2016. "Toward a Contemplative Culturally-Validating Pedagogic Imaginary." Presentation at the Mindfulness, MOOCs, and Money in Higher Education Conference, Naropa University, Boulder, CO, March.

Repetti, R. 2010. "The Case for a Contemplative Philosophy of Education." *New Directions for Community Colleges* 151:5–15.

Rice, J. S., and T. Horn. 2014. "Teaching Diversity through Service-Learning: An Integrative Praxis Pedagogical Approach." *Journal on Excellence in College Teaching* 25 (1): 139–157.

Richelle, M. 1993. *B. F. Skinner: A Reappraisal*. Hove, UK: Psychology Press.

Rilke, M. R. 1903. *Letters to a Young Poet*. Translated by R. Snell. New York: Dover.

Robbins, B. D. 2013. "Enactive Cognition and the Neurophenomenology of Emotion." In *Neurophenomenology and Its Applications to Psychology*, edited by S. Gordon, 1–24. New York: Springer.

Roberts, K. A. 2002. "Ironies of Effective Teaching: Deep Structure Learning and Constructions of Classrooms." *Teaching Sociology* 32 (2): 222–231.

Roberts, K. C., and S. Danoff-Burg. 2010. "Mindfulness and Health Behaviors: Is Paying Attention Good for You?" *Journal of American College Health* 59 (3): 165–173.

Robinson, P. 2004. "Meditation: Its Role in Transformative Learning and in the Fostering of an Integrative Vision for Higher Education." *Journal of Transformative Education* 2 (2): 107–119.

Roeser, R. W., and S. C. Peck. 2009. "An Education in Awareness: Self-Motivation, and Self-Regulated Learning in Contemplative Perspective." *Educational Psychologist* 44 (2): 119–136.

Roeser, R. W., E. Skinner, J. Beers, and P. A. Jennings. 2012. "Mindfulness Training and Teachers' Professional Development: An Emerging Area of Research and Practice." *Child Development Perspectives* 6 (2): 167–173.

Rogers, C. (1961) 1995. *On Becoming a Person: A Therapist's View of Psychotherapy*. New York: Houghton Mifflin.

Rogers, S. L., and J. L. Jacobowitz. 2015. "Mindful Ethics and the Cultivation of Concentration." *Nevada Law Journal* 15 (2): 730–743.

Rosa, H. 2003. "Social Acceleration: Ethical and Political Consequences of a Desynchronized High-Speed Society." *Constellations* 10 (1): 3–33.

Rose, E. 2013. *On Reflection: An Essay on Technology, Education, and the Status of Thought in the Twenty-First Century*. Toronto: Canadian Scholars Press.

Roth, H. D. 2012. "Developing Contemplative Studies in Higher Education: The Brown Model." Presentation at the International Symposia for Contemplative Studies, Denver, CO, April 26–29.

———. 2014. "A Pedagogy for the New Field of Contemplative Studies." In *Contemplative Learning and Inquiry across Disciplines*, edited by O. Gunnlaugson, E. W. Sarath, C. Scott, and H. Bai, 97–115. Albany: State University of New York Press.

———. 2015. "Standardization." Post to Center for Contemplative Mind in Society mailing list, August 14. "ACMHE_discussion" forum. http://lists.contemplativemind.org/private.cgi /acmhe_discussion-contemplativemind.org/2015-August/thread.html.

Royster, J. J., and G. Kirsch. 2012. *Feminist Rhetorical Practices: New Horizons for Rhetoric, Composition, and Literacy Studies*. Carbondale: Southern Illinois University.

Sable, D. 2014. "Reason in the Service of the Heart: The Impacts of Contemplative Practices on Critical Thinking." *Journal of Contemplative Inquiry* 1:1–22.

Saevi, T. 2014. "Phenomenology in Educational Research." *Oxford Bibliographies*, January 13. http://www.oxfordbibliographies.com/view/document/obo-9780199756810/obo -9780199756810-0042.xml.

Saltmarsh, J. 2010. "Sentipensante (Sensing/Thinking) Pedagogy: Educating for Wholeness, Social Justice and Liberation." *Michigan Journal of Community Service Learning* 16 (2): 90–94.

Saltmarsh, J., M. Hartley, and P. Clayton. 2009. "Democratic Engagement White Paper." New England Resource Center for Higher Education. https://futureofengagement.files.word press.com/2009/02/democratic-engagement-white-paper-2_13_09.pdf.

Sample, M. 2011. "On Reading Aloud in the Classroom." *SampleReality* (blog), September 14. http://www.samplereality.com/2011/09/14/on-reading-aloud-in-the-classroom.

Sanger, K. L., and D. Dorjee. 2015. "Mindfulness Training for Adolescents: A Neurodevelopmental Perspective on Investigating Modifications in Attention and Emotion Regulation

Using Event-Related Brain Potentials." *Cognitive, Affective Behavioral Neuroscience* 15:696–711.

Sarath, E. W. 2003a. "Case Study 4: In Programs and Departments." *Journal of Transformative Education* 1 (3): 204–206.

———. 2003b. "Meditation in Higher Education: The Next Wave?" *Innovative Higher Education* 27 (4): 215–233.

———. 2014. "What Next? Contemplating the Future of Contemplative Education." In *Contemplative Learning and Inquiry across Disciplines*, edited by O. Gunnlaugson, E. W. Sarath, C. Scott, and H. Bai, 271–286. Albany: State University of New York Press.

Sauer, S., H. Walach, S. Schmidt, T. Hinterberger, S. Lynch, A. Bussing, and N. Kohls. 2013. "Assessment of Mindfulness: Review on State of the Art." *Mindfulness* 4 (1): 3–17.

Schneider, P. 2013. *How the Light Gets In*. New York: Oxford University Press.

Schoeberlein, D., and S. Sheth. 2009. *Mindful Teaching and Teaching Mindfulness*. Boston: Wisdom.

Schön, D. 1987. *Educating the Reflective Practitioner: Toward a New Design for Teaching and Learning in the Professions*. San Francisco: Jossey-Bass.

Schroeder, C. 2007. "Countering SoTL Marginalization: A Model for Integrating SoTL with Institutional Initiatives." *International Journal for the Scholarship of Teaching and Learning* 1 (1): 1–9.

Schultz, K. 2009. *Rethinking Classroom Participation: Listening to Silent Voices*. New York: Teachers College Press.

Schweickart, P. 1996. "Speech Is Silver, Silence Is Gold: The Asymmetrical Intersubjectivity of Communicative Action." In *Knowledge, Difference, and Power: Essays Inspired by Women's Ways of Knowing*, edited by N. Goldberger, J. Tarule, B. Clinchy, and M. Belenky, 305–331. New York: Basic Books.

Scott, C. 2014. "Buberian Dialogue as an Intersubjective Contemplative Praxis." In *Contemplative Learning and Inquiry across Disciplines*, edited by O. Gunnlaugson, E. W. Sarath, C. Scott, and H. Bai, 325–340. Albany: State University of New York Press.

Shapiro, S. L., K. W. Brown, and J. A. Astin. 2008. *Toward the Integration of Meditation into Higher Education: A Review of Research*. Northampton, MA: Center for Contemplative Mind in Society.

———. 2011. "Toward the Integration of Meditation into Higher Education: A Review of Research Evidence." *Teachers College Record* 113 (3): 493–528.

Shapiro, S. L., K. Brown, and G. Biegel. 2007. "Teaching Self-Care to Caregivers: Effects of Mindfulness-Based Stress Reduction on the Mental Health of Therapists in Training." *Training and Education in Professional Psychology* 1:105–115.

Shapiro, S. L., L. E. Carlson, J. A. Astin, and B. Freedman. 2006. "Mechanisms of Mindfulness." *Journal of Clinical Psychology* 62 (3): 373–386.

Shulman, L. S. 1999. "Taking Learning Seriously." *Change* 31 (4): 10–17.

———. 2002. "Making Differences: A Table of Learning." *Change* 34 (6): 36–44.

———. 2004a. "Teaching as Community Property: Putting an End to Pedagogical Solitude." In *Teaching as Community Property: Essays on Higher Education*, edited by L. S. Shulman, 140–154. San Francisco: Jossey-Bass.

———. 2004b. *The Wisdom of Practice: Essays on Teaching, Learning, and Learning to Teach*. San Francisco: Jossey-Bass and Carnegie Foundation for the Advancement of Teaching.

Siegel, D. J. 2011. *Mindsight: The New Science of Personal Transformation*. New York: Bantam Books.

Simmer-Brown, J. 2011. "Training the Heart Responsibly." In *Meditation and the Classroom*, edited by J. Simmer-Brown and F. Grace, 107–120. Albany: State University of New York Press.

———. 2016. "Higher Education Today: Challenges, Opportunities, and Contemplative Possibilities." Panel presentation at the Mindfulness, MOOCs, and Money in Higher Education Conference, Naropa University, Boulder, CO, March.

Smith, V. P. n.d. "Contemplative Practices in Foreign Language Education at the Postsecondary Level." https://www.brown.edu/academics/contemplative-studies/sites/brown.edu.academics.contemplative-studies/files/uploads/ContemplativeFLA.pdf (accessed March 24, 2017).

Solloway, S. 2014. "Diagnostic, Formative Assessment in the Mindfulness Classroom." Presentation at the Sixth Annual ACMHE Conference, University of Washington, Seattle, October.

Solloway, S. G., and N. J. Brooks. 2004. "Philosophical Hermeneutics and Assessment: Discussions of Assessment for the Sake of Wholeness." *Journal of Thought* 39 (2): 43–60.

Solloway, S. G., and W. P. Fisher. 2007. "Mindfulness in Measurement: Reconsidering the Measurable in Mindfulness Practice." *International Journal of Transpersonal Studies* 26:58–81.

Song, K., and G. W. Muschert. 2014. "Opening the Contemplative Mind in the Sociology Classroom." *Humanity and Society* 38 (3): 314–338.

Soriano, E. 2015. *Rethinking Education for a Global, Transcultural World*. Charlotte, NC: Information Age.

Steiner, R. 2002. "The Study of Man: Lecture XIV." *Rudolf Steiner Archive*. wn.rsarchive.org/Lectures/GA293/English/RSP1966/19190905a01.html.

Stewart, T. 2011. "Opening Up Service Learning Reflection by Turning Inward." In *Problematizing Service-Learning*, edited by T. Stewart and N. Webster, 37–67. Charlotte, NC: Information Age.

Stewart, J., and M. Thomas. 1995. "Dialogic Listening: Sculpting Mutual Meanings." In *Bridges Not Walls*, edited by J. Stewart, 184–201. New York: McGraw-Hill.

Stock, B. 2012. "Education and the Humanities." Presentation at the International Symposia for Contemplative Studies. Denver, CO, April.

Strawser, M. 2009. "Assessing Assessment: Toward a Hermeneutic-Phenomenological Perspective." *InSight: A Journal of Scholarly Teaching* 4:56–68.

Suttie, J. 2015. "Can Compassion Change the World? Daniel Goleman Talks with *Greater Good* about His New Book, *A Force for Good: The Dalai Lama's Vision for Our World*." *Greater Good*, June 23. http://greatergood.berkeley.edu/article/item/can_compassion_change_the_world.

Swick, D. 2010. "Robert Coles and the Moral Life." *Mindful*, August 24. https://www.mindful.org/robert-coles-and-the-moral-life.

Taber, M. W. 2010. "I Know I Shouldn't Generalize, but . . . : A Rhetorical Critique of Ethnography in Composition Studies." Master's thesis, University of South Florida, Tampa.

Tang, Y.-Y., Q. Lu, M. Fan, Y. Yang, and M. I. Posner. 2012. "Mechanisms of White Matter Changes Induced by Meditation." *PNAS* 109:10570–10574.

Tang, Y.-Y., Y. Ma, J. Wang, Y. Fan, S. Feng, Q. Lu, Q. Yu, D. Sui, M. K. Rothbart, M. Fan, and M. I. Posner. 2007. "Short-Term Meditation Training Improves Attention and Self-Regulation." *PNAS* 104 (43): 17152–17156.

Tannock, R. 2008. "Paying Attention to Inattention." Paper presented at the Harvard Learning Differences Conference, Boston, March 7.

Teddlie, C., and A. Tashakkori. 2011. "Mixed Methods Research: Contemporary Issues in an Emerging Field." In *The SAGE Handbook of Qualitative Research*, 4th ed., edited by N. K. Denzin and Y. S. Lincoln, 285–300. Thousand Oaks, CA: Sage.

Tell, C. 2001. "Appreciating Good Teaching: A Conversation with Lee Shulman." *Educational Leadership* 58 (5): 6–11.

Thomas, J., F. Hameed, and A. Perkins. 2015. "Second Language Acquisition and Accultura-tion amongst Bilingual College Students in the United Arab Emirates." Poster presented at Annual Scholarship of Teaching and Learning Conference, Zayed University, April.

Thompson, E. 2006. "Neurophenomenology and Contemplative Experience." In *The Oxford Handbook of Religion and Science*, edited by P. Clayton, 226–235. New York: Oxford University Press.

Thompson, P. M. 2012. *Returning to Reality*. Eugene, OR: Cascade Books.

Thurman, R. 2006. "Meditation and Education: India, Tibet, and Modern America." *Teachers College Record* 108:1765–1774.

Tisdell, E. J. 2003. *Exploring Spirituality and Culture in Adult and Higher Education*. San Fran-cisco: Jossey-Bass.

Tomlin, R. S., and V. Villa. 1994. "Attention in Cognitive Science and Second Language Acqui-sition." *Studies in Second Language Acquisition* 16 (2): 183–203.

Treadway, M., and S. Lazar. 2009. "The Neurobiology of Mindfulness." In *Clinical Handbook of Mindfulness*, edited by F. Didonna, 45–57. New York: Springer.

Trotman, D. 2006. "Evaluating the Imaginative: Situated Practice and the Conditions for Professional Judgement in Imaginative Education." *International Journal of Education and the Arts* 7 (3): 1–19.

Valera, F. J. 1996. "Neurophenomenology: A Methodological Remedy for the Hard Problem." *Journal of Consciousness Studies* 3 (4): 330–334.

Van Manen, M. 1997. *Researching Lived Experience: Human Science for an Action Sensitive Pedagogy*. 2nd ed. London: Althouse.

———. 2007. "Phenomenology of Practice." *Phenomenology and Practice* 1 (1): 11–30.

Vassar College. n.d. "Vassar College Writing Center." http://ltrc.vassar.edu/writing-center (accessed June 8, 2017).

Vygotsky, L. S. 1978. *Mind in Society*. Cambridge, MA: Harvard University Press.

———. 1986. *Thought and Language*. Revised by A. Kozulin. Cambridge: Massachusetts Insti-tute of Technology.

Walker, G. 2001. "Reclaiming the Artist Within." In *Seeds of Awakening: Cultivating and Sustaining the Inner Life*, edited by P. Jamison, 103–111. Kalamazoo: Western Michigan University.

Walsh, R. 1989. "Can Western Philosophers Understand Asian Philosophies?" *Crosscurrents* 39:281–299.

Walvoord, B. 2011. "How to Construct a Simple, Sensible, Useful Departmental Assessment Process." In *Literary Study, Measurement, and the Sublime: Disciplinary Assessment*, edited by D. Heiland and L. J. Rosenthal, 335–352. New York: Teagle Foundation

Wegner, S. 2003. "Case Study 3: In the Classroom." In "Survey of Transformative and Spiritual Dimensions of Higher Education," edited by M. Duerr, A. Zajonc, and D. Dana. Special issue, *Journal of Transformative Education* 1 (3): 199–201.

Weiser, M., and J. S. Brown. 1995. *Designing Calm Technology*. Palo Alto, CA: Xerox Parc.

Welch, M., and K. Kroth. 2009. "Spirituality and Service-Learning: Parallel Frameworks for Un-derstanding Students' Spiritual Development." *Spirituality in Higher Education* 5 (1): 1–9.

Wenger, C. 2015. *Yoga Minds, Writing Bodies: Contemplative Writing Pedagogy.* Fort Collins, CO: WAC Clearinghouse and Parlor Press.

Wiggins, G., and J. McTighe. 2005. *Understanding by Design.* 2nd ed. Alexandria, VA: Association for Supervision and Curriculum Development.

Willcox, K. E., S. Sarma, and P. H. Lippel. 2016. "Online Education: A Catalyst for Higher Education Reforms." https://oepi.mit.edu/files/2016/09/MIT-Online-Education-Policy-Initiative-April-2016.pdf.

Wolcott, F. L. 2013. "On Contemplation in Mathematics." *Journal of Humanistic Mathematics* 3 (1): 74–95.

Wolf, M., and M. Barzillai. 2009. "The Importance of Deep Reading." *Educational Leadership* 66 (6): 32–37.

Wolvin, A. 2010. "Introduction: Perspectives on Listening in the 21st Century." In *Listening and Human Communication in the 21st Century,* edited by A. Wolvin, 1–5. Chichester, UK: Wiley-Blackwell.

Wright, M. C., and J. E. Howard. 2015. "Assessment for Improvement: Two Models for Assessing Large Quantitative Reasoning Requirement." *Numeracy* 8 (1). http://scholarcommons.usf.edu/cgi/viewcontent.cgi?article=1158&context=numeracy.

Wu, S. 2011. "Mindfulness in the History Classroom: Teaching as Interbeing." In *Meditation and the Classroom,* edited by J. Simmer-Brown and F. Grace, 209–215. Albany: State University of New York Press.

Zajonc, A. n.d. "Vision." http://www.contemplativemind.org/programs/acmhe (accessed June 8, 2017).

———. 2006. "Love and Knowledge: Recovering the Heart of Learning through Contemplation." *Teachers College Record* 108 (9): 1742–1759.

———. 2008. *Contemplative Practices in Higher Education: A Handbook of Classroom Practices.* Northampton, MA: Center for Contemplative Mind in Society.

———. 2009. *Meditation as Contemplative Inquiry.* Great Barrington, MA: Lindisfarne Books.

———. 2010. "Beyond the Divided Academic Life." In *The Heart of Higher Education,* edited by P. J. Palmer and A. Zajonc, 53–75. San Francisco: Jossey-Bass.

———. 2012. "Welcoming Comments." Presentation to the International Symposia for Contemplative Studies, Denver, CO, April.

Zaretsky, R. 2013. "An Appeal for Silence in the Seminar Room." *Times Higher Education,* August 8. https://www.timeshighereducation.co.uk/comment/opinion/an-appeal-for-silence-in-the-seminar-room/2006270.article.

Zeidan, F., S. K. Johnson, B. J. Diamond, Z. David, and P. Goolkasian. 2010. "Mindfulness Meditation Improves Cognition: Evidence of Brief Mental Training." *Consciousness and Cognition* 19 (2): 597–605.

Zelazo, P. D., and K. E. Lyons. 2012. "The Potential Benefits of Mindfulness Training in Early Childhood: A Developmental Social Cognitive Neuroscience Perspective." *Child Development Perspectives* 6 (2): 154–160.

Zhang, A. 2013. "Service-Learning as Civic and Spiritual Engagement." In *Re-envisioning Higher Education: Embodied Pathways to Wisdom and Social Transformation,* edited by J. Lin, R. Oxford, and E. Brantmeier, 285–297. Charlotte, NC: Information Age.

Index

PATRICIA OWEN-SMITH is Professor of Psychology and Women's Studies at Oxford College of Emory University. She holds a Ph.D. in Developmental Psychology with a concentration in child and adolescent development. In 2000 she was named a Carnegie Scholar by the Carnegie Academy for the Scholarship of Teaching and Learning for her research project focused on models of insight development in the college classroom. She founded Oxford College's Women's Studies and Service-Learning programs and continues to serve as the director for both of these programs. Dr. Owen-Smith is the recipient of the Emory Williams Teaching Award, the highest honor for teaching at Emory University.

CPSIA information can be obtained
at www.ICGtesting.com
Printed in the USA
FSOW02n0733151217
42468FS